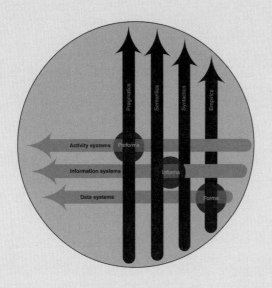

*Sign*ificance

Exploring the nature of information, systems and technology

Paul Beynon-Davies

Also by Paul Beynon-Davies and published by Palgrave

BUSINESS INFORMATION SYSTEMS
DATABASE SYSTEMS
eBUSINESS

*Sign*ificance

Exploring the Nature of Information, Systems and Technology

Paul Beynon-Davies
Professor of Organisational Informatics, Cardiff Business School, Cardiff University, UK

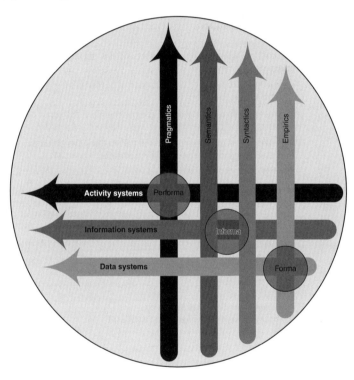

palgrave
macmillan

First published 2011 by
PALGRAVE MACMILLAN

Palgrave Macmillan in the UK is an imprint of Macmillan Publishers Limited, registered in England, company number 785998, of Houndmills, Basingstoke, Hampshire RG21 6XS.

Palgrave Macmillan in the US is a division of St Martin's Press LLC, 175 Fifth Avenue, New York, NY 10010.

Palgrave Macmillan is the global academic imprint of the above companies and has companies and representatives throughout the world.

Palgrave® and Macmillan® are registered trademarks in the United States, the United Kingdom, Europe and other countries.

ISBN: 978–0–230–27519–5 hardback

This book is printed on paper suitable for recycling and made from fully managed and sustained forest sources. Logging, pulping and manufacturing processes are expected to conform to the environmental regulations of the country of origin.

A catalogue record for this book is available from the British Library.

A catalog record for this book is available from the Library of Congress.

10   9   8   7   6   5   4   3   2   1
20 19 18 17 16 15 14 13 12 11

Printed and bound in Great Britain by
CPI Antony Rowe, Chippenham and Eastbourne

In memory of John Edward Davies

Contents

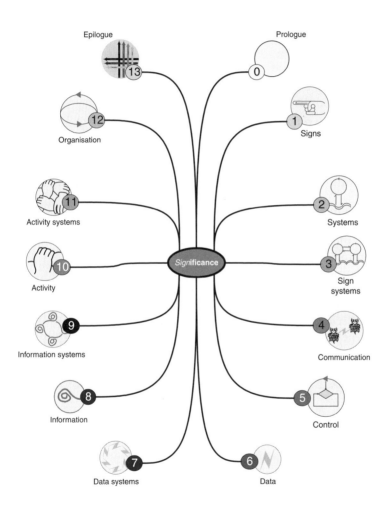

Contents

Figures

Prologue: The nature of *sign*ificance

Signs have become cool, due largely to the enormous success of a trilogy of novels by Dan Brown (*Angels and Demons, The Da Vinci Code, The Lost Symbol*). Within these thrillers archaic and religious signs open up conspiracies and offer secret, sacred knowledge. But signs play a much larger and much more mundane part in our world and are no less magical for this.

Consider the following recent case (Webber-Maybank and Luton, 2009). The orthopaedic unit at Llandough hospital in Cardiff, UK introduced a simple initiative using signs which radically improved discharge times for patients. It costs up to £400 per day to care for an average patient on a UK National Health Service (NHS) surgical ward. It is also estimated that a reduction in the length of stay for a typical patient of between 2 to 6 days could save the NHS up to £47 million per annum. Shorter lengths of stay are also associated with increased patient satisfaction and lower risk from infections related to healthcare.

On entry to hospital an expected discharge date is typically recorded and held within records maintained by administrators, clinicians and nurses, but it is never immediately available to patients. The orthopaedic unit manager at this hospital thought it would be a good idea if patients themselves were given notice of this date on arrival. The main aim was to improve the patient experience, particularly allowing them to feel more in control of their own recovery.

The unit therefore instituted a system in August 2008 which they referred to as the 'ticket home' initiative. On arrival, at the hospital unit the patient is given an A4 laminated card on which is printed the patient's name, clinical consultant and their expected date of discharge. This date is predicted on the basis of appropriate lengths of stay for specific surgical procedures and clinical diagnoses. The 'ticket' is then placed on display for all to see on the patient's locker next to the patient's bed. The various multi-disciplinary healthcare teams which care for the patient while on the hospital ward can add information to the ticket such as whether the patient needs transport home or whether their take-home X-ray and medication have been completed.

To their surprise this initiative, which had the simple intended purpose of making information more visible to patients, had an unexpected side-effect. For some reason it improved their discharge rates to a level at which over 70% of patients were discharged on their expected date. As a consequence, the average length of stay for a patient needing a hip replacement fell from 6.2 days to 5 days and the initiative also seems to have contributed to increased patient satisfaction.

The key aim of this book is to explain how and why things like this happen. Why are signs so magical? We want to argue in this work that the side-effects experienced at Llandough hospital can be commonplace, but only if we understand the ways in which the nature of significance arises at the intersection of signs and systems. It is at this intersection that significance is enacted. Signs are created within systems of activity, communication and representation but they are also resources for activity, communication and representation.

Both the concept of a sign and that of a system are what Conrad Waddington referred to over three decades ago as *tools for thought* (Waddington, 1977). Our purpose in this book is to demonstrate how understanding something of the nature of signs and systems as well as how they interact in various ways enables us to better understand the world and how it works, particularly the many and varied ways in which humans organise. The combined use of these two *tools* gives us enormous power not only for understanding how humans organise themselves as they do but how to make such forms of organisation better.

Having over thirty years of experience as an information technology practitioner, as a business analyst and as an academic, I have become increasingly concerned with a developing range of taken-for-granted assumptions underlying the nature of the modern world, particularly as it concerns the nature of information, information systems and information technology. For instance, a number of recent books in the popular genre have considered information as the stuff of the universe (Vedral, 2010) or contemporary information technology as heralding in a new world order in the way in which we produce things (Tapscott and Williams, 2006). There is a grain of truth in both these positions but neither provides the whole picture. I wish to attempt something radically different from conventional approaches to considering issues such as 'information' and the 'information society' and in the process I want to challenge conceptions and build what I hope is a more holistic or rounded picture of the way things are.

On the one hand, I want to broaden our notions of information, information systems and information technology, and in the process challenge accepted connotations of these terms. On the other hand, I want to demonstrate the universal character of these concepts based within the nature of significance. In this sense, I wish to challenge the modern notion that our contemporary society is of an order of difference from previous forms of human society. Instead, I want to argue that significance is a continuing accomplishment related closely to what it means to be human. Taken literally, it is impossible to separate man from the notion of an *information society* because man is by nature Homo Signum: the animal that signifies. We shall maintain that the defining characteristic of Homo Sapiens is its species ability as a complex user of signs. It is through such sign use that our capacity to think about things, to represent things, to communicate about such things and to organise ourselves in relation to things takes shape.

Therefore, in considering the nature of significance we shall have to provide a better basis for lots of key terms that are used very loosely within literature from a range of different disciplines – terms such as data, information, information technology and information system. Providing better definitions for these terms is important for a number of reasons. First, it allows us to demonstrate the ubiquity of significance and also the inherent inter-connections an understanding of the nature of significance provides to a large range of areas. Second, as we have mentioned, it allows us to illustrate how many of these terms refer to concepts that link closely to some universal features of what it means to be human. Third, and perhaps most importantly, providing more precision to key terms allows us to get a better grip on understanding a large number of problems in the modern world, particularly in areas such as business, management and information technology but also more widely within the economy, society and the polity.

But shifting established conceptions of things is not easy; many of the meanings we associate with terms such as data, information and information technology are 'bracketed' by our understanding of modern digital computing technology. As more and more of us use computers as part of our everyday lives it becomes more and more difficult to understand such simple questions as *what value do computers have for us*; after all, a simple piece of card on a hospital ward appears to have had just as much effect on the efficiency of this system as the introduction of any desktop computer.

This has resonance with a familiar problem experienced by social researchers such as social anthropologists who seek to understand the workings of a society of which they are a part. Such researchers are therefore provided with a number of techniques to help them make the familiar *strange*. Many such techniques encourage a breaking down or breaching of the 'methods' that people employ to act appropriately in particular social situations. In this book we use a similar approach and seek to breach over-socialised current conceptions of information, information systems and information technology.

Our overall aim then is to attempt to identify a number of universal characteristics associated with the notion of significance. Take, for instance, the concept of an information system itself. We work from the premise that information systems are nothing new. Indeed, they are a natural consequence of the need for humans to communicate and coordinate their activity. Hence, we would expect information systems to exist across time, space and human cultures. This leads us further to suggest that all information systems have a number of characteristics in common (universals) and that to determine the essence of what an information system is, we need to analyse examples of information systems used by different human societies at different historical periods.

Take also the nature of communication. We deliberately consider a number of cases of animal communication within this book and argue that this is important to help us get a grip on the essence of communication. Considering such cases allows us also to identify some crucial differences between animal and human communication. Further, it enables us to get a better handle on the nature of man-machine communication.

Therefore, to demonstrate the universality or deep structure underlying core concepts we utilise a range of examples which are deliberately *strange* in a number of senses. First, we have deliberately steered clear of much discussion of the modern information and communication technology revolution, although we do make the case for it being more an evolution rather than a revolution. Second, most such cases have not appeared in literatures that traditionally deal with the topics I shall be discussing. Hence, for instance, a close examination of Sumerian clay tokens and the Inka Khipu offer new ways of considering what we actually mean by 'information technology'. Third, and perhaps most importantly, the cases are interesting in that they demand that we step outside our own entrenched worldview of our own culture and time and consider different artefacts, forms of communication and modes of activity within situations in which they achieved significance.

In making this excursion into the realms of the 'strange' we shall assemble elements of a conceptual framework which we believe helps us unpack the nature of significance. The three main facets of our 'prism' which we use to illuminate this phenomenon are illustrated in Figure P.1. To summarise our perspective: we maintain that the issue of significance is naturally located at the intersection of signs and systems. Signs are critical to sense-making because they encapsulate issues of intentions (pragmatics), meaning (semantics), structure (syntactics) and form (empirics). Such signs are enacted through three patterns of organisation: through forma (the substance of a sign), informa (the content of a sign) and performa (the use of signs in coordinated action). Such a conception of enactment allows us to

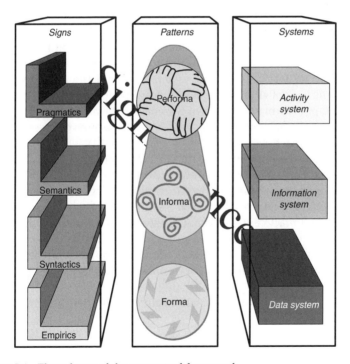

Figure P.1 Three facets of the conceptual framework

define more clearly and to relate three classes of system important to human organising: activity systems, information systems and data systems. Such systems consist respectively of the patterning of per-forma, informa and forma.

Our aim in developing this framework has not been to 're-invent the wheel'. Instead, we have attempted a synthesis of elements from a number of areas. Broadly we see no value in the intellectual gulf between the physical, psychological and social sciences and wherever possible attempt to bridge this divide. For instance, systems theory or systemics is having a renaissance in many of the physical sciences, par-ticularly biology. In contrast, semiotics is still largely positioned as a bridge across many social sciences. But semiotics as we shall see has a clear physical foundation and the systems viewpoint has much to offer an understanding of the social.

It is also difficult to discuss the interaction of signs and systems and how this interaction contributes to the phenomena of organisation without some reference to 'mind' or what we shall more broadly refer to as 'psyche'. Hence, we attempt to demonstrate how a systemic and semiotic outlook helps us better understand how the noun *information* is better expressed as the verb *in-formation* and how this process of in-formation relates to the control of action both at the individual level and at the level of groups. This is one clear example of the way in which we attempt to form better ways of considering the nature of significance not only as it concerns humans but also as it concerns other organisms and indeed machines.

Although our aim is primarily to build stronger theory, having stronger theory does not mean less relevance to practice. In fact, we would argue the opposite; as the American sociologist Kurt Lewin once said *'nothing is as practical as a good theory'*. This is because good theory guides good practice. In the final chapter we paint some of this land-scape. We consider the relevance of our framework to understanding and suggesting some solutions to a number of modern problem situa-tions, particularly in the areas of business, management and informa-tion technology.

So let us see what is significant about the enactment of significance...

Cardiff, July, 2010

References

Tapscott, D. and A. D. Williams (2006). Wikinomics: how mass collaboration changes everything. Atlantic Books, London.

Vedral, V. (2010). Decoding Reality: the universe as quantum information. Oxford University Press, Oxford.

Waddington, C. H. (1977). Tools for Thought. Jonathan Cape, St Albans, Herts.

Webber-Maybank, M. and H. Luton (2009). Making effective use of predicted discharge dates to reduce the length of stay in hospital. Nursing Times 105(15): 20–21.

1
Signs: Units of significance

Introduction

In walking down a high street in downtown San Francisco a year or so back I spotted a sign in a store window. The sign consisted of a large piece of paper with just three words written upon it in large type. It said, 'SIGNS MEAN BUSINESS'. In a sense, those three simple words, taken together, sum up what we are trying to achieve within this book. We are trying to make a case for the importance of signs within systems of various forms. Signs are critically important in all forms of activity, including business. Signs are important because they establish what it is to be human. Without signs we could not think, we could not communicate what we think and we could not ensure that we collaborate successfully in our working, home and leisure activity.

This chapter considers the nature of signs as units of significance. It is no accident that the terms sign, significant and significance in English have the same root. Very broadly a sign is anything that is significant. But what does significant mean? To help answer this question, the chapter utilises the perspective of semiotics, particularly the four-fold distinction between the pragmatics, semantics, syntactics and empirics of signs. This is sometimes referred to collectively as the semiotics ladder because the four levels act as rungs between the physical world and the social world. Within this model, pragmatics is concerned with the purpose or intentionality of a sign; semantics is concerned with the meaning or intensionality of a sign; syntactics is concerned with the structure of a sign; empirics is concerned with the physical form or representation of a sign. This semiotics ladder is one of three branches of a conceptual tree that forms the backbone to this book.

We shall begin each chapter with an interesting but non-standard case. Our purpose in doing this is to help demonstrate the relevance of a number of theoretical components that build up to form the unified conceptual framework mentioned in the prologue. In this manner, we try to keep our theoretical discussion grounded but also expanded. Our choice of examples and cases is deliberately broad because we wish to *break down* some of the conceptions that you the reader may bring to your reading of this text. In this chapter we help ground the concept of a sign by considering a case from prehistory. Over 10,000 years ago cultures in the Middle East were using clay tokens to stand for things. Many see such significant artefacts as the precursor to the invention of writing (Beynon-Davies, 2009e).

Clay tokens

Sumer was one of the earliest known civilizations and was located in southern Mesopotamia – meaning in Greek 'The land between the two rivers'. This is an area geographically located between the Tigris and Euphrates rivers, largely corresponding to modern Iraq, north-eastern Syria, south-eastern Turkey, and the Khūzestān Province of south-western Iran. The civilisation lasted from the late sixth millennium B.C. through to the rise of Babylon in the early second millennium B.C.

The cities of Sumer were not the first human cities. However, they were the first urban conurbations to practice intensive, year-round agriculture. It has been proposed that this agrarian revolution created a surplus of foodstuffs which could be stored for later consumption (Rudgley, 1999). This allowed the population to settle in one place instead of migrating with the movement of crops and herds. Intensive agriculture also allowed for a much greater population density. This, in turn, promoted developments such as forms of hierarchical social organisation, an associated division of labour, the invention of record-keeping and the development of writing.

Small clay tokens ranging between 1 and 5 centimetres across, of multiple shapes, and apparently falling into distinct categories have been found in Near Eastern sites dating between 8,000–3,000 B.C (Schmandt-Bessarat, 1978). The archaeologist Denise Schmandt-Besserat believes that such tokens represent the earliest evidence for accounting and record-keeping (Schmandt-Bessarat, 1992). Inherently she proposes that these tokens are some of the earliest examples of signs used to record economic information and were used as symbols to signify two distinct concepts. First, they served as counters and as such represented quantities of things. Second, they served to stand for some economic good or commodity. Hence, a given token signified both a type of commodity and the quantity of this commodity.

Schmandt-Besserat (Schmandt-Bessarat, 1996) suggests that the way in which tokens signified goods and quantities changed over the millennia. At first tokens were used to signify staple agricultural commodities such as wheat or maize. Later, tokens were used to signify goods manufactured by craftsmen in cities. In other words, simple tokens were initially used to signify unprocessed commodities. Over time, complex tokens evolved to signify processed commodities.

When the token system came about, circa 8,000 B.C., the first tokens consisted mainly of abstract shapes formed in clay such as cones, spheres, tetrahedrons, disks and cylinders. She suggests that these so-called *plain tokens* continued to be used until the end of the third millennium.

In about 4,400 B.C., what Schmandt-Besserat refers to as *complex tokens* started appearing in the early cities of Sumer. These tokens consisted of new shapes and the use of incised markings. She proposes that these complex tokens stood for finished products, such as bread, oil, perfume, wool and rope, and for items produced in workshops such as metal, bracelets, types of cloths, garments, mats, pieces of furniture, tools and a variety of stone and pottery vessels. It is noteworthy that these complex tokens did not replace the earlier plain tokens but were merely added to form a larger system (Figure 1.1).

The clustering of tokens at various archaeological sites suggests that a given token typically signified a small quantity of a given commodity. Tokens are frequently found in clusters varying in size from two to about one hundred. This suggests that there appears to have been a one-to-one correspondence between a given token and one unit of the commodity signified. Hence, one jar of oil could be represented by one ovoid, six jars of oil by six ovoids and so on. There were apparently only a few tokens that stood for a collection of items. For example, the lentoid disk probably signified a flock of perhaps ten animals. This meant that the token system did not allow the user to express numbers abstractly. In other words, there was no token for the concepts of one, two and three independently of the commodity counted.

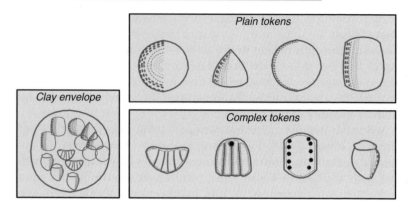

Figure 1.1   Examples of a clay envelope and clay tokens

In about 3,250 B.C., tokens started to be enclosed in hollow clay balls which Schmandt-Besserat refers to as *clay envelopes*. Initially, the 'signatures' of parties engaging in the economic transaction being recorded were imprinted on the clay envelope. Then impressions of the tokens contained in the envelope were impressed in its outer layer. After the envelope was completed it was baked, making the record persistent or difficult to alter.

The evolution of the token system appears to reflect an ever increasing need for accuracy. For example, in tokens dealing with livestock, early plain cylinders and lentoid disks apparently stood for heads of livestock. In contrast, in the fourth millennium B.C. complex tokens signified different species such as fat-tail sheep, the sex of the animal such as a ewe and the age of the sheep such as a lamb (Schmandt-Besserat, 1996). This increase in the number of token types and subtypes, which occurred in large cities of Sumer about 3,500 B.C., seems therefore to indicate a concern for more precise data and consequently a more sophisticated form of record-keeping.

Schmandt-Besserat argues that tokens were a conceptual leap, constituting a new means of encoding data (Schmandt-Besserat, 1992). The essential purpose of tokens was to keep records of things: an accounting. The shape of the token signified the thing about which the record was made. Hence, a conical type of token probably stood for a small measure of grain, while a spherical token stood for a larger measure of grain. In contrast, a cylinder token probably stood for a domesticated animal, a tetrahedron token for a unit of labour and an ovoid token for a jar of oil.

Since tokens of different kinds and in different quantities could be stored together, it has been proposed that they were used as one of the earliest forms of accounting record. Such records precluded the need for any individual to memorise the accounts. They could be referred to and understood at any future time by someone who knew what the token represented. The token system was also open-ended in that an accounting of new types of commodities merely required the addition of a new type of token to the token system, consisting of a new shape or an existing shape with new or distinctive markings (Rudgley, 1999).

Another advantage of the system was that people speaking different languages found it easy to adopt this system based on physical artefacts. The evidence of extremely wide distribution of such tokens throughout the Near East in Neolithic times seems to support this inference. Also, because of the one-to-one correspondence between the token and the commodity represented, it was relatively easy to apply operations such as addition or subtraction within the system. However, when the numbers of things to be counted was large such operations could be time-consuming and tedious.

Evidence from archaeological investigation suggests that the use of tokens for keeping accounts followed an annual cycle of activity associated with agriculture (Mattesich, 1989). Tokens appear to have been discarded after the harvest and threshing, when the crops would be stored. This suggests that transactions were made in the course of the year to be completed at the time of the harvest. If this was so, the usual length of keeping accounts in archives was less than a year.

Signs and sign-systems

Very broadly a sign is anything that is significant. In a sense, everything that humans have or do is significant to some degree. Sometimes not having or doing anything is regarded as significant. The world within which humans find themselves is therefore resonant with systems of signs. Signs are the core element serving to link issues of human intentions, meaning, the structure of language, forms of communication transmission, data storage and collaborative action.

For Charles Pierce (Pierce, 1931), signs relate people, objects and ideas: *'A sign is something which stands to somebody for something in some*

respect or capacity'. For Charles Morris (Morris, 1946), signs relate stimuli to behaviour: *'If something, A, controls behaviour towards a goal in a way similar to (but not necessarily identical with) the way something else, B, would control behaviour with respect to that goal in a situation in which it were observed, then A is a sign'*.

Signs therefore relate for some actor the symbol which stands for some referent: something that is referred to. We deliberately use the term actor here rather than person because we wish to focus on the issue of how signs are used in action. An actor is any entity that can act and thus includes, as we shall see, humans, animals and machines.

Consider the example in Figure 1.2. A particular type of clay token is illustrated here and represents a symbol. This symbol was probably produced by some actor working probably for one of the temples of ancient Sumer. It was created by this actor to stand for some referent – a commodity. In this case probably an amphora of wine.

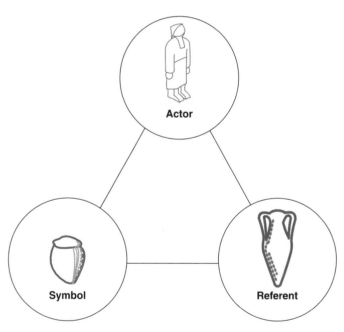

Figure 1.2   Actors, symbols and referents

But signs don't exist in isolation. They normally form parts of an organised system of representation. Steven Pinker (Pinker, 2001) argues that our genetic makeup predisposes humans to be excellent manipulators of sign-systems. A sign-system is any organised collection of signs and relations between signs. Everyday spoken human language is probably the most readily identifiable example of a sign-system.

However, the concept of a sign-system is much broader than spoken human language. Signs exist in most forms of human activity since signs are critical to processes of human communication and understanding. For example, within a face-to-face encounter, humans communicate through non-verbal as well as verbal sign-systems; colloquially referred to as 'body language' (Morris, 1979). Hence, humans impart a great deal in the way of information by facial expression and other forms of bodily movement. Such movements are also signs. The importance of such signs to human communication is evident in the recent explosion of business and personal development books purporting to reveal the 'secrets' of such body language.

But signs are also important to non-human communication such as in animal communication and in man-machine communication. In Chapter 4, for instance, we shall consider the case of a fascinating system of communication evident amongst European honeybees; while in Chapter 7 we shall consider what signification means in relation to communication in and with machines.

Note the link between the words *sign* and *significant* in English; they have the same root. Hence, the significance of signs cannot be divorced from actors. Different actors find different things significant. Many such differences in significance are due to differences in the context of communication. Within the human sphere, such context is defined by the concept of culture: a set of conventions relating to behaviour.

Consider the clay tokens of ancient Sumer. Schmandt-Bessarat (Schmandt-Bessarat, 1996) identifies sixteen main types of tokens based primarily upon shape (Figure 1.3). These include cones, spheres, discs, cylinders, tetrahedrons, ovoids, rectangles, triangles, biconoids, paraboloids, bent coils and ovals/rhomboids. She also identifies a number of sub-types based upon variations in sizes and markings. For example, cones, spheres, disks and tetrahedrons are typically represented in two sizes – 'small' and 'large'. Many shapes also have incised markings consisting of lines, notches, punches and pinched appendices. As a

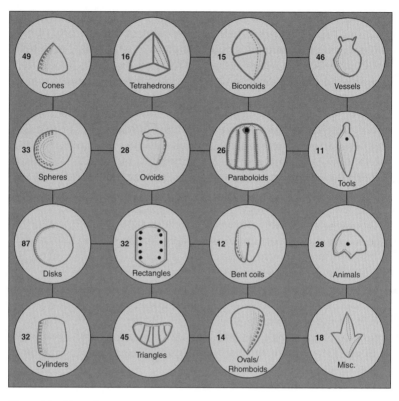

Figure 1.3   The token system as a sign-system

whole, the token system can be considered a sign-system. The numbers assigned to each type in Figure 1.3 represent the number of sub-types in each category identified by Schmandt-Bessarat.

In essence then a sign consists of a significant pattern: a pattern being a set of elements that repeat in a predictable manner. Such an idea is central to many disciplines. For instance, the American architect Christopher Alexander (Alexander, 1964) proposed that architectural design is based on a number of archetypal patterns which encapsulate fundamental principles of building design. This idea has had much influence within other disciplines such as software engineering where design patterns are proposed as general solutions to programming problems.

We shall exploit an idea due to the biologist Gregory Bateson (Bateson, 1972) and argue that a pattern is a coherent set of differences perceived as such by a community of actors. As humans, patterns may be directly observed with any of our five senses. Hence, as we shall see, patterns constitute *modulated* aspects of the world that are regarded as significant by some actors.

Inherent in the idea of a pattern is the idea that it repeats or is reproduced across more than one situation. Signs are key examples of such repeating patterns treated by two or more actors as significant. Clay tokens are clear examples of such repeating patterns. Actors in ancient Sumeria consistently produced similar shapes in clay. From the archaeological evidence and the wide distribution of such artefacts we can infer that such actors clearly regarded these shapes as significant.

Most signs are conventional patterns. Ruth Millikan (Millikan, 1984) argues that not all patterns are conventional. A pattern is only conventional if it is reproduced purely by weight of precedent and only if it is unlikely to emerge or re-emerge in the absence of such precedent. Conventional patterns are thus arbitrary patterns. Conventional patterns are patterns for which other patterns might well be substituted except for historical accident.

Certain clay tokens were meant to look like what they represented, such as in the case of the clay token which stood for an amphora of wine. These particular shapes hence could be regarded as non-arbitrary and non-conventional. However, most clay tokens constituted abstract shapes in which there is no obvious association between the shape and what it represented. Hence, there is no obvious association between a cylindrical clay token and a domesticated animal. Therefore, in the case of this majority of token types, we would say that the tokens consisted of conventional patterns. They constituted signs to which a conventional meaning was clearly assigned by groups of actors.

Semiotics and the semiotics ladder

The term semiotics or semiology is used to refer to that area devoted to the study of signs and sign-systems. Pierce (Pierce, 1931) referred to semiotics as the *'doctrine of signs'* and Morris (Morris, 1946) described semiotics as the *'science of signs'*. One of the founding fathers of modern linguistics Ferdinand De Saussure (de Saussure, 1964) used the term semiology to refer to '*a science which studies the role of signs as part of social life...*' while the anthropologist Margaret Mead (Mead, 1962) proposed the use of the term semiotics to cover '*patterned communications in all modalities*'. The eminent scholar of signs Umberto Eco (Eco, 1977), characteristically, defines semiotics as '*the discipline studying everything which can be used in order to lie*'. This is because signs are not only used to inform; they may also be used to mis-inform.

Following Pierce, Charles Morris maintained that three types of relation are important within any sign-system: the relation between signs and actors; the relation between signs and objects; the relation between signs and other signs. This led him to propose three branches to semiotics: pragmatics, semantics and syntactics. Stamper (Stamper, 1973) in his application of semiotics to issues of human organisation proposed the addition of an empirics level.

This layered model of semiotics, sometimes referred to as the semiotics ladder, serves to connect the social world with the psychological world with the physical world (Figure 1.4), and is the approach adopted here. Within this model, pragmatics is interested in the relations between signs and actors, semantics is interested in the relations between signs and objects, syntactics is interested in the relations between signs and other signs and empirics is interested in the relation between signs and matter or energy.

At the level of the social, signs are produced and used within social systems. The social layer is important because it forms the general context for communication. For communication to occur between actors, signs must exist in a context of shared understanding: what we shall refer to as collective intentionality and intensionality (Chapter 8). In terms of human actors, much of this social layer can be considered the study of culture as it affects communication – the common expectations underlying human communicative behaviour in a particular context. The reverse is also true – the way in which signs are used within social systems both reproduce and help to change such social systems.

Pragmatics links signs to actors within such social systems and is concerned with the purpose to which communication is put by such actors. Pragmatics therefore links the issue of signs with that of intention. The focus of pragmatics is on the intentions of actors engaged in communicative behaviour. In other words, intentions link sign-systems to action.

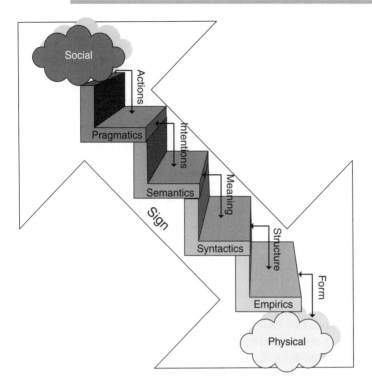

Figure 1.4   The semiotics ladder

Semantics links signs to objects and is concerned with the content or <u>meaning</u> associated with a sign. Semantics is the study of the association between signs and the 'world' and hence can be considered the study of the link between symbols and their referents or concepts.

Syntactics links signs to other signs and is therefore concerned with the <u>structure</u> of signs. Syntactics as an area studies communication in terms of the logic and grammar of sign-systems. Hence, syntactics is devoted to the study of how signs relate together within their encompassing sign-system.

Empirics links signs with matter or energy and is the study of the <u>form</u> of a sign. Empirics is concerned with the physical form of a sign; how signs are represented and stored as well as how signs are transmitted along communication channels.

Therefore, empirics relates signs to physical or technical systems. In such systems, each sign has a material or physical form independent of the creator and user of the sign.

The precise nature of the rungs of the semiotics ladder may be difficult to comprehend at this early stage. Bear with me. In Chapters 6 through 11 we shall cover each of these rungs in far greater detail – starting with empirics and ending with pragmatics.

Clay tokens as signs

Sumerian clay tokens were utilised in support of human activity at the dawn of civilisation. However, many of the patterns evident in the creation and use of these signs have recurred across human history and human cultures.

We clearly have no direct access to the social systems within which clay tokens were used and to the purpose (pragmatics) to which such tokens were put. Nevertheless, based upon an interpretation of the existing evidence, Schmandt-Besserat proposes that clay tokens were used as one of the earliest forms of accounting within one of the first human societies characterised by organised religion and social hierarchy (Schmandt-Bessarat, 1992).

The evidence for this is three-fold. First, the creation of the token system coincided with a new settlement pattern characterised by larger communities. In other words, the rise of the first tokens coincides with the advent of a hierarchical or rank society and the emergence of a new type of leadership overseeing community resources. Second, the tokens recovered in the tombs of prestigious individuals suggest that, from the Neolithic to the Bronze Age (6,000–3,500 B.C.), the use of clay tokens served as an instrument of power for an elite controlling access to commodities. Third, in all the major ancient Near Eastern cities such as Uruk and Susa complex tokens occur in archaeological levels in which seals featuring the ruler have been discovered. They also occur in public buildings built according to an identical plan and decorated with typical mosaics and containing grain measures. In other words, the administrative centres that yield complex tokens were the seats of a large bureaucracy, housed in similar buildings, using the same administrative devices (complex tokens, seals and grain measures) and, most importantly, were headed by the same powerful ruler. The complex tokens can be considered, therefore, being an essential element of an emerging temple bureaucracy used by Sumerian rulers to govern and control the distribution of commodities in the first city-states.

Human memory is sufficient to support cooperative and simple activities between individuals in small communities. As communities grow, activities, particularly those reliant on economic exchange, need to take place between strangers and generally are more complex in nature, reliant typically on some division of labour. At some point in human development signs started to be used to make records of things. The key purpose of records is to extend and compensate for the limitations of human memory. Records of economic transactions institutionalise memory of past economic exchanges and the obligations placed upon individuals engaged in such exchange. Accurate record-keeping is also critical in establishing and sustaining trust between strangers engaging in economic exchange. Records account not only for the types and quantities of commodities exchanged, they are also important for supporting social relationships of ownership and debt (Mattesich, 2000).

It is therefore likely that the clay tokens could have fulfilled a number of distinct purposes within these early societies. The creation of a clay token might have been used to make commitments such as that a given actor promised to hand over one unit of cloth as tribute to the temple. It might also have been used to declare that the signified tribute had been paid to the temple. Finally, it is likely to have been used to assert that a given quantity of a particular commodity was held in the temple stores.

The American philosopher John Dewey (Dewey, 1916) suggested that a word is three things: a fence, a label and a vehicle. The same could be said more generally of the concept of sign. A sign is a 'fence' in the sense that it sets a conceptual boundary around some thing and is used to distinguish one thing from another. A sign is a 'label' in that it acts as a convenient reference standing for something else. Finally, a sign is a 'vehicle' in the sense that used with other signs as a sign-system it is a means for describing and debating with the world as well as acting upon it. Pragmatics is particularly interested in the sign as a vehicle – as a means for supporting action. Syntactics is particularly interested in the sign as a fence – how conceptual boundaries are created with symbols. Semantics is particularly interested in the idea of the sign as label and as such is the study of what symbols refer to.

The collection of both plain and complex tokens constituted as a whole a sign-system. The physical makeup of the tokens themselves and

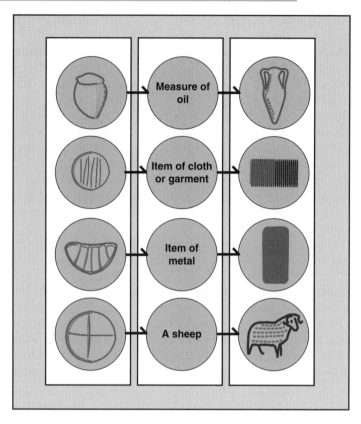

Figure 1.5   The meaning associated with particular token types

the ways in which the features of each token allowed the user to distinguish between one type of token and another constituted the syntax of the sign-system.

Given the demise of the human community that used this particular sign-system, the semantics of tokens is subject to interpretation. As we have seen, Schmandt-Besserat argues that a token was used to stand for two concepts through its existence and shape: the quantity of some commodity and the type of commodity. Hence, there was meant to be a one-to-one correspondence between the token itself and what it represented within the sign-system. For example, one token of a given shape represented one item of a commodity such as grain or livestock. Schmandt-Besserat believes that there is sufficient evidence for a number of associations such as those illustrated in Figure 1.5 for particular types of plain and complex token.

Collecting together a group of tokens and wrapping them in a clay envelope is also likely to have had some distinct intent. The impressions on the outside of many clay envelopes contain impressions of the objects contained inside. There are also other markings which have been interpreted as some 'signature', perhaps of the actors involved. Enveloping tokens in this manner is therefore likely to have stood for a discernable transfer of commodities from one actor to another. From this we can infer some of the pragmatics of clay tokens.

Conclusion

Signs then are units of significance. Signs mediate between the social world on the one hand and the physical world on the other. Semiotics or semiology is used to refer to that area devoted to the study of signs and sign-systems. Semiotics has four branches which offer four perspectives on the sign and act as a 'ladder' between the physical world on the one hand and the social world on the other. Pragmatics is concerned with the purpose of a sign; semantics is concerned with the meaning of a sign; syntactics is concerned with the structure of a sign; empirics is concerned with the physical representation of a sign.

Our case from prehistory, the Sumerian clay token, is a classic example of a sign. As a token it has an empirical or physical form consisting of a shape formed in clay. The physical makeup of the tokens themselves and the ways in which the features of each token allowed the user to distinguish between one type of token and another constituted the syntax of this sign-system. We clearly do not have direct access to the human community that used this particular sign-system and therefore the semantics or meaning of tokens is subject to much interpretation. There is clearly however sufficient evidence from the archaeological record to suggest the use of tokens to signify quantities of specific commodities. Such tokens appear therefore to have been used to represent the accumulation of agricultural and manufactured products by a community and to account for this collective wealth for the purposes of economic re-distribution.

William Rowland (Rowland, 2003) summarises a number of suppositions gleaned from the historical study of communication. The first supposition is that all communication technologies (or what we would refer to as information and communication technologies) are extensions of basic, innate human communication capabilities. The second supposition is that different communication 'technologies' impact upon the cognitive structures of human beings over time, influencing changes in social organisation.

The work of Schmandt-Besserat in relation to clay tokens supports such reasoning. In her research, an inherent association is proposed between the use of tokens for record-keeping purposes and the rise of social hierarchy, centralised religious places of worship and the development of writing in ancient Sumeria. She states, '*Tokens and clay tablets functioned as an extension of the human brain to collect, manipulate, store and retrieve data. In turn, processing an increasing volume of data with more complex tokens brought people to think with greater abstraction*' (Schmandt-Besserat, 1992).

Each chapter within this book is provided with a unique logo. A logo is usually some form of graphic used by organisations, groups and individuals to aid and promote instant recognition. Our logos are designed to promote the fundamental concepts underlying the framework described in this book.

The logo used at the beginning of this chapter stands for the general concept of a sign. The arrow, embodied in the idea of the pointing hand, is used to emphasise the properties of a sign as a 'vehicle' and a 'label'. In other words: a sign 'points'. When a human forms her hand in this way she is using it to direct the gaze of some other actor to some other thing.

Therefore, a sign is anything that stands for something else. Signs used by humans tend to be mostly arbitrary in nature. By this we mean that there is no inherent association between a particular sign and what it stands for. In the case of clay tokens as discussed in this chapter, although certain tokens were meant to look like what they represented, most were merely abstract shapes to which a conventional meaning was assigned by groups of people.

Here we have a clear example of the power of signs and sign-systems. Certain elements of the world can be chosen to be significant and manipulated independently of what they stand for. This means further that complex order or organisation can be assembled or generated from simple units by the application of recursion to the relation of standing for or pointing to. In other words, a sign can be taken by convention to stand for a further sign which stands for something else, and so on.

Hence, signs are magical because they act as conceptual 'glue', allowing us to understand interconnections between various forms of order or 'organisation' in the world. They not only represent things, they communicate things and through such communication they impact upon psychological and social structures. Signs, as we shall see, interconnect conventional patterns of order in three domains which we shall refer to as forma, informa and performa.

Any such patterning of order we generally denote with the label system – as we have already done so in referring to the patterning of signs as a sign-system. Therefore, it is to this concept of a system that we turn next.

References

Alexander, C. (1964). Notes on the Synthesis of Form. Harvard University Press, Harvard, Mass.

Bateson, G. (1972). Steps to an Ecology of Mind. Balantine books, New York.

Beynon-Davies, P. (2009e). Neolithic informatics: the nature of information. International Journal of Information Management 29(1): 3–14.

de Saussure, F. (1964). Course in General Linguistics. Peter Owen, London.

Dewey, J. (1916). Essays in Experimental Logic. University of Chicago Press, Chicago.

Eco, U. (1977). A Theory of Semiotics. Macmillan, London.

Mattesich, R. (1989). Accounting and the input-output principle in the prehistoric and ancient world. ABACUS 25(2): 74–84.

Mattesich, R. (2000). The Beginnings of Accounting and Accounting Thought. Routledge, London.

Mead, M. (1962). Keynote Address. Approaches to Semiotics: transactions of the Indiana University Conference on Paralinguistics and Kinesics. Indiana University, US.

Millikan, R. G. (1984). Language, Thought and Other Biological Categories: New Foundations for Realism. MIT Press, Cambridge, Mass.

Morris, C. W. (1946). Signs, Language and Behavior. Prentice-Hall, New York.

Morris, D. (1979). Manwatching: a field guide to human behaviour. Harry N. Abrahams, London.

Pierce, C. S. (1931). Collected Papers. Harvard University Press, Cambridge, Mass.

Pinker, S. (2001). The Language Gene. Penguin, Harmondsworth, Middx.

Rowland, W. D. (2003). Foreword. Communication in History: technology, culture, society. D. Crowley and P. Heyer. Boston, Pearson Education.

Rudgley, R. (1999). The Lost Civilisations of the Stone Age. Simon and Schuster, New York.

Schmandt-Bessarat, D. (1978). The Earliest Precursor of Writing. Scientific American 238(6).

Schmandt-Bessarat, D. (1992). Before Writing. The University of Texas Press, Austin, Texas.

Schmandt-Bessarat, D. (1996). How Writing Came About. The University of Texas Press, Austin, Texas.

Stamper, R. K. (1973). Information in Business and Administrative Systems. Batsford, London.

2
Systems: Patterns of order

Introduction

We are surrounded by systems. Our bodies are made up of various systems such as a digestive system and a central nervous system. We live on a planet that is part of the solar system. We engage with people in groups that form social, political and economic systems. We are educated in the use of number systems. Various forms of human organisation would collapse without information systems.

At first sight these varied systems appear to have little in common. However, on closer examination we see that all these examples represent what we might describe as a patterning or ordering of things. Systems theory, systems thinking or as we prefer to call it – *systemics* – is the attempt to study the generic features of such patterning.

Signs take their shape within a number of different types of system and form patterns of significance in such terms. This chapter utilises concepts from systemics to help us understand the way in which such patterns of significance emerge and how such patterns bridge between the social, the physical and the psychological worlds. Within human organisation we are particularly interested in the way in which signs are used to express intentions and generate action. This is clearly the realm of the social world or social action. However, we are also interested in the relationship between signs and the physical world – particularly in the ways in which signs are represented and manipulated using 'technology'. Finally, we are interested in the role of signs both as physical and social constructs within in-formation and the way in which this process is critical to decision-making and control. This falls clearly within the realm of the psychological world.

Therefore, we use the term system not only to encapsulate the notion of the organisation of signs but also to denote the organisation of activity, communication and representation. Thus, the semiotics ladder discussed in Chapter 1 can be seen to capture the nature of signs as socio-physical or sometimes socio-technical phenomena. This means that signs inter-relate between and within three different patterns of order, which we shall refer to as forma, informa and performa.

Forma consists of the substance or representation of signs, informa the content or communication of signs and performa the use of signs in coordinated action. These different domains of patterning allow us to more clearly define three levels of system of interest to human organisation: activity systems, information systems and data systems.

To help ground our discussion, we move our lens across time and space and consider a case from the Victorian period in industrial Britain – the Railway Clearing House (Campbell-Kelly, 1994). This case helps illustrate how signs take shape within systems of activity, information and data and how this interaction creates and re-creates patterns of significant order.

The railway clearing house

The British railway network first began to be developed during the 1830s (Wolmar, 2007). By 1840 some 1,500 miles of railway track had been laid and many problems, such as that associated with standardisation of railway gauge, had been resolved. It therefore became possible for railway passengers to embark upon long journeys such as that between London and Newcastle. However, such journeys required passengers to use the railway lines of several different railway companies. Such companies not only managed and operated their own trains, carriages and freight wagons; but they also managed and operated their own sub-network of railway lines.

Hence, for long passenger, parcels or goods journeys that crossed the networks of two or more railway companies, the revenue from a journey had to be divided appropriately amongst the railway companies involved (Bagwell, 1968). Initially, private arrangements between companies for such through traffic enabled the division of a composite fare. However, as the number of railway operators grew, this 'accounting'

challenge proved monumental for individual companies. Also, companies were frequently unable to agree on the terms of a composite fare. This led to passengers being turned out of their railway compartments at the junctions between the networks of railway operators. Passengers then had to purchase tickets for the next leg of their journey. The same happened in the case of goods traffic. Philip Bagwell cites the case of a wealthy horse owner who had to send a servant to a particular station simply to lead his horse from one train to another.

The idea for a Railway Clearing House is generally attributed to George Carr Glyn and Kenneth Morrison (Campbell-Kelly, 1994). Glyn was the partner of a banking firm and chairman of the London and Birmingham railway. Morrison was chief accountant of the same railway and was to become the first executive secretary of the Railway Clearing House. The idea for this organisation appears to have been modelled on the Bankers' Clearing House on whose executive committee Glyn sat.

In 1841, Glyn persuaded his own railway and that of eight others to jointly subscribe to a railway clearing system. The initial focus of the endeavour was upon establishing an intermediary organisation that would handle information associated with through-passenger traffic. Under this system, passengers would be able to book a journey from any station to any other station amongst the network of participants. The Clearing House would then be responsible for distributing revenue from fares to its participants. In time, the Clearing House would also assume responsibility for clearing the transport of parcels and goods on the railway network. Parcels were carried in the goods van of passenger trains; the transport of goods demanded special freight wagons.

The Railway Clearing House began operation on 2 January 1842. Initially, its staffing consisted of George Carr Glyn as chairman, Kenneth Morrison as a part-time secretary and six full-time clerks. By 1845, 16 companies had joined the system and details of over a half a million passenger/journeys were being processed in that year. By 1848, 43 companies had joined, raising the scale of the network to some 887 stations. This demanded an increase in staffing to 45 clerks and a change of accommodation to offices in Seymour Street, near Euston station in London. These offices were eventually substantially re-modelled and extended to create the famous 'long office', which was the largest single office in Britain at the time of its completion in 1855.

As the railway network of the country continued to expand, the Clearing House grew to meet the increased demand for its service. By 1861, 500 clerks worked in the Clearing House and were organised into a number of working divisions. In 1864, the Railway Clearing House had 873 clerks and processed a total of 1.6 million settlements between participating railway companies. By 1874, the number of settlements totalled 4.9 million. However, staff numbers had not increased in proportion and comprised only 1,325 clerks. This was presumably because of increasing productivity amongst the workforce.

In 1876, the Railway Clearing House was at peak capacity and became an organisation that was respected worldwide. At this time, its staff comprised over 1,000 clerks and 500 so-called 'number-takers' which we describe below. Staff were organised into three large divisions: the Coaching department with 352 clerks; the Mileage and Demurrage department with 276 clerks and 500 number-takers; and the Merchandise department with 720 clerks. In addition, there was a small Lost Luggage department with a complement of 16 clerks.

The Coaching department had responsibility for dividing up receipts from passenger and parcel traffic between member companies. The department was headed by an assistant secretary and divided into seven sections. Three Passenger sections with 55 clerks each, dealt with receipts from passenger traffic. Similarly, three Parcel sections, again with 55 clerks each, dealt with receipts from parcels traffic. The final section was a Ticket section with 25 clerks that processed passenger tickets. Each section was headed by a senior clerk and subordinates were graded and paid in a scale usually based upon experience. It took approximately three months for a clerk to achieve 'novitiate' status and they were only considered experienced after five or more years of service.

The largest division in the Railway Clearing House was the Merchandise department, which was responsible for dividing revenues from goods traffic. It was divided into 16 sections each with 44 clerks.

The Mileage and Demurrage department was the smallest department but handled the most complex activities. By the 1870s, it was possible for any railway company to transport a wagon-load of merchandise on any of the lines of the railway network using any suitable vehicle, whether or not the company actually owned the vehicle. The mileage function of this department divided the revenue between many different actors who participated in this process: the company that organised the train, the company that owned the wagon, the companies that owned the railway lines and the companies that provided terminal facilities. A system of fines, known as demurrage, was enforced to ensure that unused rolling stock was returned to its owner promptly.

Clearly the 'systems' of the three departments of the Railway Clearing House worked differently. For our purposes, we shall focus on describing the systems underlying the work of the Coaching department, since they were the simplest of those used by the Clearing House.

The principle underlying the work of this department was straightforward. Any fare paid for a through-journey needed to be divided amongst the companies involved and a levy raised to help fund the operation of the Clearing House. The complexities lay in dividing up a given journey into its constituent parts and handling the vagaries of different fare structures. This took the monthly returns from booking offices and the tickets collected from passengers at the end of their journey and transformed them into payments made to railway companies.

The Railway Clearing House supplied all through-passenger tickets to member companies. These tickets were printed on 6 cm by 3 cm green card. Tickets were issued to each booking office on the railway network and were pre-printed with all the common destinations available on the network. Tickets were issued in batches of one hundred and within each batch an individual ticket was printed with a serial number by machine. Serial numbers continued between batches.

Tickets were sold in strict ascending serial number order from within a batch. At the end of each day, the booking office clerk would record the serial number of the lowest-numbered unsold ticket in each batch and send these numbers with the cash collected to the head office of the railway company. At head office these numbers were used to check the cash received against tickets sold. They were used to compile a monthly summary of tickets sales and receipts for the Railway Clearing House.

Tickets were collected at the end of each passenger's journey, usually at railway stations. These were sent on in batches to the head office of the railway where staff would sort them by destination. The batches of sorted tickets, along with a summary of ticket sales, constituted a monthly return from a railway company to the Ticket section of the Coaching department.

In the Ticket department 25 boy clerks would arrange the incoming tickets into serial order sequence and reconcile them with the monthly summaries of sales. Frequently, such reconciliation identified anomalies. For instance, there might be a missing half-fare ticket for a child within a batch. In such cases, a senior clerk was called in and a standard form was completed inviting explanation from the offending railway company. Ticket clerks were also responsible for determining the actual route taken by a passenger from a number of possible routes taken. This was determined by inspection of the punches made in a given train ticket by train conductors. Each railway company used a distinctive set of 'snippers' to make this possible. In 1876, there were approximately 3.3 million tickets processed in this manner.

After all the tickets from relevant batches had been verified the results would be tabulated on another standard form and passed on to the appropriate passenger section. In the passenger section the proceeds from an individual ticket needed to be divided between participating companies. To do this, clerks had to inspect a complex set of fare structures. The simplest fare structure was the 'ordinary fare' which consisted of the sum of local fares applicable for the individual legs of a passenger journey. In contrast, for certain discounted fares a division had to be made on the basis of the total mileage between all the junctions in the railway network covered by a passenger journey. Hence, maps of the railway network, detailing such junctions and the mileage associated with branches of the network had to be inspected.

In terms of each passenger ticket sold in the railway network, the company that sold the ticket was classed as the 'debtor' of the transaction. All other companies involved in the passenger journey became 'creditors' in the transaction. A months-worth of tickets generated thousands of debits and credits against each of the 80 companies in the railway network. Processing this volume normally took a couple of weeks work by clerks. At the end of this activity, the total debits and credits were summed for each company and on this basis a single transfer of funds was made between the Railway Clearing House and the railway company. The aggregate result of these financial transfers had to balance. Hence, clerks normally worked in pairs, each checking the work of the other.

Systemics

It has become popular in numerous aspects of life to refer to problems as systemic. But what actually underlies a systemic approach to things?

Three key principles are significant: that of holism, emergence and purpose.

The ancient Greek philosopher Aristotle's dictum that *the whole is more than the sum of its parts* implies that it is important to investigate and understand phenomena holistically – as a whole. Early ideas in Systemics can be seen as a reaction against the reductionism inherent in what is commonly referred to as the scientific method. *Reductionism* involves dissecting a problem into its smallest parts, attempting to understand the workings of parts and building up a conception of the whole from this understanding. Reductionism has been extremely successful at developing natural scientific understanding. However, a major criticism is that a reductionist approach frequently fails to provide an adequate understanding of the whole from the interaction of parts. This approach is hence often accused of 'not seeing the forest for the trees', particularly in relation to understanding human psychological and social phenomena. In contrast, *holism* takes the whole as the primary focus of investigation. Holism is interested in studying how the complex interaction of parts creates and sustains the identity and behaviour of the whole.

Systemics is therefore interested in how the behaviour of the system emerges from the interactions among system parts. From this viewpoint, a system is a complex entity that has properties that do not belong to any of its constituent parts, but emerge from the relationships or interaction of its constituent parts. This is really what is meant by: *the whole is more than the sum of its parts.*

The concept of a system is normally seen as a teleological entity – an entity with a purpose. This means that the defined purpose of some system normally equates to defined or observed goals and the behaviour of the system is designed to fulfil such goals. The goals frequently set clear measures of performance in terms of what we shall refer to in Chapter 5 as a control process. This is part of some system that steers it in the direction of its goals.

Consider what it means to describe the Clearing House case as systemic. First, to understand the case we need to consider this example of human organisation as a whole. This means that we need to describe how its parts – actors such as railway company employees, passengers, rolling stock and so on – interacted with the staff of the Clearing House. Second, we need to understand how this interaction created order in the sense of regularities or patterns of behaviour. Third, we need to see how such regularities or patterns fulfilled collective goals – both in terms of the Clearing House itself and the railway system it served.

Core concepts of systems

The term *system* has a Greek origin; derived from *syn* meaning together and *histemi* meaning to set. In very broad terms, and from a static point of view, a system can be seen to consist of a collection of objects that are related or set together. But by setting together is also meant that a system is dynamic in the sense that the objects potentially influence each other: they behave.

Our very general definition of a system clearly encompasses a vast array of phenomena. For a certain interesting class of systems (open systems) on which we shall focus, a popular way is to specify certain types of objects and relations to be of interest. Systems of this type are generally portrayed in terms of an input-process-output model existing within a given environment. In this view, systems can be seen as being composed of the following elements: one or more operational *processes* or mechanisms of transformation; one or more sets of *inputs* from and *outputs* to actors in the environment; one or more *control* processes.

The *inputs* to a system are the resources it gains from actors in its environment; some of which may be other systems. The *outputs* from a system are those things that it supplies back to actors in its environment.

Processes represent the dynamic elements of systems and constitute mechanisms of transformation. A process consists of an inter-connected set of actions (behaviour) necessary to transform some input(s) into some output(s).

It is possible to define two major types of processes relevant to any system: operational processes and control processes. Operational processes achieve the defined purpose or transformation of some system. Control processes (see Chapter 5) maintain the behaviour of operational processes in desired directions and hence maintain the overall identity of the system.

Consider the Coaching department within the clearing house in light of our definition of a system. The key inputs into this 'system' were the monthly returns from booking offices and the tickets collected from passengers. The key outputs from the system were payments made to railway companies. The key operational processes within this system involved activities such as the batching and sorting of tickets, the totalling of fares upon forms and the calculation of creditors and debtors. What is not discussed in the case but which can be inferred is that managers within the Coaching department monitored the work of clerks to ensure the smooth flow of activity. This would have been the critical control process for the system.

As can be inferred from our description above, defining a system means deciding what is to be included in a system and what is to be included in its *environment*. This means defining a boundary for the system. It means drawing the figure (the system) against its ground (the environment). The decision as to what to include as within a system and what to exclude is a decision for the system modeller. A system is a key 'tool for thought' and systemic thinking is necessarily a process of abstraction – a process of resolution of what is environment, system and sub-system.

Hence, it is possible to consider the clearing house as a whole as a system and its environment as the railway network of Great Britain at the time. Or, as we have done above, we can treat each department within the Clearing house as a system, such as the Coaching department. In this case, the environment expands to include actors both within and without the Clearing house, such as the Mileage and Demurrage department.

This example illustrates that hierarchy is an inherent property of most systems. In viewing systems we frequently use a recursive lens. In other words, we can view a system on various levels, each level of which can be conceptualised in terms of a system. Hence, the environment of a system may be viewed as a system in its own right and a process, which is part of one system, may be treated as a system in turn, and so on.

The behaviour of a system can be defined in terms of the notion of *state* or more precisely in terms of changes of state. The state of a system is defined by the values appropriate to the system's attributes or state variables. Theoretically, at any point in time a value can be assigned to each of such variables.

The set of all values assumed by the state variables of a system at one time defines a system's state. *Variety* is a measure of the complexity of a system (Ashby, 1956). Using the idea of a system's states, variety may be defined as the number of possible states of a system. For many systems the variety of the system may be incomprehensibly large in the sense that the number of possible states may not be precisely countable.

Hence, the complexity or variety in any system of human organisation such as the Clearing House is potentially enormous. This is because such a system consists not only of a multitude of actors and relations between actors; it also consists of complex patterns of activity, communication and representation. Hence, within the clearing house a multitude of actors such as passengers, train guards, booking clerks, railway company clerks and clerks within the various departments of this organisation communicated not only through the spoken word but also through a large range of formal communications such as tickets, booking forms and waste forms. It is through interaction between such patterns of action, communication and representation that the complex order of human organisation which was the Clearing House emerged.

We can illustrate this complexity using a simple example (Beer, 1966). Consider a collection of actors, each of which we represent as a node labelled A-F in the diagram illustrated in Figure 2.1. We assume that

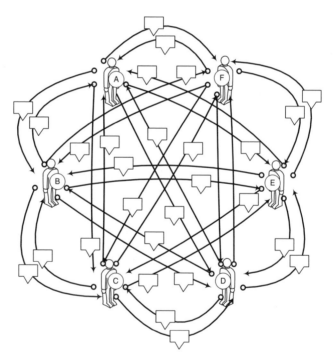

Figure 2.1 The variety of a simple system

each actor can theoretically communicate with each other actor in the group. We draw arrows between nodes to represent such communication and draw such arrows in both directions between any two nodes to indicate that, for instance, relation A → B is different from B → A. In other words, actor A can make an utterance to actor B and actor B can make an utterance to actor A; each is a separate speech act. In this sense, each relation or communication channel is effectively a 'switch' that may be turned on or off, perhaps indicating the effect of one node in the network on another. Here we have a simple system in which a collection of things now interacts; it operates or behaves.

Hence, we could consider this as a simple model of a human communication network in which perhaps we wish to study the movement of communication around the network; perhaps the way in which some bit of gossip travels amongst the group. In this system, one state of the system is when the communication channel A → B is open and all the other channels closed. Another state is when B → C is open and all other channels are closed and so on.

As we have seen, using the idea of a system's states, variety may be defined as the number of possible states of a system. Hence, since there are 2 possible communication relations between each of the 6 actors in the network, there are n(n-1) or 6 times 5 possible relations between nodes, which is 30 possible relations (Figure 2.1). If we regard a state of the system as being a particular configuration of active and inactive communication relations then there are over 2^{30} (1,073,741,824) possible states for the entire system. This is a measure of the variety inherent in this comparatively simple system. Hence, for many actual social systems in which there are many more actors and relationships than in our example, the variety of the system may be incomprehensibly large.

Patterns of order

Jan Dietz (Dietz, 2006) uses the root of the Latin verb *informare*, from which the English word *information* is taken, to define three perspectives on the sign: forma, informa and performa. These three perspectives act as the 'glue' between semiotics on the one hand – which we considered in Chapter 1 – and systemics on the other – which is the topic of the current chapter (Figure 2.2).

Forma refers to the 'substance' that carries a sign. Forma deals with the physical nature of signs and therefore crosses the physical/technical

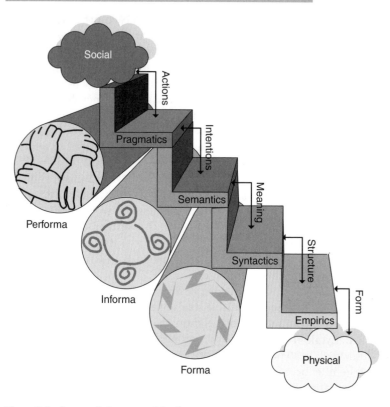

Figure 2.2 Forma, Informa and Performa

and empirics levels on the semiotics ladder. Informa deals with the content and meaning of signs. It concerns the use of signs in communication and therefore crosses the syntactics and semantics levels of signs on the semiotics ladder. Performa refers to the use of communication to make decisions and to take appropriate social action. Performa therefore crosses the pragmatics and social levels of the semiotics ladder.

Three symbols are used within Figure 2.2 to stand for forma, informa and performa. Forma is represented by a cycle of signal symbols used within electronics to indicate the patterning of physical transformations required to communicate and is the topic of Chapter 6. Informa is represented by a cycle of speech glyphs familiar to the Aztec or Mexica peoples of mid-America. This cycle of informa represents the patterning of communication between two or more actors, and is the topic of Chapter 8. Performa is represented by a cycle of entangled hands to indicate the patterned coordination of action. Coordinated action is the binding of one actor's actions to those of others, and is the topic of Chapter 10.

We introduce the term *enactment* to relate systems of signs to systems of representation, communication and activity. This term is frequently used to refer to the bringing into force of some piece of legislation. We use it in one of its alternative senses; that used within drama. Enactment in this context refers to the action in which the text of the drama is given expression. Enactment is to act out, represent or perform as if in a play. It is the process of acting the part of a character on stage; dramatically representing the character by speech, gesture and action.

We would claim that the patterning of order characteristic of human organisation is enacted through three inter-related forms of action. Formative acts amount to the enactment of forma: acts of data representation and processing. Informative acts constitute the enactment of informa: acts of communication involving message-making and interpretation. Performative acts constitute the enactment of performa: the performance of coordinated action within human groups.

A performative act consists of an actor at a given time and in a given space undertaking some transformation of the world. There are many examples of performative acts in the case of the Clearing House. For instance, booking clerks issuing train tickets, passengers undertaking train journeys, train drivers driving trains on particular journeys, railway workers loading and unloading goods and parcels onto and from trains, train guards checking tickets and station guards collecting tickets.

For coordinated performance actors have to communicate mutual intention through informative or communicative acts. However, as we have seen in Chapter 1, one should not assume that all communicative acts involve acts of speech. For instance, within the Clearing House a passenger might assert her intention verbally to wish to take a particular train from a particular embarkation point to a particular destination. However, during her journey she hands over her railway ticket to a railway conductor. This physical act suffices to communicate an assertion of her right to travel on the particular train.

Performative acts rely upon communicative acts for effective coordination. Communication is built upon formative acts: acts of data representation and processing. Within the clearing house such formative acts were particularly devoted to the creation, updating and retrieval of business forms of various types.

The operation of the Clearing House is an exemplar of the rise of the office and its associated 'technology' as a solution to the control crisis caused by the increasing complexity of activities associated within developing industrial society. Alan Delgado (Delgado, 1979) defines an office in terms of its minimum function, *'which is to direct and coordinate the activities of an enterprise. In an office information is received, recorded, arranged and given out. It is a place where information can be safeguarded'.* During the early years of the industrial revolution, offices were initially small, family affairs in which the internal operations of industrial firms were controlled and coordinated through informal communication. Oral communication was used for immediate purposes and letters for communications distant in space and time.

By the mid-1800s under the impetus of a new systematic philosophy of management *'the informal and primarily oral mode of interaction gave way to a complex and extensive formal communication system depending heavily on written documents of various sorts'.* Martin Campbell-Kelly (Campbell-Kelly, 1994) claims that large-scale offices developed in Britain during the 1840s. In the period between 1850 and 1870 clerical work within such offices experienced rapid growth. As we have seen, such offices began to employ hundreds of clerks processing millions of business transactions.

Within such offices systematic management emphasised and promoted the use of standard and formal communications ('forms') for numerous purposes such as the issuing of managerial orders, tracking of worker activity and the production of summary reporting (Yates, 1989). We tend to forget that the use of the 'form', consisting of a set of defined and named areas for representing things, is as a communication convention a comparatively recent invention. This conventional pattern of forma appears to date back only a few hundred years.

Not surprisingly perhaps, many of the early manuals on management focused specifically upon issues surrounding the design of such forms. The clearing house case includes description of a multitude of office forms used to record or physically represent aspects of communicative acts. For instance, the form illustrated in Figure 2.3 was used to compile

						Classes									
Progressive Numbers				Stations	Route	Single.				Return.				Rate	1st & 2nd Class	3rd Class.	Party.	Total.
From	To	Children	Non-issued			1.	2.	3.	Party.	1.	2.	3.	Party.					

P. 1.

_____Railway

RAILWAY CLEARING HOUSE

RETURN of Passengers' Fares Booked at the_____Station.

Month of_____187_

Figure 2.3   Form P.1

a monthly abstract of ticket sales from each booking office run by a railway company.

Types of system

Within our framework, therefore, the term system is used not merely to encapsulate the notion of the organisation of signs. It is also used to denote the organisation of activity, communication and representation. Thus, the semiotics ladder can be seen to conceptualise signs as socio-physical or socio-technical phenomena. We further argue that signs inter-relate between and within three different levels of system of interest to human organisation: activity systems, information systems and data systems (Figure 2.4).

At the level of the physical, signs are used within systems of representation. We use the term *data system* to refer to such systems of forma. Data systems consist of patterns of formative acts. As we shall see, human speech analysed at the level of phonemes can be considered a data system as can the Incan artefact of the khipu and an image stored as pixels on a modern peripheral storage device.

At the level of the social, signs are used within systems of activity. We use the term activity system to refer to such systems of performa. Activity systems consist of patterns of performative acts. As we shall see,

33

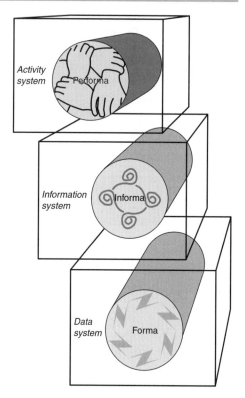

Figure 2.4   Types of system

any form of coordinated activity can be considered an activity system. When the dominant actors in such an activity system are humans we refer to it as a human activity system.

An information system is a mediating construct between activities (activity system) on the one hand and representation (data system) on the other. We thus use the term information system to refer to systems of informa. Information systems consist of patterns of informative or communicative acts. As we shall see, communicative acts rely on a collective background of significance.

Consider another example from the Clearing house case in this light. To refresh, the Mileage and Demurrage department was the activity system within the Clearing House which enabled the rolling stock of participating companies to be pooled. Such rolling stock at this time comprised as many as a quarter of a million vehicles consisting of loco-motives, carriages and wagons. The department enabled the owners of such rolling stock to be compensated, the users of such rolling stock to be charged and also encouraged the prompt return of vehicles to their owners.

Every item of rolling stock in the network was given a unique ser-ial number. When a goods train was assembled, a card was fixed to each vehicle in the train which detailed this serial number, the name of the owning company, its destination and its contents. As the train moved around the railway network it picked up and dropped off wag-ons. Hence, the Clearing House not only had to monitor a goods train's movements, it also had to monitor its changing composition during its journey. This was achieved through two types of return: the weekly returns of staff known as number-takers and the weekly returns of the railway companies themselves.

At each junction between the individual networks of railway compan-ies a number-taker was employed by the Clearing House. Each number-taker had the responsibility for recording the destination of each train passing through as well as the details of an average of 30 vehicles mak-ing up the train. The number-taker recorded such data into a small blue-book provided for this purpose. In the intervals between trains arriving he would then transcribe the details carefully onto a weekly abstract sheet that would be sent to the Clearing House. This information was supplemented by a weekly return from each railway company listing all 'foreign' vehicles passing through its stations.

From the 276 clerks employed within the Mileage and Demurrage department one or more account clerks were assigned to each railway company within the network that had put rolling stock into the system. It was the responsibility of this account clerk to track all the vehicles for his company and to debit the companies that used them.

This meant that the weekly abstract sheets sent in by number-takers needed to be visually scanned for events at which an item of rolling stock had left its parent network and entered the network of another company. This also needed to be checked against the weekly returns from the railway companies.

Once such an event was detected the account clerk would create a movement record for the vehicle on a 'waste sheet': a large form ruled into vertical columns and on which details were recorded in a

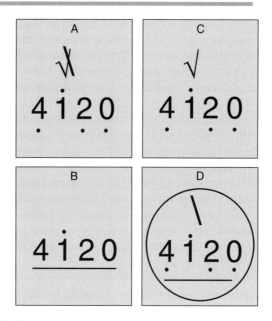

Figure 2.5   Coding on waste sheets

specialist short-hand. Figure 2.5 illustrates aspects of a form of coding used by clerks in the Mileage and Demurrage department for this purpose. The various symbols were used to signify distinct states a train went through on one particular journey undertaken on the railway network. On the basis of this signification, further actors calculated charges to be made for mileage and demurrage against particular railway companies.

Hence in exhibit A, this piece of forma signified that the vehicle identified by serial number 4120 had been subject to both a mileage and a demurrage charge (coded as a tick and a dash). The dots below the serial number signified the number of days taken for the return journey of the vehicle – in this case, three. The dots above the serial number indicated the number of days taken in the outbound journey – in this case, one. In exhibit B, the line placed under the serial number indicated that the wagon had a tarpaulin. In exhibit D the circle indicated that the wagon was lightly loaded or empty and hence was not subject to a mileage charge.

In this description we have examples of patterns making up systems of activity, information and data. Waste sheets comprised a complex data system in which symbols were used to represent both the composition of wagons and wagon movements. Such waste sheets were used by clerks to communicate their understanding or 'accounting' of the state of this world over a particular period of time. In these terms, the patterning of this communication was a critical information system which accounted for or modelled its encompassing activity system: wagon movements around the railway network.

Hence, a particular entry on a waste sheet such as that in exhibit D in Figure 2.5 represented a key example of forma in this case. This forma served to communicate informa, namely that wagon 4120 had a tarpaulin and was lightly loaded. It was hence not subject to a mileage charge for the journey which took one day for the outward journey and three days for the return journey. It was however fined for demurrage, presumably because the wagon was not returned to its owners promptly enough. This informa hence served to model or represent a number of complex activities or performa undertaken in the wider activity system.

Conclusion

The logo placed at the beginning of this chapter is meant to stand for a system interacting with its environment. The arrowed circle is meant to emphasise the way in which systems consist of continuous and cyclical patterns. Through the accomplishment of such patterns a system sustains itself; it maintains identity. To enable their continuity, a certain class of systems with which we are primarily concerned can be seen to interact with their environment. They receive inputs from such an environment and they output to this environment.

We would argue that much of this interaction between system and environment is modified through or mediated by signification: the use of signs. Hence, we have used two of our sign arrows to indicate that a system, in the language of control which we shall consider in more detail in Chapter 5, can be said to attenuate its environment through signs and amplify itself to its environment through signs. The wavy lines on the logo therefore stand for the environment of the system; they are wavy to indicate that the environment, just like the system it surrounds, is itself in continuous flux. This flux serves to continuously perturb the system and causes it to continuously adapt.

Signs, therefore, take their shape within systems of various forms and such systems can be seen to constitute the continuing patterning of order or organisation in the world. The term system is therefore used to refer not only to the patterning of signs, but also to denote the patterning of activity, communication and representation.

This means that signs inter-relate between and within three different patterns of order which we have introduced as forma, informa and performa. Forma constitutes the substance or representation of signs, informa the content or communication of signs and performa the use of signs in coordinated action. These three patterns of order allow us to more clearly define three levels of system of interest to human organisation: activity systems, information systems and data systems. Activity, information and data systems are by definition all systems. They can hence all be considered in terms of core systemic concepts such as inputs, outputs, processes and control.

Our account of the clearing house case demonstrates the sociotechnical nature of systems within human organisation. A coherent account of any information system cannot be provided without considering the information technology used, the communication this enables and the activities supported. Our account of the Railway Clearing House clearly demonstrates this. The account entangles the activity of the early railways, the information required to support the work within this system and the 'technology' employed in support of communication.

Another way of viewing this is to say that the patterning of order characteristic of human organisation is enacted through three interrelated forms of action. Formative acts amount to the enactment of forma: acts of data representation and processing. Informative acts constitute the enactment of informa: acts of communication involving message-making and interpretation. Finally, performative acts consist of the enactment of performa: the performance of coordinated action within human groups.

Activity systems then consist of the patterning of performa. They are systems of performance and consist of regular and repeating patterns of performative acts. The key output from such systems is therefore action or activity. As such, performa takes place at the level of the social on the semiotics ladder and includes consideration of pragmatics in action. As an example, the key activity system of the Victorian railways consisted of the movement of trains, passengers and goods around the railway network. The key problem for this activity system was that the railway network of the time consisted of a multitude of competing actors. This meant that a passenger wishing to make a long journey which crossed the lines and used the trains of a number of different train companies had to purchase a number of separate railway tickets. The solution to this control crisis was the invention of an organisation, namely the Clearing House, which facilitated coordinated 'performance' across the railway network.

Data systems consist of the patterning of forma, are systems of symbols and consist of regular and repeating patterns of formative acts. Data systems naturally output data. Forma crosses the physical, empirics and syntactics levels of the semiotics ladder and is concerned with the representation and manipulation of symbols. Within this chapter, the Railway Clearing House case has been used as a way of emphasising the critical invention of the business form as an information technology underlying office communications during the Victorian era. This particular genre of forma proved so successful that it is still evident in the design of modern 'information technology': the digital computing systems of the modern day.

Information systems mediate between activity and data systems and consist of the patterning of informa. Information systems are systems of communication and consist of regular and repeating patterns of informative or communicative acts. The key output from such systems is information. Therefore, informa crosses the semantics and pragmatics levels of signs and is concerned with the meaning of symbols and their use within human action.

For instance, the information system of the Railway Clearing House involved various people involved in collective communication such as railway company clerks, number-takers and Clearing House clerks. The case of the Railway Clearing House highlights the central role of information systems in the control of performative action. To engage in such control an information system must serve to 'model' critical aspects of its encompassing activity system. The records written on forms within the Railway Clearing House served to model not only objects such as trains, wagons, passengers and parcels; they also modelled the movements of trains and passengers around the national railway network. Such a model was used to make decisions as to the amounts owed to particular railway companies for passenger and train traffic. In this sense, the Clearing House as an information system served to 'control' the performance in the wider activity system.

The collision of signs, the concept discussed in Chapter 1, with systems, the concept of the current chapter, produces a sign-system. Sign-systems are particularly important because they cut across these three ways in which the patterning of order is enacted within human organisation. In other words, signs are enacted in three entangled ways – through forma, informa and performa. In this way signs act as a systemic glue relating issues of action, communication and representation together.

So let us begin to examine this concept of a sign-system in detail...

References

Ashby, W. R. (1956). An Introduction to Cybernetics. Chapman Hall, London.

Bagwell, P. S. (1968). The Railway Clearing House in the British Economy 1842–1922. Allen and Unwin, London.

Beer, S. (1966). Decision and Control: the meaning of operational research and management cybernetics. John Wiley, Chichester.

Campbell-Kelly, M. (1994). The Railway Clearing House and Victorian Data Processing, in Information Acumen: the understanding and use of knowledge in modern business, L. Bud-Frierman, Editor. Routledge, London.

Delgado, A.. (1979). The Enormous File: a social history of the office. John Murray, London.

Dietz, J.L.G. (2006). Enterprise Ontology: Theory and Methodology. Springer-Verlag, Berlin.

Wolmar, C. (2007). Fire and Steam: a new history of the railways in Britain. Atlantic Books, London.

Yates, J. (1989). Control through Communication: the rise of system in American management. John Hopkins University Press, London.

3
Sign-systems: Patterns of significance

Introduction

In her Earthsea quartet of fantasy novels (Le Guin, 1993) Ursula Le Guin describes a world in which magic is a reality. Wizards perform such magic through the use of special words, and the use of these words allows wizards to manipulate things in the world of Earthsea. In a sense, this use of words is not entirely remote from our use of words in the real Earth. Word use in this fantasy world is an extension and exaggeration of our own everyday relationship with words and language.

This is because words as signs are Janus-like; they have two faces. Our use of word-signs allows us to describe and reflect upon reality. But when we use words we also 'create' major aspects of the reality we are describing. This means that we all generate sign-magic on a daily basis, particularly within our working life.

Take a key instance. Medical practitioners are prime examples of professionals that use signs as 'magic'. They first diagnose your illness on the basis of signs. In other words, they read your symptoms as a means of highlighting what may be wrong with you. They then use some esoteric term (usually with Latin roots) to stand for your illness. On the basis of this signification they will prescribe perhaps a range of treatment, probably including drugs, again with many weird and wonderful names, some proprietary: some generic.

Signs are also critical to many aspects of management. Managers issue instructions or directives using signs. They also receive reports or assertions of what is happening in their business. This may cause them to signal commitments as plans for action. Signs are hence critical not only to communication but also to control of action. This is because signs help stitch together organisation of activity, communication and representation.

However, signs do not exist in isolation. They form part of complex wholes which we referred to in Chapter 1 as sign-systems. A sign-system is any organised collection of signs and relations between signs. Sign-systems amount to the patterning of signification in the world: distinct domains of signs which interact and inter-relate.

Therefore, signs are important to any form of communication: to non-human communication such as animal communication and to man-machine communication. As a key example, and in an attempt to make the topic 'strange', we treat the interesting case of human facial expressions as a sign-system. Such a sign-system is interesting both because of its apparent universal basis in the biology of Homo Sapiens and because it appears to be also used by some of our closest evolutionary relatives: the higher apes.

Facial expressions

Consider the illustrations of a person's face in Figure 3.1. The figure is meant to illustrate the same person performing a number of different facial expressions. The key question is: can you 'read' these illustrations

Figure 3.1   Four common facial expressions

of facial expressions? In other words, can you work out what is being conveyed by each of these facial expressions; what does each facial expression stand for?

When people are asked what these facial expressions 'mean' across the world, they generally come up with the same answers. Facial expressions such as these are generally associated with some common human emotions. Facial expression 1 is normally seen to stand for something like 'happiness' while facial expression 2 stands for 'sadness'. Facial expression 3 stands for something like 'anger' and facial expression 4 stands for 'disgust'.

Emotions are mental states and we can use words, such as I have done in English, to refer to particular emotions. But the words of course differ which language you use – there is an arbitrary association between the set of symbols used and the thing being referred to. However, if we treat a facial expression as a symbol, the relationship between symbol and mental state appears non-arbitrary. Indeed, if we also treat the entire set of facial gestures as a sign-system, there appears a commonality of meaning across human cultures which suggests that this is in some way 'hardwired' into our makeup as a species.

2009 was the 150th anniversary year of the publication of Charles Darwin's ground-breaking work, *The Origin of the Species*. Twenty years after its publication, Darwin published another book of which he was equally proud: *The Expression of the Emotions in Man and Animals*. In this book Darwin described his pioneering investigation of emotive facial expressions in humans and their closest evolutionary relatives. His key conclusion was that '...*the young and the old of widely different races, both within man and animals, express the same state of mind by the same movements*' (Darwin, 1998).

Darwin's proposition that emotive facial expressions are common across all human races and cultures was confirmed by the later work of Paul Ekman (Ekman, 1998). Up until the mid-20th century most anthropologists believed that facial expressions were entirely learned and should therefore differ among cultures. Pioneering work by Ekman and others eventually supported Darwin's belief to a large degree, particularly for expressions of anger, sadness, fear, surprise, disgust, contempt, happiness and caring.

For instance, in a study by Ekman, a 'stone age' native tribe of New Guinea were chosen as subjects (Ekman, 2003). The study consisted of 189 adults and 130 children from among this very isolated population.

Participants were told a story in their native language that related to one particular emotion. They were then shown two or three pictures of facial expressions and asked to match the picture which best expressed the emotion within the story. Most of the sample identified the correct emotion, except for some mis-interpretation between fear and surprise. This led Ekman to the conclusion that a common range of emotions relate to a common range of facial expressions regardless of cultural background.

But facial expression is not unique to humans. After many years of study, Darwin concluded that there was a marked similarity between such expressions in apes and humans (Darwin, 1998). The muscular physiology of the face determines what expressions can be made by humans and what by apes. Chimpanzees, for instance, can reproduce all of the standard facial expressions found amongst humans except frowning. Hence, Darwin implicitly proposed the existence of a deep structure for such a sign-system which crosses species situated on the same evolutionary branch.

Systems of signs

The term language is frequently used as a synonym for a sign-system. In its broadest sense the term language refers to an agreed system of signs used to convey messages between a set of communicative agents. Language is important for humans because as Stephen Pinker states, *'a common language connects the members of a community into an information-sharing network with formidable collective powers'* (Pinker, 2001). This suggests an inherent relationship between information, communication, language and action.

We prefer to use the term sign-system rather than language for a number of reasons. First, the use of the term language tends to carry with it connotations of human language, particularly human spoken language. As we have argued, human spoken language is only one example of a sign-system; albeit probably one of the most complex sign-systems we know of. For example, in traditional forms of face-to-face communication, we know that humans communicate a great deal through non-verbal sign-systems of various forms. Hence, humans communicate a great deal by way of facial movements and other forms of bodily expression. Such expressions are also signs. Second, we wish to utilise the same concept of a sign-system in consideration of other forms of communication such as animal communication and man-machine communication. Examination of simpler forms of such systems of signs within non-human communication can help to illuminate some of the essence of communication and in particular can help to provide tentative answers to the question of the nature and function of communication (see Chapter 4).

So what is a sign-system? As a system, a sign-system consists of some organised pattern of signs. By organised we mean that:

- Each sign within the sign-system has coherence. By this we mean that it is relatively easy to distinguish one sign from another by users of the sign-system. Such an accomplishment normally involves perceiving clear conceptual relations between the signs in a sign-system, particularly the relation of difference.
- A sign-system displays a certain stability of signification. By this we mean that there is a reasonably stable relationship between the symbols and what they stand for within the sign-system as used by a group of communicants. Without such stability signs would not be able to communicate anything between actors.
- Stability implies that signs can be expressed and interpreted in a standard way amongst some group of actors. Communicants are able to express a certain sign and other communicants are able to both recognise the sign and infer or interpret its intended meaning.

Take the example of human emotive facial expressions. Does it pass the test of criteria we have set for a sign-system? First, and as we shall see in a later chapter, humans are extremely good at distinguishing one facial expression from another, relying on some significant differences in the way in which the muscles of the face are used in different facial expressions. Second, facial expressions seem to be relatively universal across human cultures and are associated, within such cultures, with a stable set of meanings. Human actors tend to produce facial expressions in an unconscious way; other actors are able to interpret these expressions in a standard way and respond in terms of such interpretation.

Types of sign-system

Sign-systems can be distinguished on a number of levels, such as in terms of the actors involved, the medium or mode of communication, the level of formality and the level of complexity associated with the sign-system.

It is conventional to distinguish between those sign-systems involved in human communication and those involved in non-human communication. This implies that different sign-systems are needed to facilitate communication between different types of actor: human-human communication, animal-animal communication, human-animal communication, machine-machine communication and human-machine communication. There is much debate about the similarities between animal – animal communication and forms of human-human communication. However, we frequently forget that machines such as computer systems are significant actors in the modern world and that much communication within current society is either directly between man and machine or is augmented by machine in the sense that communication between human actors is facilitated through some form of technology.

Given that signs are used to communicate, sign-systems can be distinguished in terms of their modality or communication channel. For instance, within the human domain, it is conventional to distinguish between spoken and written forms of languages. As already mentioned, there are also the non-verbal or body 'languages', consisting of non-verbal cues, expressions and gestures which convey meaning within human interaction.

Sign-systems can also be distinguished in terms of their level of formality. For example, it is possible to distinguish between natural/ informal and artificial/formal sign-systems. Certain sign-systems such as spoken English are described as natural sign-systems in that they have grown or evolved 'naturally' amongst a speech community and hence as a matter of course are continuously changing. Certain other sign-systems are invented, created or designed. Most natural sign-systems have a complex, continuously changing syntax and semantics and as such they are best described as informal sign-systems. Other sign-systems are designed in the sense that they have a highly specified and normally limited formal syntax and semantics. Hence, they are referred to as formal sign-systems. A key example here is the set of programming languages, used to communicate with and instruct computers.

There is clearly a vast difference between the complexity associated with a collection of facial expressions and the complexity of spoken English as a sign-system (Chapter 3). Hence, it is possible to place sign-systems along a continuum of complexity. One measure of complexity is the *variety* of the sign-system. We might define this as the number of distinct symbols possible for use within the sign-system. Another feature which distinguishes the complexity of languages as sign-systems is *compositionality*. Within human languages, signs such as words can be combined in various ways to form new units of meaning such as phrases and sentences.

It is important to recognise that a given act of communication may be made up of messages drawn from more than one sign-system. For example, when we say a human actor 'speaks', we are normally referring to an act of communication made up of more than just words. Much meaning will be expressed by such features as the intonation of a person's voice and through bodily movement. This explains how in a typical telephone conversation much of the 'information' that would be conveyed when speaking to another person face-to-face is lost.

Let us revisit the example of human emotive facial expressions in terms of these features. This particular sign-system is reasonably simple but actually has all the elements of a sign-system. First, it is clearly a collection of signs. As we have seen, it is possible for human actors to clearly distinguish one instance of a facial expression from another. The collection is organised in the sense that each symbol within the sign-system has a stable meaning amongst a collection of actors and actors are able to produce and distinguish one sign from another. There is hence an observable order to the expression and interpretation of these signs. They recur in use across different actors and situations.

Facial expressions as sign-systems appear to be used in both human-human communication and animal-animal communication, at least as far as the great apes are concerned. There is also evidence of its use within human-animal communication. For instance, domesticated dogs seem able to 'read' human facial expression with some proficiency. Also, there is a developing use of such a sign-system in man-machine communication. For example, computer animation systems now contain routines for generating appropriate facial expression by animated characters and some progress has been made in building recognition systems for a range of common facial expression.

As mentioned previously, facial expressions are a prime example of a non-verbal sign-system. As such, when a person is making a facial expression he is using part of what in system terms we would refer to as his *effector apparatus* to produce the symbol and signal the emotion felt to some other actor. Unlike spoken language which relies on manipulating the human vocal tract and mouth, the effector apparatus in this case consists of the complex musculature of the human face. Facial expressions also rely upon the human *sensory apparatus*; particularly the human sense of sight and the transmission of light. This sensory apparatus is critical for perceiving the distinct features of particular facial expressions (Figure 3.2).

Mediating between the sensory and effector apparatus of an actor is some form of internal environment. This must act to take the inputs generated by the senses and make decisions as to appropriate outputs (actions). We begin discussing some of the features of this internal environment in Chapter 5.

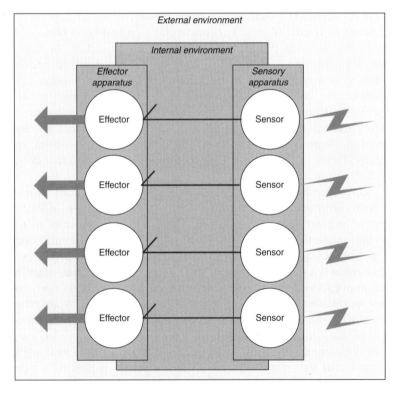

Figure 3.2   Sensory and effector apparatus

Facial expressions clearly act as symbols in that they stand for or are about something else. The range of facial expressions stand for, or are about, a common range of human emotions. Each facial expression, taken as a whole, is a symbol which relates to the idea or concept of a particular emotion. In this mode, facial expressions serve as what we shall refer to in Chapter 8 as expressive communicative acts. The creation of a particular facial expression serves to signify to other actors the emotion called out in the actor making the expression.

As we discovered in Chapter 1, most signs are arbitrary. In other words, there is a conventional or cultural association between a symbol and what it stands for. Take the example of the hand gesture illustrated in Figure 3.3. The same gesture (forming an 'o' with the first finger and

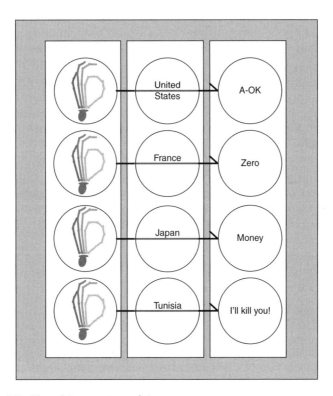

Figure 3.3   The arbitrary nature of signs

thumb of the hand and holding it up with palm facing outwards) can be used to communicate different things, depending on the cultural context. To actors in the USA it means a-ok. In France it means zero. In Japan it means money. In Tunisia it means I'll kill you! (Morris, 1979)

Facial expressions are however particularly interesting in that they are what we might refer to as natural signs. This is why we have deliberately referred to these symbols as facial expressions rather than facial gestures. Gestures such as that illustrated in Figure 3.1 can stand for almost anything (they are arbitrary signs), involve all parts of the body and are typically learned through social experience. Expressions stand only for emotions, normally restrict themselves to facial movement and appear to be part of our makeup.

Facial expressions are therefore not arbitrary: the production and interpretation of facial expressions seems part of our biological inheritance. Hence, people from different cultures are able to interpret facial expressions in a common way. What is also interesting about facial expressions is that many such expressions are involuntary or unintentional. In other words, the person does not purposefully make the facial expression. Indeed, what is even more interesting is that when actors consciously attempt to control facial expression, observers can frequently distinguish between involuntary and voluntary expressions. For example, people are able to distinguish between a 'natural' smile and a 'false' smile.

As we have mentioned, as a collection of symbols, the range of human emotive facial expressions is a relatively simple sign-system. Calculating the variety of this sign-system is clearly related to the debate as to the nature of human emotion and the number of distinct emotional states. Unfortunately, there is no agreement as to the list of mental states that constitute emotions and there have been various attempts to build taxonomy of emotions. Some common English words that act as labels for emotional states include: agony, anger, confusion, contempt, desire, disgust, excitement, fear, frustration, happiness, sadness and surprise. However, different languages label emotions differently; some cultures apparently lack words for particular emotional states. Ekman (Ekman and Friesen, 1971) maintains that most agree that humans manifest at least five distinct emotions: anger, disgust, happiness, fear and sadness. The common facial expressions associated with these emotions, along with the neutral expression (that used not to convey any emotion or to hide emotion), are illustrated in Figure 3.4.

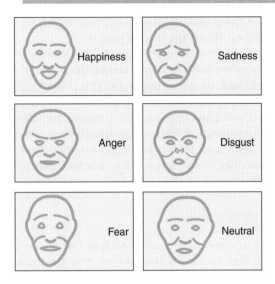

Figure 3.4 Facial expressions and emotions

Sign relations

A sign-system is a system. It can hence be seen as a collection of symbols related to other aspects of the world in various ways. Within Chapter 1 we talked of four such types of relations as being important. First, symbols relate to actors. Second, symbols relate to the world. Third, symbols relate to other symbols. Fourth and finally, symbols relate to physical representation as matter or energy.

Symbols must form part of the common understanding of some group of actors. Such actors must be able to create such symbols and to be able to interpret such symbols appropriately. In other words, symbols must be about something; they must have some intent. This is the level of pragmatics on the semiotics ladder.

Symbols must be able to stand for something else. That something else we refer to in Chapter 8 as an intension. The set of common intensions amongst a group of actors forms the bedrock for any communication. This is the level of semantics.

Symbols must relate to other symbols if only in being distinguishable from other symbols. However, within any reasonably useful sign-system

51

symbols can be composed into larger structures which have meaning in and of themselves. This is the level of syntax.

Finally, symbols must have physical characteristics. Actors must be able to use their own body or some external 'technology' to form symbols from some form of matter or energy. This is the level of empirics.

Hence, any sign-system should be analysable in terms of pragmatics, semantics, syntactics and empirics. For instance, facial expressions are clearly about imparting emotional state (pragmatics); a particular facial expression is associated with a particular emotion (semantics); facial expressions are distinct and recognisable symbols (syntactics) and consist of the manipulation of the musculature of the face (empirics).

Actors and sign-systems

One facet not covered in an earlier section but which clearly serves to distinguish sign-systems is the type of actor involved in using the sign-system. Zoosemiotics is the application of semiotics to the study of animal communication. One of its founding fathers, Thomas Sebeok, (Sebeok, 1972) argues that communication through sign-systems is an inherent feature of all living entities – from solitary cells through to entire organisms and collections of organisms. In recent years, the study of communication amongst varied organisms has shed light on the nature of communication, as we shall see in the next chapter. Sebeok also distinguishes between internal communication within an organism, which he refers to as *endogenous communication* and communication between organisms, which he refers to as *exogenous communication*.

Zoosemiotics is typically contrasted with anthroposemiotics: the application of semiotics in the study of human communication. However, key linkages are possible between zoosemiotics and anthroposemiotics. The central argument within much of this literature is that specific modes of communication have evolved within different species to contribute to the survival of such species. Hence, human communication is considered an extremely sophisticated evolution from animal communication; essentially a development from primate communication. On the one hand, anthroposemiotics can be seen to be an evolution from or a specialisation of zoosemiotics. On the other hand, anthroposemiotics can be seen to be substantially different from zoosemiotics. This perspective particularly focuses upon the distinctive nature of human language as compared to modes of animal communication.

Our focus is primarily upon exogenous communication between organisms; particularly exogenous communication supporting social behaviour. However, exogenous and endogenous communication are clearly related and the degree to which exogenous communication is reliant upon endogenous communication will be touched upon at various points within this work. The degree to which an organism can 'communicate' with itself is related to the contentious issues of mind and intentionality which we cover in Chapters 5 and 8.

Our focus is also mainly on anthroposemiotics, and particularly on the role of human sign-systems within forms of human organisation. However, we take the position that an understanding of human signification is only really possible upon a bedrock of signification in the animal world. On the one hand, we work with the assumption that an examination of animal communication, as we shall see in the next chapter, helps illuminate the essence of communication in general. Our perspective is also based in the assumption that study of simpler forms of signification evident in the animal world helps us better understand the nature of human communication. This allows us to discern a clear relationship between forms of animal communication and human communication. On the other hand, we examine the degree to which human semiosis (the use of signs) differs from modes of animal semiosis. This allows us to highlight what is distinctive about human as compared to animal communication.

Consider the case of the 'language' of prairie dogs – a species of ground squirrel found in North America. Prairie dogs are highly social animals that live in large colonies or 'towns' consisting of collections of prairie dog families and which can span hundreds of acres on the North American plains. Gunnison's prairie dog is one of five species of the prairie dog, whose mode of communication has been the subject of close study. The biologist Con Slobodchikoff and his team has been researching the behaviour of prairie dogs for over twenty years and has become convinced that these animals *'have one of the most advanced forms of natural language known to science'* (Slobodchikoff, Perla et al., 2009).

Prairie dogs use a variety of warning barks to indicate the presence of different types of predators such as badgers, coyotes, weasels and raptors. Each bark is a combination of one or two high-pitched audible syllables, with the second syllable typically lower and deeper than the first. Such warning calls can be considered signs that contribute to the survival of members of this species because such signs serve to inform other prairie dogs that danger lurks nearby. Each call can last for as long as thirty minutes and can be heard for nearly a mile away; the intensity of the signal increasing as danger moves closer and only ending when danger has passed.

How to tell a lie

Animal communication, such as that of Gunnison prairie dogs, tends to be framed as any behaviour on the part of one animal that has an effect on the current or future behaviour of another animal. *'The essence of animal communication is that one animal influences another in some way'*. Richard Dawkins and John Krebs (Dawkins and Krebs, 1978) in an influential paper published in the late 1970s went so far as to suggest that communication is more a matter of one animal manipulating another than of information transmission. Hence, they argued for study of the purpose of communication, since much animal communication is designed to deceive. Umberto Eco (Eco, 1977), as we have seen in relation to his theory of semiotics, defines a sign as anything that can be used to lie. This is an attempt to sum up the notion that it is in the nature of signs not only to enable what we shall refer to in Chapter 8 as in-formation but also to act as a resource for mis-in-formation.

Facial expressions are signs and hence can potentially be used to lie or deceive. A facial expression can be used not only to in-form but also to mis-in-form. In terms of emotive expressions, such signs are not only used to transmit felt experiences of a person to some other person, but they may also be used to deceive.

Lying or deception is not unique to the human species. Many other species of animals attempt to deceive other animals through signalling. But what is lying? Broadly, at least within the human domain, it amounts to a mis-match between what an actor intends (an actor's mental state) and what the actor is communicating.

As we have indicated, facial expressions are interesting because many such expressions appear involuntary, meaning they are not available to conscious control. This means that it is not possible to lie with such expressions. Signifying sadness through a facial expression must correspond with the mental state of feeling sad.

The difficulty of attempting to lie using facial expressions can be illustrated using the facial expression of the smile. As indicated above, a sincere or involuntary 'Duchenne' smile involves contraction of the zygomatic major muscle (lip corner puller) and inferior part of orbicularis oculi muscle (cheek raiser). This smile is an external expression of a person experiencing joy or happiness. In contrast, an insincere and voluntary smile typically involves contraction of the zygomatic major muscle alone. Such a smile is frequently used in social occasions to ease social interaction but is unlikely to represent a joyous internal state in the actor producing the facial expression.

However, it is evident from our description of sign-systems above that in any communication situation between two human actors more than one sign-system is likely to be used to communicate. Hence, lying may also be evident in the mis-match between what is being communicated via two or more sign-systems at the same time.

For example, when actor A asks 'how are you feeling?' actor B person might reply 'I am feeling great!' However, this verbal communicative act does not match with the facial expression made by actor B, which in fact is signifying sadness. The non-verbal channel is actually communicating one mental state of actor B, while the verbal channel another. The verbal communication channel is being used, at least technically, to deceive.

Conclusion

The logo at the start of this chapter is inherently a composite of the two logos from Chapters 1 and 2. It is meant to emphasise that the flow of signs (represented by arrows) occurs not only between system and environment, it also occurs between systems themselves. Hence, human actors as systems are not only interacting with their physical environment through natural signs, but also with their social environment through arbitrary signs. In both cases we can speak of the presence of a sign-system.

Signs amount to structural and meaningful differences within complex wholes which we have referred to as sign systems. We defined a sign-system as any organised collection of signs and relations between signs. Sign-systems amount to the patterning of signification in the world: distinct domains of signs which interact and inter-relate. The term sign-system is used to refer to any resource used in communication. It encompasses all forms of such resource within all forms of communication such as human communication, animal communication and machine communication.

As a system, a sign-system consists of some organised pattern of signs. By organised we mean that each sign within the sign-system has coherence. A sign-system also displays a certain stability of signification. This means that signs can be expressed and interpreted in a standard way amongst some group of actors.

Human facial expressions were considered in this chapter as a sign-system. Each facial expression, taken as a whole, acts as a distinct symbol. Each facial expression serves to stand for the idea or concept of a particular human emotion. In this mode, facial expressions serve to communicate feelings or emotional expression in a standard and consistent way between two or more actors. The creation of a particular facial expression serves to signify to other actors the emotion called out in the actor.

Sign-systems such as this can be distinguished on a number of levels: in terms of the actors involved, the medium or mode of communication, the level of formality associated with the sign-system and the level of complexity of the sign-system. Some sign-systems such as human facial expressions appear near universal across a species and hence might be regarded as 'natural' sign-systems.

In organisms with a more complex cognitive apparatus a distinct and revolutionary jump appears to have been taken. Most sign-systems within the human sphere are arbitrary. In other words, the relationship between symbols and what they signify relies not on some natural association but upon convention. When we say that a pattern is conventional we mean that regularity in the behaviour of a population from some species is evident but that this behaviour is not inherited. Instead, the regularity relies on tradition, precedent or culture. This implies that signs are not a given in the sense of being innate but are learned.

However, the distinction between natural and arbitrary signs is not a dichotomy but more a continuum. For instance, there is some evidence to suggest that many higher mammals such as the Gunnison prairie dog use signs which have many arbitrary features. Infant prairie dogs are not born with ability to reproduce alarm calls. Instead they appear to learn to gradually refine their alarm calls to match those of adults. There is also some evidence of differences in the structure of calls between distinct prairie dog colonies, leading some to suggest the existence of distinct dialects amongst prairie dog 'language'.

We have used the term communication at a number of points in this chapter, since sign-systems are inherently used to communicate. For this reason, in Chapter 4 we consider this issue in greater detail. When we speak of communication it is conventional to speak of it in terms of the transfer of information. But as we have seen sign-systems may also be used to mis-inform and hence to deceive. This highlights one of the facets of information that make it difficult stuff to get to grips with; it probably is not even 'stuff' at all, as we shall see in Chapter 8.

References

Darwin, C. (1998). The Expression of Emotions in Man and Animals. Oxford University Press, Oxford.

Dawkins, R. and J. R. Krebs (1978). Animal Signals: information or manipulation. Behavioural Ecology: an evolutionary approach. J. R. Krebs and N. B. Davies. Oxford, Oxford University Press.

Eco, U. (1977). A Theory of Semiotics. Macmillan, London.

Ekman, P. (1998). Afterword. The expression of emotions in man and animals. C. Darwin. Oxford, Oxford University Press.

Ekman, P. (2003). Emotions Revealed: understanding faces and feelings. Weidenfield and Nicholson, London.

Ekman, P. and W. V. Friesen (1971). Constants across cultures in the face and emotion. Journal of Personality and Social Psychology 17(2): 124–129.

Le Guin, U. (1993). The Earthsea Quartet. Puffin books, London.

Morris, D. (1979). Manwatching: a field guide to human behaviour. Harry N. Abrahams, London.

Pinker, S. (2001). The Language Gene. Penguin, Harmondsworth, Middx.

Sebeok, T. A. (1972). Perspectives in Zoosemiotics. Mouton, The Hague.

Slobodchikoff, C. N., B. S. Perla, et al. (2009). Prairie Dogs: Communication and community in animal society. Harvard University Press, Cambridge, Mass.

4

Communication: The medium is not the message

Introduction

In the 1960s, Marshall McLuhan famously coined the phrase, *the medium is the message* (Mcluhan, 1994). By this he meant that communication media rather than the content of messages conveyed should be the focus of study. This influential statement has acquired something of the status of an aphorism: a universal statement of truth. But in our terms it makes a fundamental mistake: that of treating knowledge of communication media as equivalent to a complete understanding of communication. This chapter begins the process of explaining why communication is much more than media or channels of communication.

The nature of significance clearly relies upon communication. The standard way of discussing communication is in terms of a classic model due to Claude Shannon (Shannon, 1949), which focuses solely on the medium of communication. In this chapter we discuss some of the limitations of this model and introduce an augmented model of communication closely coupled to the layered model of signs introduced in Chapter 1. Within this augmented model, human communication is seen as a process involving the interaction of a number of elements: actors, intentions, messages, signals and communication channels.

Norbert Wiener originally subtitled his classic book on Cybernetics – *Control and communication in animal and machine* (Wiener, 1948), and implied by this that the issue of communication was central to understanding the 'control' of behaviour amongst animals, humans and machines. To help ground our discussion, we examine a classic case from animal communication or zoosemiotics – that of the 'dances' of the European honeybee (Beynon-Davies, 2010). An analysis of this case in terms of our developing framework helps highlight some of the essence of what communication means and how this relates to the concept of a sign-system. It also helps highlight some critical differences between animal and human communication.

The dances of the European honeybee

In the 1950s and 1960s the Austrian scientist of animal behaviour (ethologist) Karl Von Frisch carried out a series of studies which revealed evidence of communication amongst European honeybees (Gould and Gould, 1995). He found that when a honeybee scout discovers a useful source of nectar it flies back to its hive and then performs a 'dance', observed by other bees. The details of this dance appeared to communicate a number of things including the distance to the food source from the hive and the direction of the food source. A number of further studies have extended knowledge of communication amongst this particular species of insect.

The honeybee dance was first documented by Aristotle and has been cited by numerous and eminent authors from a variety of disciplines including Carl Gustav Jung, John Haldane and Charles Morris. It is frequently used as a critical resource within a number of linked debates such as those over the nature of animal mind (Chapter 5) and the nature of language. Here, we use it primarily as a resource for unpacking ideas about communication and its relationship to activity and representation.

The diagram in Figure 4.1 illustrates the bee dance as a performative pattern: a coherent, structured and repeating sequence of performative acts (Beynon-Davies, 2010). Within the figure each box represents a performative act while the dotted arrows indicate the sequencing or precedence of such acts. It is through observing regularities in such performance that Von Frisch and others were able to infer the presence of some form of communicative process. In other words, observation of such behaviour demonstrated the mutual patterning of performance amongst two or more bees. When one bee danced in a certain way, the behaviour of other bees was affected in a predictable pattern.

One should note that this performative pattern is only one amongst many in the life cycle of a worker bee. Other patterns include resting,

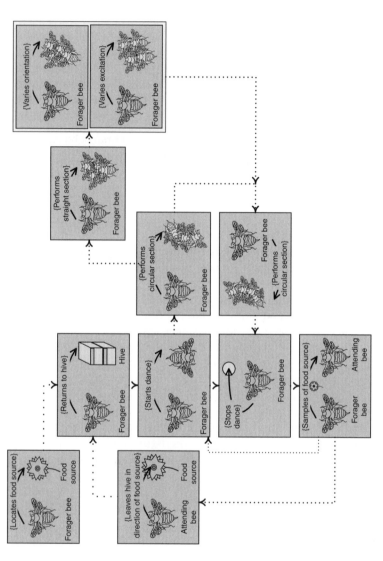

Figure 4.1 The performative pattern within the bee dance

patrolling, cleaning cells of the hive, eating pollen, tending the hive brood, building honeycomb, capping cells in the hive, packing pollen, guarding the hive, making orientation flights, following the dances of other bees and foraging.

Honeybees are continually attempting to find new sources of food. When one such source is found the foraging bee returns to the hive and her odour signals her identity as a member of the hive. She then moves to a particular part of the surface of the honeycomb, which ethologists refer to as 'the dance floor', and emits a sound by flapping her wings. These sounds help other bees within the hive to determine where she is and how she is moving. These sounds also allow attending bees to judge their position in relation to the dancing bee.

The bee then actually performs one of two forms of 'dance' (Figure 4.2). When food is within 50–75 metres of the hive, bees dance a 'round' dance on the surface of the honeycomb. When the food source is further than 75 metres away, the bees turn the round dance into a 'waggle' dance. The main difference between the 'round' and 'waggle' dance lies in the performance of a straight section in which the bee waggles from side to side.

Attending bees signal they are aware of the dance by emitting sounds that vibrate the surface of the honeycomb. The dancing bee senses these

Figure 4.2   The round and waggle dance

vibrations through her feet and at this point stops her dance. She then delivers samples of food she has collected to the attending bees. These food samples signal to them the taste, smell and quality of the food at the source.

Within a 'waggle' dance a number of aspects of performance are typically varied within the straight section of the dance by the forager bee. The forager bee may first vary the level of excitation of the performance, which indicates the quantity of nectar. The greater the level of excitement then the more nectar there is at the source and hence the more bees are needed to collect it.

The forager bee may also vary the degree of orientation of the straight section relative to the rest of the dance. This degree of orientation signifies to attending bees the position of the food source relative to the sun and the hive. The orientation of the 'straight' part of the figure-eight represents the direction of the source with respect to the position of the sun. For instance, if the 'straight' section is oriented at 80 degrees to the left of straight up then the bees are instructed by this to fly toward a point 80 degrees towards the left of the sun (Figure 4.3). Finally, the elapsed time the dancing bee takes to complete the waggle part of the

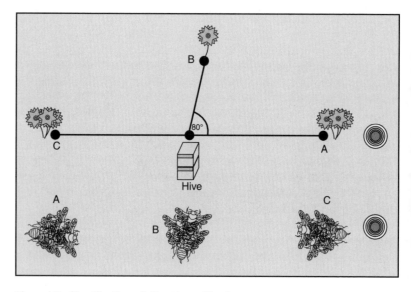

Figure 4.3   Signification of direction of food source

dance indicates the distance to the nectar source. The greater the duration of this part of the dance: the longer the flight to the source.

After completing a cycle of the dance the bee checks for a response from other bees. This pattern may then be repeated a number of times. Bees that are 'recruited' to a food source by the dancing leave to locate the food source signalled. Provided they find the source and like what they find they return to the hive and also perform a dance. In this way, a virtuous cycle or positive feedback loop (Chapter 5) is established in which the best food source initiates the most dances and so will attract the most bees. If the dance has been successful then attending bees will start leaving the hive in the direction of the indicated food source. This will signal to the foraging bee that her message has been delivered.

Classic model of communication

The honeybee dance is clearly an example of animal communication. But what is communication? In other words, what do we mean when we say that one actor such as a scout bee communicates with another actor, such as an attending bee?

The most cited model of communication is one due to Claude Shannon and Warren Weaver (Shannon, 1949). In this model, communication is treated as an 'engineering' problem. As Shannon himself stated, *'the fundamental problem of communication is that of reproducing at one point, either exactly or approximately, a message selected at another point'*. In this model (Figure 4.4), a source generates a message. This message is then encoded and transmitted as a signal along some communication

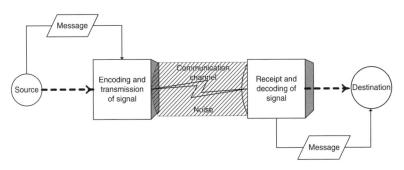

Figure 4.4   Classic model of communication

channel. The signal may be subject to noise in the environment, meaning that the received signal at the destination may not be identical to that transmitted from the source. Hence, the process of decoding a signal may involve correcting errors introduced by noise to produce the original message.

Any form of energy propagation can be used for communication through signals: a signal being a physical pattern which travels along some communication channel. For instance, speech travels as a signal consisting of a pattern of sound waves. Modulation is the process by which variety is introduced into a signal. If we are unable to modulate the pattern of a signal then no information can be communicated between sender and receiver along a communication channel. Once we can vary the signal then it becomes possible to code certain messages using variations in the signal. Coding is thus the translation of a signal from one medium into the same pattern expressed differently in some other communication medium.

Consider the example of a bee that has returned from a foraging trip to the hive. Bees carry with them a pouch of material from the hive which they release as they re-enter. The odour emanating from this pouch indicates to guarding bees at the entrance to the hive that they are part of the hive and provides them with safe entry. In this example, the foraging bee is the source and the guarding bee is the destination of the message. The message is coded as a signal in terms of a series of pheronomes or odours and transmitted through the air by diffusion. The distinct patterning of pheronomes constitutes modulation along this communication channel.

Augmented model of communication

The Shannon and Weaver model has been criticised on a number of grounds as a model of human and somewhat of animal communication, primarily because it is designed to address only what we have referred to in previous chapters as the empirics level of signs. The base model considers communication solely as a problem of physical energy transmission. It therefore excludes consideration of the well-formedness of messages (syntax), the meaning of messages (semantics) and the purpose of communication (pragmatics).

There are a number of additional problems, associated with the way in which communication is controlled between two or more actors.

First, the model assumes that communication is inherently linear, whereas human and animal communication normally is transactional in nature. Human verbal communication, for instance, typically occurs in the form of dialogue, discourse or 'conversation'. Within such discourse actors adjust their messages in response to a history of previous messages conducted within a particular dialogue. Second, the model tends to focus upon a limited subset of communication practice – dyadic communication – communication between two actors. In contrast, human and animal communication frequently occurs within and between groups of communicants. Finally, the model under-emphasises the role of records and record-keeping within human communication. We shall argue that, when human communication occurs between more than two people and particularly when messages have to be transmitted across time and space, the persistent record is an essential feature of much human communication. This last factor we see to be a significant difference between human and animal communication.

Another way of looking at this is that the four levels of semiotics define elements of a *protocol* between actors in communication activity. A protocol is a convention or a set of conventions which controls (Chapter 5) the communication process. This means that both sender and receiver must agree or negotiate a protocol for communication before such communication can occur. In terms of this communication protocol, pragmatics concerns the intentions conveyed in a message, semantics the meaning of a message, syntactics the formalism used to represent the message and empirics the signals used to code and transmit the message.

Within our classic example of an intra-species animal communication system, the actors are European honeybees. Multiple channels are used in this communication system including vision, taste, touch and smell. The incoming or forager honeybee is the primary sender of messages; the primary receivers of messages are those bees in closest proximity to the dancing bee (attending bees). Messages form a dialogue between the forager bee and attending bees and are coded primarily in terms of distinct elements of the dance engaged in by the forager bee. The main intentions wishing to be conveyed by the incoming bee is the direction of the food source in relation to the hive and the sun and the likely quantity of food at the source. Sensing bees decode the messages expressed in terms of this enacted sign-system and act on the basis of this: they fly off in the direction of the food source.

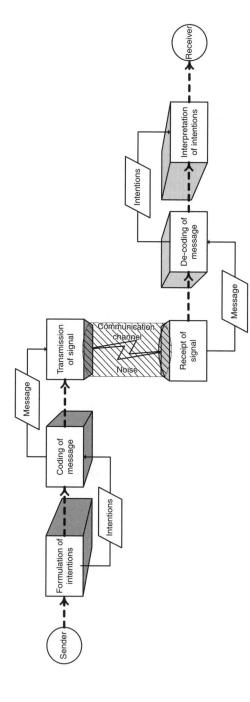

Figure 4.5 Augmented model of communication

Hence, to serve as a satisfactory baseline model of actor communication a number of elements have to be added to the Shannon and Weaver model, as illustrated in Figure 4.5. Within this augmented model communication is seen as a process involving the interaction of actors, intentions, messages, signals and communication channels. Actors are the senders of communication or the receivers of communication. The intentions of a sender will be encoded in a message using elements from a particular sign-system. The message will be transmitted by the sender in terms of signals along some communication channel. One or more of the other parties will be a receiver, which have the ability to decode signals to reveal the meaning of the message.

Fundamentally then, this augmented model of communication presumes the existence of a sign-system. The honeybee dance(s), as we have described it, clearly satisfies the characteristics of a sign-system, discussed in Chapter 4. Clear differences can be identified between elements of behaviour in European honeybees. Units of behaviour regularly repeat and are performed consistently by multiple actors. There is also clear identifiable coordination of action associated with particular patterns of performance.

Sensory modality

Studies of animal communication frequently work with something approaching the augmented model of communication described in the earlier section. However, they append to this model two linked concepts: that of a sensory modality and a sensory apparatus (Slater, 1983), terms we have implicitly used in both the current chapter and in previous chapters. The key emphasis within this literature is that the physical and behavioural makeup of the organisms involved in some communication process has a bearing on the nature of communication between such organisms.

There is a clear synergy between the idea of a communication channel and what within zoosemiotics is referred to as a sensory modality. Within animal communication and face-to-face human communication a given communication channel effectively corresponds to a sensory channel. Forma can be modulated and coded as signals using such a sensory channel.

The physical makeup of the actors in some communication determines a limited range of sensory modalities. These modalities determine what the actors are capable of sensing: the range of phenomena that can be discriminated using a particular sense. This sets the perceptual and cognitive background for what actors in any communication can use as symbols. There is thus a close relationship between symbols, signals and sensing (see Chapter 6).

Various sensory modalities include vision, audition, olfaction and electroreception. Which sensory modality is used for a particular signal depends on the nature of the information being conveyed and the nature of the environment within which the signalling takes place.

Scientists of animal behaviour argue that the signals employed by animals of a specific species are subject to evolutionary principles. In other words, they assume that the signals they observe are the result of natural selection, in the sense that the properties of particular signals make them the most effective at conveying information within the particular ecological environment in which the organism lives.

A key assumption within this literature is that the nature of signalling evolves to produce a signal which will travel through a particular environment and reach recipients as efficiently as possible and with as little distortion as possible. Hence, larger animals will tend to use an auditory modality – sounds. This is because sounds move more rapidly, can travel around objects and can be detected at great distances. Smaller animals such as ants cannot achieve a sufficient intensity of sound and so may use pheronomes (odours) which travel on the wind.

The notion of sensory modality is clearly closely related to the idea of sensory apparatus. An actor's sensory apparatus refers to the entire range of sensors that the organism can use to receive signals. Hence, it tends to be associated with the characteristics of a receiver. An actor's sensory apparatus allows the actor to attend to and be aroused by a signal in some sensory modality. It detects and filters the signal in the presence of noise in some communication channel. It also frequently allows the receiver to identify the location of the signal in space.

For instance, honeybees use sounds as a limited part of the performative pattern illustrated in Figure 4.1. The vibration of air created by the flapping of wings or through the actions of feet is used to direct and signal attention between scout and attending bees. But signals are also transmitted along other communication channels such as an olfactory channel. Pheronomes are particularly used to signal identity in this regard.

The symbols within some communication process are reliant upon the sensory modalities and associated sensory apparatus of particular communicative actors. Take the case of the honeybee. The honeybee relies primarily on four key sensory modalities for communication: smell, sight, taste and touch. There is also some evidence that honeybees have a form of hearing and an undefined ability to sense the Earth's magnetic field.

As we have seen, bees use odours to communicate many different things. For instance, guard bees which locate near the entrance to a hive 'smell' other bees trying to enter. If the bees don't have a recognisable odour appropriate to the particular hive they are expelled. New virgin queens produce a sex pheromone to attract drones during the mating flight. When a bee stings, she releases an alarm pheromone to alert others to the danger. The queen also maintains behavioural control of the colony by a pheromone known as the 'queen substance'. As long as it is being passed around, the message to the colony is that *'we have a queen and all is well'*.

Honeybees, like most insects, have compound eyes made up of some 4500 individual light sensors known as ommatidia (Gould and Gould, 1995). These eyes produce images of relatively low resolution as compared to humans but enable them to sense a fairly broad range of colour. Although bees do not see red, they can differentiate between six major categories of colour, including yellow, blue-green, blue, violet and ultraviolet. They also see a colour known as 'bee's purple': a mixture of yellow and ultraviolet. Honeybees taste, smell and touch using their antennae which are covered with odour and taste receptors. Hence, they have been found to be able to distinguish between sweet, sour, bitter and salt 'tastes'. They also use their antennae to gauge the width and depth of cells while constructing honeycomb. Bees communicate via both touch and 'hearing' during bee dances. Sounds are received by attending bees through organs located on the legs and on antennae.

Communication and sign-systems

We have deliberately used a well-publicised case of animal communication within this chapter because of our wish to generalise the concept of sign-system from a concern purely with human spoken language. Many attempts have been made to highlight significant differences between animal communication, as in the example of the honeybee dance, and communication within the species Homo Sapiens Sapiens. Much of this debate has now moved on from a simple assumption that human spoken language is unique. Instead, modern animal communication studies have pioneered the viewpoint that human language evolved from simpler forms of animal communication, but is distinctive as a medium for communication on a number of dimensions associated with the complexity of our sign-systems.

One influential example of this position is the work of Charles Hockett who published an important paper in the 1960s delineating 13 features which he believed were characteristic of all human languages (Hockett, 1963). The aim of the paper was to distinguish the idea of human languages from non-human forms of communication. In a subsequent article, Hockett added a number of other features to his list to make a list of some 17 features. The entire list of such features includes:

- *Vocal auditory channel.* Human communication primarily uses the vocal/auditory channel for communication rather than other channels such as the use of gesture or expression. Hockett postulates that this channel has the advantage for primates of leaving much of the body free for other activities.
- *Broadcast transmission.* Because of the way in which sounds propagate through air a vocal sign can be heard in all directions by listeners within earshot.
- *Directional reception.* Those listeners having bi-aural direction finding will also be able to interpret the sign as coming from one specific direction.
- *Rapid fading.* The sound made by speech diminishes quickly after being released; it does not persist for any length of time.
- *Interchangeability.* The speaker has the ability to reproduce any message he can understand.
- *Total feedback.* Individuals are able to hear and internalise a message they have sent.
- *Specialisation.* Speech is produced for communication, not chiefly for some other function, such as echolocation.
- *Semanticity.* Speech sounds can be linked to specific meanings.
- *Arbritrariness.* There is no direct connection between a speech sign and its meaning.
- *Discreteness.* Each unit of communication can be separated and discriminated by a hearer.
- *Displacement.* The ability to talk about things that are not physically present.

- *Productivity.* The ability to create new messages by combining already-existing signs.
- *Traditional transmission.* Language is acquired through learning within social groups.
- *Duality of patterning.* Meaningful signs (morphemes) are made up of, and distinguished from one another by, meaningless constituent parts (phonemes).
- *Prevarication.* Language can be used to deceive: to make false statements (to lie).
- *Reflexiveness.* Language can be used to refer to (i.e., describe) itself.
- *Learnability.* Speakers of one language can learn to speak another.

From this list of 'design features', Hockett maintained that the first 9–10 features were characteristic of communication amongst all primates. The last 7 features in the list were what distinguished human languages from forms of animal communication. Charles Snowdon (Snowdon, 2002), for instance, finds clear evidence of the following 'design features' in primate communication such as among vervet monkeys: vocal auditory channel (vervet monkeys use alarm calls as communication); broadcast transmission and directional reception (vervet calls are broadcast through the environment); rapid fading (vervet calls rapidly decay with time); interchangeability (vervet senders and receivers can use the calls interchangeably); total feedback (one can argue that vervet monkeys are able to hear and internalise a message they have sent); specialisation (vervet calls seem specialised only for the communication of alarm); semanticity (each call is associated with a different referent, namely a type of predator); arbitrariness (each call does not resemble any vocalisation of the predator; discreteness (each type of predator-call differs from another). There is also some evidence of the duality of patterning and syntax within primate communication. Some New World primates such as cotton-top and capuchin monkeys combine individual calls into sequences that retain the meaning of individual elements. Simple examples of syntactic structure have been reported in several non-human primates. For instance, cotton-top tamarins have an alarm call. After the threat is over monkeys combine the alarm call with a relaxed contact call in a sequence which appears to signal 'all clear'. This leaves only displacement, productivity, traditional transmission, prevarification, learnability and reflexiveness as characteristic of human communication as compared to animal communication.

From our perspective, the main limitation of this approach is its focus on a comparison with human *spoken* language. Because of the way in which Hockett limits his classification to this sensory modality he excludes other forms of sensory modality from consideration. The more general concept of sign-system allows us to consider how signs are given physical form using different modalities within what we shall refer to as a data system employed by actors within the same species. Hence, as we have seen, in the case of the data system associated with the honeybee dance(s), communication occurs along a number of different sensory modalities.

Utilising the concept of a sign-system directly also allows a better understanding of the relationship between facets as well as the complexity associated with the sign-system. For instance, it is possible to see a clear relationship between most of Hockett's design features and the levels of the semiotics ladder described in Chapter 1. Interchangeability and total feedback relate to the physical characteristics or capabilities of the actors involved in communication. Certain features such as vocal auditory channels, broadcast transmission, directional reception and rapid fading are features at the empirics levels and relate to the physical characteristics or properties of speech and hearing. Other features such as discreteness, the duality of patterning and productivity seem appropriate as syntactic properties of speech signs. Some features such as semanticity and arbritrariness are classic concerns of semantics. Finally, features such as prevarication, reflexiveness and displacement are concerns of the pragmatics of language, while traditional transmission and learnability are social characteristics of language.

Conclusion

So what is the fundamental role of communication? The Shannon model of communication is interested purely in the transmission of forma: the substance of a sign. Within the logo at the start of this chapter we have represented the way in which the transmission of forma is enacted via signals supporting communication between two actors – in this case, two honeybees.

A particular theme within animal communication is the study of the physical characteristics of animal signalling. Effectively this works at the empirics and syntactics levels of the semiotics ladder. Biologists take an evolutionary position focusing upon the question of why animal signals form as they do. The key background theoretical assumption adopted is that signals are selected that will travel through a particular environment as effortlessly and with as little distortion as possible. Hence, for instance, within a hive a dance cannot be seen by other bees because the interior of the hive is pitch-black. Other sensory modalities such as touch, taste and sound are therefore employed within signification processes by European honeybees.

But communication also concerns both informa and performa. The philosopher John Austin was one of the first to argue in his famous book – *How to Do Things with Words* (Austin, 1971) – that communication is an act in and of itself. When we communicate we normally wish to impart some intentions from ourselves to some other actors. Many such intentions involve the attempt to influence the behaviour or performance of others. Communication is thus a critical process for ensuring organisation or order within social systems. This is why animal communication is typically defined as any behaviour on the part of one animal that has an effect on the current or future behaviour of another animal. Some researchers of animal behaviour have even gone so far as to suggest that communication is more a matter of one animal manipulating another than of information transmission. Hence, they argue for study of the purpose of communication – since some animal communication is designed to deceive. Zoosemiotics might also be seen to be the study of everything that can be used to lie (Eco, 1977), since deception appears commonplace amongst animals.

Significance clearly relies upon communication, since communication involves the use of signs for information transmission. As we have seen, the standard way of discussing communication is in terms of a classic model due to Claude Shannon, which focuses solely on the medium of communication. As argued in this chapter, an augmented model of communication must include other layers of the semiotics ladder. Within this augmented model communication is defined not only as a matter of forma but also as a matter of informa and performa. The forma-tion of messages within communication are used not only to in-form but to per-form.

Within this conception, communication is thus seen as a process involving the interaction of a number of elements: actors, intentions, messages, signals and communication channels. Actors are the senders of communication or the receivers of communication. The intentions of a sender will be encoded in a message using elements from a particular sign-system. The message will be transmitted by the sender in terms of signals along some communication channel. One or more of the other parties will be a receiver, which have the ability to decode signals to reveal the meaning of the message.

The focus within this chapter has been upon embodied or what in human terms is frequently referred to as face-to-face communication. This form of communication is entirely reliant upon the physical makeup of the actors involved. Such human and animal communication is therefore framed by the sensory modality and sensory apparatus of the communicants. In further chapters we shall establish the idea of disembodied communication or communication through the use of persistent artefacts. This is a critical defining characteristic of much human communication, particularly recent human communication reliant upon technology.

In one sense, human communication is more limited than forms of animal communication. The sensory modalities we typically use as humans are limited primarily to vocal and visual modalities, because of the constraints imposed by our sensory apparatus. In comparison the dance of the European Honeybee uses four to five different sensory modalities to communicate. In another sense, aspects of human communication are clearly much more sophisticated than animal communication. The complexity of human spoken languages (as measured in terms of aspects such as the variety of the sign-system) is clearly much greater than all extant animal sign-systems.

But human spoken language is only one of the sign-systems used by man. In certain areas there are clear points of overlap between sign-systems employed by humans and those employed by animals. As we have seen in the previous chapter, there are clear similarities between non-verbal communication amongst humans and the non-verbal communication utilised by our closer relatives: the higher apes.

But one area not considered explicitly in the literature is the way in which *techne* or craft is critical to human as opposed to animal communication. One comparison under-represented in the discussion of the differences between human and animal communication is the use of signs for the representation of persistent records of things. Animal communication does not use anything like what we shall refer to as a persistent data system. The sensory modalities in communication determine symbols that are not persistent. Hence, the concept of a record does not exist in animal communication. There is evidence of natural persistence amongst signs in the animal world, but such 'records' have marginal persistence. A trail of pheronomes produced by ants, for instance, might be considered persistent and hence to constitute a record in that it persists beyond the act of communication itself. However, the creation of such a scent 'record' relies on ant embodiment not on techne (Chapter 6).

Hence, the ability to create and use persistent symbols should perhaps be added to Hockett's list of distinguishing features of human communication. Homo Sapiens is a species best signified as both Homo Signum and Homo Habilis. As a species we are accomplished users of sign-systems for communication on many levels. Some levels of human sign-system have similarities with forms of animal communication. Spoken language is a critical breakthrough accomplishment, but the ability we have to externalise such language using techne is an equally significant accomplishment.

So to provide a tentative answer to the question of the purpose of communication we must point to its role as a critical element in the process by which a system ensures organisation or order. By organisation we mean that the system is able to maintain identity and viability through time. To ensure this some form of control is necessary. In the case of a system being a single actor, then internal communication is essential for the regulation of the behaviour of the actor. In the case of a system being multiple actors, then external communication is critical to ensure effective coordination of behaviour amongst and between actors.

It should therefore come as no surprise that the issues of communication and control of behaviour have been associated for some time, particularly within the field of cybernetics. It is this issue of control that forms the topic of the next chapter.

References

Austin, J. L. (1971). How to Do Things with Words. Oxford University press, Oxford.

Beynon-Davies, P. (2010). Dances with bees: exploring the relevance of the study of animal communication to informatics. International Journal of Information Management 30(1): 185–198.

Eco, U. (1977). A Theory of Semiotics. Macmillan, London.

Gould, J. L. and C. G. Gould (1995). The Honey Bee. Scientific American, New York.

Hockett, C. F. (1963). The Problem of Universals in Language. Universals of Language. J. H. Greenberg. Cambridge, Mass., MIT Press.

Mcluhan, M. (1994). Understanding Media: the extensions of man. MIT Press, Cambridge, Mass.

Shannon, C. E. (1949). The Mathematical Theory of Communication. University of Illinois Press, Urbana.

Slater, P. J. B. (1983). The study of communication. Animal Behaviour: Volume 2: Communication. T. R. Halliday and P. J. B. Slater. Oxford, Blackwell.

Snowdon, C. T. (2002). From Primate Communication to Human Language. Tree of Origin: what primate behavior can tell us about human social evolution. F. B. M. deWaal. Cambridge, Mass., Harvard University Press.

Wiener, N. (1948). Cybernetics. Wiley, New York.

5
Control: Remaining viable

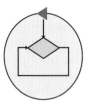

Introduction

Are you the same person you were ten years ago? At the level of yourself as a complete organism you would certainly say you were. At the cellular level however you are probably not since virtually every cell in your body has renewed itself over this period. So as a system your component parts have changed but as a whole you have maintained identity and remained viable. This process of ensuring the identity and viability of organisms is exercised through many layers of control.

Now consider order at the social level – order involving the interaction between multiple organisms. How is order sustained in coordinated action between multiple actors? Well, imagine a world without watches, or more worrying still, any standard measures of time. Since no time measure exists, how do you schedule a business meeting? Well, you probably calibrate action against the constants of the physical world such as the movement of the Earth in relation to the Sun. You suggest perhaps that the meeting begin at sunrise, at midday (when the sun is at its peak) or at sunset. In doing so you are inherently using common experience to create a measure of time based on natural signs and through this to control mutual performance. The concept of time and its measure is hence essential for the control of mutual human performance; there is an inherent association between control, the use of signs and mutual performance.

At a high level, the issue of control is inherently associated with the discipline of Cybernetics. As we have seen, Norbert Wiener defined Cybernetics as the *'entire field of control and communication theory, whether in the machine or in the animal'* (Wiener, 1948). The ancient Greek work Kybernetes, from which the term cybernetics is derived, means the art of steersmanship. At the time, the word was naturally used to refer to the art of piloting a maritime vessel. However the ancient Greek philosopher, Plato, used the word to refer to steering the 'ship of state'. The English word governor is derived from the Latin word gubernator, which in turn is derived from the Greek word Kybernetes. This word governor in modern English is used to describe both a mechanical mechanism and a political role. A governor is part of a steam engine, which uses a self-adjusting valve mechanism to keep the engine working at a constant speed under varying conditions of load. A governor of state is a public steersman or political decision-maker, tasked with steering some aspect of the political system.

Systems of whatever sort must maintain their identity through time through processes of continuous re-creation. Control is the steering process which ensures that a system remains viable at the current time and sustainable through time. Therefore, the idea of control and control processes has relevance for understanding how order or organisation emerges not only in systems of performance, communication and representation but also within intentional systems of mind or what we shall refer to as psyche within the current chapter and in Chapter 8.

In Chapter 2 we described a system as being the patterning of order. Control is the process by which such patterning of order is created and maintained. To help us understand the link between control, communication and action we consider what at first glance might seem like a simple human accomplishment: that of walking through spaces or perambulation.

Perambulation

Norbert Wiener, the founder of cybernetics, was an academic for much of his life at the Massachusetts Institute of Technology (MIT) and was famous there as a compulsive walker of the corridors of this institution. Being a creature of habit, he walked a particular route around the university campus, talking to everyone he met regardless of status and academic discipline. This route became known as the Wienerweg in his honour – *weg* being German for way or route. At one time along this route Wiener met a student at around midday. At the end of their conversation he asked the student to tell him which way he had been walking when they first met: towards the canteen or away from it. It was only the response from the student that enabled Wiener to remember whether he had yet had lunch!

Locomotion is a characteristic of all animals and consists of the process by which the animal moves itself from one geographic position to another. The majority of mammals are quadri-pedal meaning they walk on four legs. A crawling human infant reproduces the behaviour of a slowly walking quadruped in which three limbs are always in touch with the ground at any one time. However, within a short span of time the human infant loses the stability of the tripod inherent in four-legged locomotion and learns to adopt bi-pedal or two-legged locomotion. Bi-pedal locomotion might to an observer look to be less complex than its quadri-pedal cousin. In fact, bi-pedal locomotion demands greater neuronal control than quadri-pedal locomotion because of the need to continuously control the stability of the organism; some of this control being instinctual in nature and some of it learned.

The act of walking is an accomplishment we all take for granted everyday; although many people in Western societies do not walk enough, contributing to health issues such as obesity. Although significant aspects of this accomplishment are learned, much of this accomplishment is unconscious. We only become aware of the difficulties underlying this accomplishment when aspects of it breakdown. For instance, when we trip up or accidentally collide with a fellow walker.

All of us walk differently, largely caused by differences in our anatomy. Hence, tall people walk differently from short people, and fat people walk differently from thin people. This underlies our ability to use the 'signature' of a person's walking style as a partial cue to recognising the identity of a person at a distance. Also, the way in which we walk can frequently reflect internal mood. Hence, we walk differently when we are exhilarated as compared to when we are depressed.

All human walking is based upon a common and cyclical pattern referred to as the double pendulum (Rose and Gamble, 1994) (Figure 5.1). During forward motion, the leg that leaves the ground swings forward from the hip. This sweep is the first pendulum. The leg then strikes the ground with the heel and rolls through to the toe in a motion described as an inverted pendulum. The motion of the two legs is coordinated so that one foot or the other is always in contact with the ground. The process of walking is an efficient form of locomotion in that it recovers

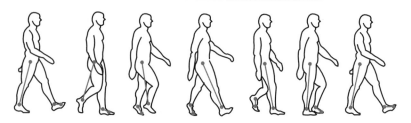

Figure 5.1 The act of walking

approximately 60% of the energy used due to the dynamics of the double pendulum and ground reaction force.

But the act of walking is far more than the physical act of locomotion. Hence, we should distinguish between mere locomotion and perambulation or the act of walking through some space. Perambulation is a complex individual and social activity which demands higher aspects of control and even the need for external or exogenous communication.

As an individual accomplishment perambulation involves an actor in navigating through some space. In such terms, the individual must sense the presence of objects within the space and plan strategies of locomotion to avoid collision with such objects. The individual must also adjust facets of her behaviour such as the speed or pace of walking depending on the nature of the surface walked upon. Hence, an individual is likely to slow her pace in icy conditions or when walking up a slope.

Perambulation is also a social activity. When walking through certain spaces we frequently inter-act with other actors, also perambulating. The act of navigation must now involve calculation of the likely trajectories of other moving and frequently intentional objects. Therefore, as a social accomplishment, walking can be considered on a number of levels.

Consider an individual walking down a pavement at the side of some street. A number of other actors are walking along the same pavement, some going in her direction, some coming at her from the opposite direction. The process of navigating along this pavement is clearly a social accomplishment for this actor. She clearly has to adjust her speed and direction in response to 'calculations' she makes about the likely trajectory not only of individuals coming towards her, but also individuals possibly overtaking her on the pavement. Frequently this accomplishment breaks down as in the case of two individuals who make different assumptions about each others' likely actions. For instance, actor A assumes actor B will move and pass on her left and therefore veers to the right; actor B assumes that actor A will pass on his right and hence veers to his left. They are hence clearly on a collision course and are likely to resolve the situation through a typical manoeuvre such as stopping and issuing an apology, before attempting another passing move. This will continue until a successful traversal of each other is achieved.

Sometimes we even walk together with other actors, making it a collective accomplishment (Ryave and Schenkein, 1974). Walking together involves us not only in avoiding other actors walking towards us; it also involves us in adjusting our walking to match that of other members of the group with which we are walking. Consider now the more complex activity of two or more persons walking together, perhaps also engaging in other acts of performance such as talking. Such actors have to continuously adjust their behaviour not only in terms of other actors as above but also in terms of the movement of actors of their walking-together group. This is particularly important to be able to maintain the possibility of speech. Hence, each actor within the group has to continuously adjust their position, speed and direction to facilitate joint communication.

The meaning of control

Control is effectively the process by which the order within some system is built and sustained. Systems (Chapter 2) are by their very nature entities of organisation. Systems are different from aggregates or collections of things. A collection is merely a set of objects. To be a system the set of objects must be related in some ways. Hence, a system is both a set of objects and a set of relations. By using the term organisation we imply that the continuous interaction between things/objects is important to sustaining order.

Within the physical theory of thermodynamics the natural state of the universe is one of disorder – known in more formal terms as *entropy*. Systems (or more specifically open systems) are islands of order – negative entropy or *negentropy* – in a universe of disorder. Systems of this form display characteristics of organisation, order or this characteristic of negentropy (Stonier, 1994).

Claude Shannon (Chapter 4) used a particular conception of entropy to help define 'information'. Within 'information' theory, binary decisions expressed as logarithms to the base 2 are used as a measure of the degree of uncertainty associated with a message, based upon probabilities calculated from the relative frequency of elements of a message. The more infrequent the elements of a message, the more 'information' the message conveys. As we shall see in Chapter 6 this phenomenon actually relates to the degree of differences or variation in some signal and can be used to calculate the degree of orderliness associated with such a signal.

Following Stonier and others, we therefore link the idea of order or organisation with the degree of patterning or negentropy within some system. Therefore, we know that something is ordered or organised if we see evidence of patterning. In other words, we observe a common pattern across situations. Such patterns may be examples of representation as in the case of signals, communication as in the case of elements of a conversation or of behaviour or activity such as in routines found in organisations.

Control is the process by which such patterning of order is created and maintained across situations. We recognise something as having a distinct identity – as being a system – through some patterning in the world. *Control* is the process by which a system ensures continuity through time. It is thus the means by which system identity is sustained and the system maintains its viability in terms of changes in its environment. Control is the means by which system behaviour is reproduced. In our terms, control produces the patterning evident in systems of activity, communication and representation amongst groups of actors.

For example, walking is a recurring pattern in the sense it is reproduced by actors across situations. Walking is an accomplishment of a particular actor and as a patterned accomplishment it can be considered a system. The accomplishment of walking or perambulation thus relies on control; actually on many layers of control.

Control can be conceived both as a process of regulation and as a process of adaptation applicable to systems. The typical connotations of the term *control* are stability and conservation. This side of control is frequently referred to as *regulation*. Regulation is the conservative side of control and is typically concerned with the internal operations of some system. In terms of regulation, control ensures that a system will recover some stability after a period of disturbance and maintain its viability over time.

Walking is actually a bodily movement which continually introduces the potential for the actor undertaking this accomplishment to fall over. Certain cognitive and bodily processes allow the actor unconsciously to continuously recover his or her stability in the process of moving forward. It is therefore possible to think of such perceptual and cognitive processes as regulating the physical system of walking.

However, there are alternative connotations embedded in the principle of organising. This side of control is frequently referred to as *adaptation*. Adaptation is the evolutionary side of control and is concerned with the external relationships between the system and its environment. Systems generally exhibit some form of control that enables the system to adapt to changes in its environment; changing its behaviour to ensure a degree of 'fitness' between system and environment.

Perambulation, as discussed above, is not only the physical act of moving forward: it is also the activity of an actor moving from point A to point B. In achieving this goal the actor needs to continually adapt the accomplishment of walking in terms of the constraints imposed by the environment being walked through. Hence, the actor will adjust elements of this physical activity to avoid obstacles, climb stairs or traverse a steep incline.

The physical act of walking can thus be considered the reproduction of a physical pattern, dependent on one level, upon sensori-motor control. This means that it relies upon the individual sensing its own movement and effecting continuous change in muscle tension throughout the body to regulate both forward movement and balance. On another level, the more encompassing idea of perambulation relies upon navigational control. Here, the individual is sensing its immediate environment and effecting changes to its performance of walking to avoid collision with objects within this environment. The individual adapts her behaviour to what she finds in the environment. On yet a further level, as a social activity, *walking together* demands forms of social control. Here, the actors performing together as a group must sense and interpret the movements of other actors and make continual and situated adjustments to their own behaviour in order to maintain a level of proximity to their group.

Control as a process

As the example of walking should suggest, control can be viewed in terms of a monitoring sub-system, or a hierarchy of such sub-systems, that 'steers' the behaviour of other operating sub-systems. Hence, this monitoring sub-system is frequently referred to as a control mechanism, sub-system or process.

In terms of systems 'designed' by human beings, such as certain organisations, control can be considered an imposed process. In the process of designing and constructing a system, necessary processes of control for regulation have to be established. In contrast, control in natural or physical systems is usually not designed but emerges through processes of self-organisation. For a branch of systemics known as complexity theory, 'control' (although it is not referred to as such) emerges from the system itself. Coherent patterns of order or control emerge from the complex interaction of the multiple parts of a system.

Take one example from the physical world and one from the social world. Within biology the process of natural selection can be seen to emerge from evolution and provides the control mechanism for species change. A concept of emergence familiar in classical economics is the

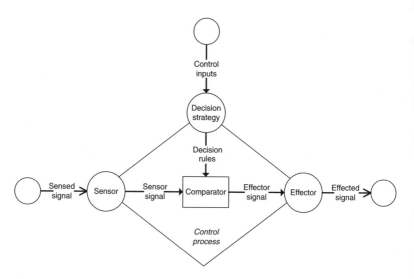

Figure 5.2   Control process

concept of price. The price of a good or service such as the price of oil in a pure economic market is not fixed but emerges from the continuous interaction of supply and demand.

The systems theorist Brian Wilson (Wilson, 1990) argues that any coherent element of a system must inherently have a control mechanism or process embedded within it. In other words, a system with operational or productive processes must have at least one controller for such processes. Applying the idea of systems hierarchy, we can refine the idea of a control process within some system as consisting of inputs, outputs and processes (Figure 5.2). For a control process to work effectively it must have three things: resources to deploy to regulate the behaviour of the system in a particular direction; control inputs which implement the 'purpose' of the system; control signals enabling the process to monitor and instruct operational processes.

The control process ensures defined levels of performance for the system through use of a number of control inputs. This sets the key decision strategy for the controller. Such a decision strategy then works in interaction with three other key elements of a control process: sensors, comparators and effectors. *Sensors* are processes that monitor changes in the environment of some system or in the system itself (sensed signals) and send further signals to comparators. *Comparators* compare signals from sensors against some decision strategy and on this basis make some decision to send signals to effectors. Sometimes referred to as actuators or activators, *effectors* cause changes to a systems' state. In other words, they introduce changes to system variables by sending signals to particular parts of a system.

Consider one example of a technical system. In a security system sensors are likely to be placed at points of entry into a building such as windows and doors. If a window is opened when the system is activated then a sensor sends a signal to the control unit. This control unit is likely to identify the point of entry and through its decision strategy to send signals to effectors such as alarms.

Some elements from this conception of control have already been introduced in the last chapter, where we introduced the ideas of the sensory and effector apparatus of some actor. We argued that embodied communication is reliant on these two types of apparatus. But all action is reliant upon some notion of control in which actors continually sense their environment and effect changes in their behaviour in response to such sensations. For instance, walking is an accomplishment because it demands continual adjustment in terms of some set goal. The sensory apparatus of the individual senses the environment through touch, hearing and sight. The comparator apparatus of the individual compares the actor's current position with his intended goal. He then effects actions to move closer towards his goal. Such action is again reassessed within the cycle of movements from which walking is composed.

From this discussion it should be evident that the process of control and the concept of information are inherently inter-linked. For instance, in order for a control process to work effectively it must continually monitor the state of the system it is attempting to control. Such monitoring occurs through sensing signals in its environment. The control process must also contain a model of the system it is attempting to control. Critical to this model will be some 'measures' of performance. Signals transmitted from the monitoring process are compared against this model and further signals are transmitted back to the system to maintain the system's performance within parameters defined by this model.

Thus there is an inherent association between control, performance and measurement. In order to control the performance of a system a control process must 'measure' its environment against its goals. In such terms, all forms of measurement can be considered in terms of a sign-system. Points on a temperature scale, for instance, can be taken to stand for ambient energy in the environment. Particular points on this scale are likely to be calibrated to certain natural signs – perhaps associated with certain discernible changes in the organisation of matter (Stonier, 1994). Hence, in the centigrade scale zero degrees C stands for the freezing point of water while 100 degrees C stands for the boiling point of water. These particular signs therefore serve to stand for distinct changes in the organisation of water: from solid through liquid to a gas.

A control process makes decisions about appropriate action by comparing signals from the environment against its decision strategy. Decision-making is the activity of deciding upon appropriate action in particular situations. Decision-making is reliant on communication in the sense that communication is seen as reducing uncertainty in decision-making. Hence, to use the example of the social nature of perambulation: if each person walking towards each other shouts their intended direction to others when within earshot, then each actor is assured of navigating his or her course with certainty.

Control and communication

Therefore, control relies upon both internal/endogenous communication and external/exogenous communication. Peter Senge believes that one of the most important and valuable characteristics of systemic thinking is its ability to handle cycles of cause and effect. This is inherently what is meant by *feedback* (Figure 5.3). Control is normally exercised within a system through some form of feedback. Control outputs from the process of a system are fed back to the control process. The control process then adjusts the control signals to the operating process on the basis of the signalling it receives.

Feedback has two major forms – positive and negative feedback – terms that should not imply any value-connotation. We may also distinguish between those feedback processes involved primarily with regulation (single-loop feedback) and those involved with adaptation (double-loop feedback).

Control is normally exercised through a negative feedback loop. Sometimes known as a balancing loop or damping feedback it involves the control process monitoring the outputs from the operational process through its sensors. The comparators in the monitoring system detect

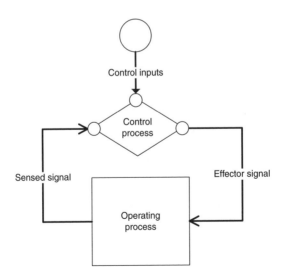

Figure 5.3   Single-loop feedback

variations from defined levels of performance provided by control inputs. If the outputs vary from established levels then the monitoring sub-system initiates some actions that <u>reduce</u> or decrease the variation through its effectors.

For example, in a thermostat, if the temperature falls below some specified level then the thermostat initiates an action such as opening some hot water valve. A company maintaining cash flow can be conceived of as a system with negative feedback in which the cash balance continually influences company decisions on expenditure and borrowing.

The navigational side of perambulation can be considered reliant upon some control process that implements negative feedback. The goal for the actor is to walk from point A to point B. In taking paces towards its goal the actor continually monitors the distance left to cover. When it has reached its destination, pacing forward ceases.

Commonly known as a 'vicious circle' or reinforcing loop, positive feedback involves the control process monitoring the outputs from the operational system through its sensors. If the outputs vary from established levels then the monitoring sub-system initiates some actions that <u>increase</u> the discrepancy between desired and actual levels of performance. In other words the variation is increased through its effectors.

The 'arms race' that occurred during the 'cold war' period is a classic example of a system characterised by a positive feedback loop. At the time, the United States increased its level of armament to improve its security. This prompted the USSR to increase its level of armament because of a perceived greater threat to its security. The United States responded by increasing its levels of armament, and so on. This positive feedback loop was eventually terminated with the collapse of the Soviet Union and a new form of international political world-order emerged to take its place.

The examples of feedback cited above are examples of single-loop feedback. Single-loop feedback is primarily concerned with regulation. In this type of feedback a single control process monitors variations in the state of an operational process, compares this state against some planned levels of performance and takes corrective action to bring performance in line with plan. In single-loop feedback the plans for performance (the control inputs) remain relatively unchanged (Figure 5.4). Sensors only monitor the behaviour of internal processes and effectors only act upon such internal processes.

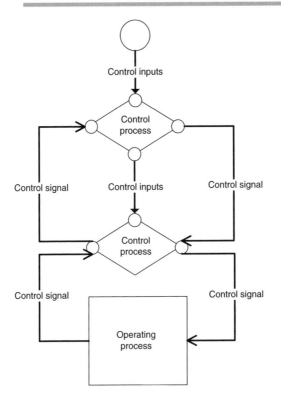

Figure 5.4 Double-loop feedback

In terms of the individual actor the physical act of walking can be seen to be reliant on single-loop feedback. Some cognitive process must continually monitor the effect of each step after another and adjust its next step in terms of that taken before.

Double-loop feedback is primarily concerned with adaptation. In this type of feedback the control process must not only monitor variations in the state of an internal process, it must also monitor changes in its environment. Hence, there are two control loops involved and the feedback from the higher-level controller will cause adjustments to the decision strategies of lower-level controllers.

Double-loop feedback is consequently a higher-level form of control. William Ross Ashby insists that double-loop feedback is essential to ensure that a system adapts effectively to changes in its environment. Double-loop feedback is that form in which the monitoring of lower-level single-feedback control systems as well as monitoring of the environment triggers examination and perhaps revision of the principles on which the control process is established.

Psyche as control

Implicitly in some of the examples we have used, we have built the case for an actor to be considered an operational system in which the action or behaviour of the actor is determined by some control process. Within higher organisms this control process is clearly enacted by the central nervous system. The operation of this control process, or more likely a complex hierarchy of such control processes, produces an emergent effect which is generally referred to as 'mind'.

We shall use the term *psyche* to refer to this emergent phenomenon rather than mind for a number of reasons.

The term *mind* carries with it a bag of unfortunate associations. It is particularly associated with human perceptual and cognitive abilities and as such is used as a major characteristic to distinguish humankind from the rest of the animal kingdom. One reason for using the term psyche rather than mind is that the concept of mind, just like the concept of language considered in the previous chapter, has been seen by many to be the sole preserve of humans. Whenever some evidence of signifying capability or cognitive activity is found amongst non-human animals the concept of language or mind is re-defined in terms of purely human behaviour. Dennett (Dennett, 1996), like Varela and Maturana (Maturana and Varela, 1987), the Russian psychologist Vygotsky (Vygotsky, 1986) and the theoretical biologist Tom Stonier (Stonier, 1997) challenge such a viewpoint, proposing that psyche is not a fixed entity but a continuum that evolved amongst the vast variety of the animal kingdom. In such terms, psyche can be seen to be an emergent effect of the increasing complexity of the nervous system amongst organisms. Psyche is considered an internal environment that emerged and developed in order to make interaction with the world more successful for such organisms.

The concept of mind is also inherently associated with the so-called mind-body problem which is still much argued within philosophy. Within this debate the term mind is used in a rather vague way to encapsulate inner, subjective experience, particularly consciousness, and distinguish it from outer, objective experience. One is seen to be amenable to independent study while the other is only available to introspection. We take the position here of attempting to avoid this duality by specifying psyche in terms of a series of directly observable functions which implement various layers of control in actors. By implication, psyche is not an all or nothing thing. We follow a growing body of supposition which proposes that psyche is best regarded as a continuum of accomplishment.

This means that it becomes possible to suggest various relationships between forms of animal psyche and human psyche. Indeed, we suggest that the human psyche is in itself a layered continuum built upon layers of psyche found more widely in the animal kingdom. Considering psyche as a continuum allows us to better unpack the much-cited problem of *agency*. It also allows us to consider the degree to which machines, perhaps as forms of artificial life, are ever likely to display such agency.

Psyche is therefore a more useful term to encapsulate the range of operation characteristic of what we have referred to in Chapter 3 as the internal environment of some actor. Hence, it includes not only cognitive functions such as decision-making and perceptual abilities such as symbolic recognition but also matters of self and self-awareness. Psyche, or the operation concerned with an actor's internal environment, can be contrasted with *techne,* concerned with activities in which an actor transforms aspects of the external environment. This distinction is particularly important to defining aspects of forma in the next chapter.

As we have seen, the sensory apparatus of the actor determines what the actor is able to react to. The effector apparatus of the actor determines how the actor can act; what it can do. The comparator apparatus of the actor probably corresponds with what Fred Dretske (Dretske, 1981) refers to as one of the key functions of psyche. Perception and cognition are distinct but related aspects of psyche associated with its function as a control system. In simple terms, perception turns sensory inputs into categories. Perception attenuates the complexity of the environment by assigning a limited range of categories to certain signals emanating from the ambient environment. Cognition operates upon such categories and makes decisions about appropriate action.

Maturana and Varela (Maturana and Varela, 1987) argue that humans tend to assign the ability to move (or locomote) as one of the key characteristics of living beings. The ability to perform complex movement is also associated with the complexity of the nervous system of the organism. For example, a primitive organism known as a protozoan consists of a cell body to which is attached an appendage known as a flagellum. The flagellum beats in such a way that it is able to pull the body of the cell behind it through some fluid medium. When the organism hits some obstacle within the medium it is travelling through the flagellum is the first part of organism to impact with the obstacle and it bends. This bending triggers changes in the flagellum's base that is embedded in the cell. Such changes trigger an associated change in the cytoplasm (the main body of the cell) which causes it to slightly rotate. This means that when the flagellum begins beating again it moves the protozoan off in a different direction. Varela and Maturana explain this behaviour in terms of a coupling between a sensory surface (a structure capable of maintaining certain perturbations) and a motor surface (a structure capable of generating movement). This corresponds quite closely to the ideas of a sensory and effector apparatus.

Between the sensory apparatus of some organism and its effector apparatus there must be some neuronal apparatus which serves to couple particular sensations with particular actions. This is what is normally referred to as a nervous system. Such a nervous system serves to 'control' the behaviour of the organism. It is from this nervous system that various forms of psyche emerge.

Levels of psyche

Daniel Dennett (Dennett, 1996), amongst a growing body of other scholars, proposes that there are various forms of psyche, ranging from the least to the most complex. The purpose of such psyche is to generate future. In other words, the purpose of psyche is to generate decisions as to possible actions and tests of such actions to determine the most optimal action to take in terms of some environmental situation. We follow this approach and propose a number of levels of psyche based upon an amalgam of work from philosophy, cognitive science and artificial intelligence. Each level subsumes the functions contained in the levels below it.

We first have to set the lower limit for the development of psyche. Here, an entity can be distinguished from its environment in the sense of having a body. A clear boundary can hence be drawn between this body and its environment. The body is also self-sustaining, as indicated

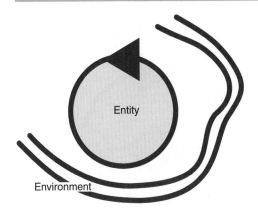

Figure 5.5 An embodied entity

by the arrow in Figure 5.5. However, there is no interaction between this body and its environment. No psyche therefore exists at this level; but in having a body it sets the baseline for the development of psyche. An isolated chromosome is an example of an entity at this level.

The next level is where there is evidence of a sensory and effector apparatus as part of the entity. The sensory and effector apparatus are also connected together by a set of invariant functions. At this level we have the emergence of an actor. However, such an entity is able to act but only in terms of fixed responses to given stimuli. In other words, it has a fixed decision strategy. The entity lacks any function of memory and hence has no capacity to learn. This means that behaviour is controlled through a closed, single-feedback loop. A virus or simple, single-celled bacteria are examples of entities at this level of psyche (Figure 5.6).

Dennett argues that the invariant functions making up the decision strategy of the entity may not be modified within an individual but may be modified over time amongst a population of such individuals through external processes of natural selection. Such simple forms of reactive psyche are evident in what Dennett refers to as *Darwinian creatures*, after Charles Darwin. Such simple organisms are blindly generated by processes of recombination and random mutation of genes. The psyche, and particularly the decision strategy, of such creatures is hardwired into the organism at birth and consists of simple stimulus and response mechanisms that are not amenable to change; there is

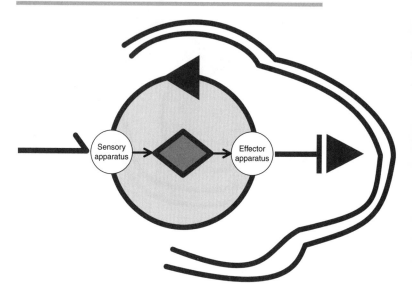

Figure 5.6   A reactive entity

no ability to learn in the sense that their decision strategy can change. Hence, natural selection determines which types of psyche survive and reproduce in terms of some environment. The actions of such organisms are tested against their natural environment and the best 'designs' survive in the sense that they multiply within the environment (Figure 5.7).

Examples of Darwinian psyche are evident in single-celled bacteria such as protozoa as we have already described. In certain other types of protozoa the cell is able to rotate its flagella rather like a propeller to enable it to move through its fluid environment. When a grain of sugar is dropped close to such bacteria they can be observed to move towards this source by rotating their flagella in a particular direction. This process, referred to as *chemotaxis,* can be explained in terms of the way in which the membrane of the bacterium (its sensory surface or aparatus) contains certain molecules capable of interacting with sugar. The presence of a concentration of sugar within its immediate fluid environment causes changes to be made within its internal environment which in turn make the flagellum rotate (its motor surface or apparatus) in the direction necessary to produce forward motion.

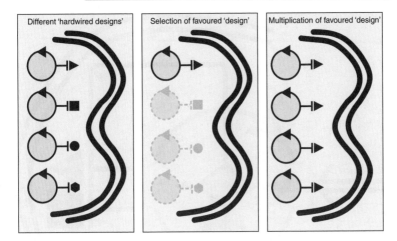

Figure 5.7   Evolution of favoured psyche

The next level of psyche is characterised by entities which possess some form of memory. Such memory allows different forms of decision strategy to be stored. This means that the actor can evaluate the result of a particular action and on the basis of such evaluation reinforce a particular decision strategy over another within its memory. The earthworm is an example of an entity at this level of psyche.

Dennett refers to this particular level in the evolution of psyche as *Skinnerian Creatures*, after the notable behavioural psychologist B.F. Skinner. Individual organisms of this type are not wholly designed at birth (Figure 5.8). They are said to have a degree of plasticity in the sense that their action may change depending on the previous experiences of the organism. In other words, they are able to sense the results of some action they take and on the basis of feedback are able to reinforce those behaviours that achieve favourable outcomes. Such organisms tend to use simple trial and error to establish how best to deal with a new situation and adopt behaviours through so-called operant conditioning. Favourable actions are reinforced within memory and then tend to be repeated in future action.

The computer scientist Raul Arrabales (Arrabales, Ledezma et al., 2010) adds an additional important function to this adaptive psyche: that of attention. This means that the actor is able to exercise some

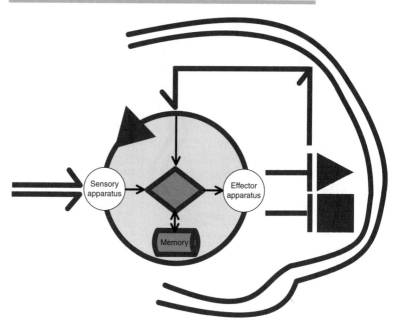

Figure 5.8   Adaptive psyche

form of selective control over both its sensory and effector apparatus. The actor is able to select specific content from the total amount of such content available in memory or through its sensory apparatus. Such content is evaluated in terms of some primitive emotive mechanisms, enabling the entity to develop action directed towards specific external objects. Hence, organisms are able to chase, follow or run away from such objects. Such emotive mechanisms are therefore used not only to select what objects to which to pay attention, but which behaviours to store in memory. Quadruped mammals are said to be examples of this level of psyche, as are most forms of fish.

At this level we are beginning to see the ways in which the conglomeration of functions making up the psyche starts to provide an inner environment for the actor which it can exploit in making better decisions about appropriate action. The development of a more complex memory enables entities at this level to be able to work with multiple goals and also to be able to shift between such goals. This requires the

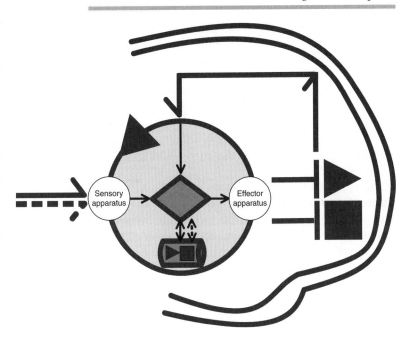

Figure 5.9   Executive psyche

ability to shift attention between tasks (Figure 5.9). The entity is also able to evaluate performance against goals and to reinforce learning in terms of emotions. In other words, it is able to perform basic emotional learning.

Dennett refers to this level of psyche as *Popperian creatures*, named after the philosopher Karl Popper. Such actors have the ability to pre-select among a variety of possible behaviours or actions. They are able to do this because they have an inner environment which can be used to select amongst possible actions by testing such actions against the inner environment and observing results. For this to work the inner environment must contain sufficient information about the outer environment and its regularities. This requires the psyche to contain some form of model of the external environment. The organism behaves in terms of decisions made in relation both to what it senses from aspects of the external environment and predispositions embedded in its internal environment. Popperian creatures would be expected to make much smarter moves than their Skinnerian counterparts because they can pre-select from possible actions, weeding out the truly stupid actions before risking them in the environment. Mammals, birds, reptiles and fish can all pre-select their behaviour before acting in this manner.

There is clearly much debate about when the levels of psyche previously discussed break through into a so-called *theory of mind*. One of the first such functions generally accepted as constituting 'mind' is represented by the capability of holding basic mental states such as emotions and being able to use such states to make decisions as to behaviour.

The next level up clearly arises when an entity becomes self-conscious. Here, the entity is able to *know that it knows*. This makes it possible for the entity to consider its own future behaviour and to plan for its behaviour – to undertake intentional action. The entity is also able to distinguish itself from aspects of its environment, which opens up the possibility of using parts of this environment as *tools* in pursuit of its goals.

Tomasello (Tomasello, Carpenter et al., 2005) and his team provide more detail on the functions required of the inner environment required by this level of psyche. Here crucially is the idea of an intention as a plan of action, distinguishable from some goal – some form of mental state underlying instrumental action.

Suppose some human has the internal goal of opening some box (Figure 5.10). This person may formulate some intention (or plan of action) to achieve this goal. In making some decision as to the most appropriate intention the actor will consult both its existing knowledge and skills and its model of the environment. Hence, depending on the way in which the box is constructed the actor might decide upon the most appropriate tool for the job – a knife, a pair of scissors and so on.

The intention of some actor results in some action using its effector apparatus – in this case, the hand. After the action is complete, the state of the world is transformed in some way. The result of the action is directly observable by the actor through its sensory apparatus. This result may or may not match the original goal. A successful result is one in which the resultant state matches the goal state. A failure results when the resultant and goal state do not match. This may be due to accident in which an unintended result is achieved. In both such cases a further cycle of decision-making and action is likely to occur.

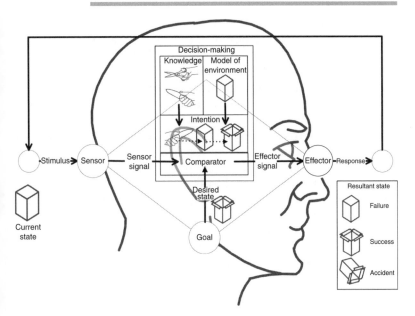

Figure 5.10   Popperian psyche

Therefore, crucial to any intentional action is the way in which an actor continuously monitors the situation: first, to determine the state of the environment; second, to perform the action itself; third, to monitor the resultant state. This is inherently a process of feedback.

Tomasello et al. (Tomasello and Carpenter, 2007) implicitly propose three levels of intentional action. These are related closely to levels of psyche we have discussed and to a development sequence evident amongst human infants.

In a Darwinian creature there is a straightforward direct route between a sensor signal and an effector signal in pursuit of some goal. The actor performs a simple comparison of the state of the world with a delimited goal. The organism has no internal model of the world and no plan of action is formulated prior to action in the psyche of the organism. Hence, this form of psyche as control can operate simply with a form of single-loop feedback. In a Skinnerian creature certain ways of acting may become reinforced by a form of double-loop feedback in terms of the consequences or resultant state of some action. The ability to

99

perform intentional action begins to emerge with Popperian creatures. Such creatures are able to adjust their behaviour in terms of an internal model. They plan their action in terms of this internal model of the environment and knowledge of alternative ways of acting.

For true human-like psyche three further functions are required. First, the entity is able to recognise other objects as intentional systems: *I know you know*. This makes social behaviour possible. It also opens up the possibility of constructing and using more complex tools, in cooperation with other intentional entities. Second, the psyche must have the capacity to support an advanced theory of mind: *I know you know I know*. This is the fundamental basis of *inter-subjectivity* and opens up the full range of social behaviours including communication and use of complex sign-systems. Actors with such a level of psyche are not only able to communicate but also to exercise Machiavellian strategies such as lying/deceit. Third, the possibilities afforded by inter-subjectivity and communication open up the role of the social environment along with the physical environment in the shaping of behaviour. Behaviour is modulated by culture, particularly the use of external tools for knowledge transmission.

Dennett refers to entities having this level of psyche as Gregorian Creatures (Figure 5.11), named after the biologist Richard Gregory. These are organisms whose inner environments are informed by designed parts of their outer environment. Gregorian creatures are particularly able to import mind-tools (signs) from the outer environment and to create through manipulation of these mind-tools an inner environment which improves control.

This has a resonance with the distinction made by the Russian psychologist Lev Vygotsky who argued that human beings never interact with the world directly. Instead, such interaction is mediated by tools which come in two forms: physical or technical tools such as hammers and psychological tools or signs which help people affect themselves or others, such as a map. Both physical tools and psychological tools are mediators which help change the structure of activity.

A common set of such mind-tools amongst organisms of the same species opens up the possibility of communication between organisms. Aspects of the behaviour of the organism then become adapted to the attempt to influence the behaviour of other organisms, which of course, now form a significant part of the environment of such organisms.

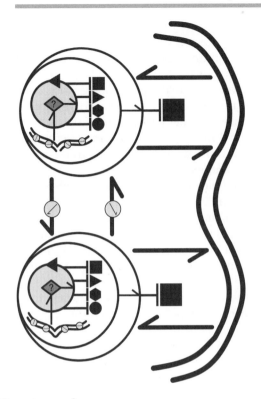

Figure 5.11   Gregorian psyche

Conclusion

We began this chapter with a close analysis of walking or perambulation. Norbert Wiener, perhaps not surprisingly given his interest in this activity, used walking as a popular example of control in action. He posed the question of how was it that humans did not fall over when they walked forward (Wiener, 1950). His solution to this puzzle was to propose the idea that parts of the human nervous system continuously exercised control of this activity through negative feedback.

Both individual and social cases of perambulation are commonplace examples of social action. Both types of action rely on forms of control and will also undoubtedly rely on forms of both internal and external communication. In both cases, actors will be interpreting the forma in

101

the situation: in this case the movements of their own body and the movements of other actors as natural signs. Further, they will also be calculating or planning their own manoeuvres in terms of their interpretations of such forma.

In Chapter 2 we argued that organisation consists of the patterning of order. The key question is how does such patterning persist: how does it remain viable and how does it sustain itself through time? We are particularly interested in the concept of control because it contributes to our understanding of how such patterning in the world is created and re-created across multiple situations.

However, the term control has acquired something of a negative connotation in modern, everyday usage. This chapter has been an attempt to establish a more informed understanding of control and to explain its role as a critical, systemic concept. Control is an essential part of a viable system. This implies that every system has to have some form of control in the sense that control fulfils the system purpose of ensuring viability and sustainability.

Therefore, the logo for this chapter is meant to suggest control through feedback. Systems of whatever sort must maintain their identity through time through processes of continuous re-creation. Control is the process by which a system remains viable at the current time and sustainable through time. We have argued that the idea of control and control processes has relevance for understanding how order or organisation emerges not only in systems of performance, communication and representation but particularly in the intentional systems of mind.

A given control process can be seen to be made up of sensors, comparators and effectors and works with feedback. Such control processes are evident in communication, learning and decision-making. Most signs used in the animal world and in the machine world are 'programmed' or 'hardwired' into the makeup of the animal and machine. Hence, we might argue that the decision strategy 'designed' to work in the presence of such signals is built into the actor from 'birth' and is used to implement processes of regulation through single-loop feedback.

There is hence a tendency to infer from this that the behaviour of an individual actor is deterministic. This is the typical argument in relation to much animal behaviour such as the honeybee dance as described in Chapter 4. An attending honeybee senses the actions of the foraging honeybee and responds to this dance in terms of a decision strategy defined within the genetic makeup of the honeybee. Some aspects of human behaviour have similarities to this reactive psyche, such as the production of facial expressions as the result of some emotional state (Chapter 3).

Generally, however, human behaviour is much more flexible in nature because decision strategies are not hardwired but are acquired and continually revised through double-loop feedback: through learning. Within some higher species of animal and particularly within the human sphere signs tend to be learned. This means that the 'model' embedded within the control process is amenable to change through double-loop feedback processes.

The flexibility and non-deterministic nature of much human action means that the human psyche must enact much more complex control. Humans need to build mechanisms for in-formation (Chapter 8): for ensuring that multiple actors accomplish common representations of the world and use such representations to achieve coordinated action. Sign-systems prove themselves as significant resources within such collective accomplishment.

Communication and control are therefore two aspects of the context for sign-systems that we shall return to at a number of points in the discussion which follows. The eminent science fiction writer Philip K. Dick (Dick, 1978) in one of his most famous novels once claimed that *'The basic tool for the manipulation of reality is the manipulation of words. If you can control the meaning of words, you can control the people who must use the words.'* If we substitute *sign* for *word* in this quote it aptly sums up the inherent relationship between signs, meaning and the control of action which we shall return to in further chapters.

Let us first turn to the nature of signs as physical form: as data...

References

Arrabales, R., A. Ledezma, et al. (2010). ConsScale: A pragmatic scale for measuring the level of consciousness in artificial agents. Journal of Consciousness Studies 17(3/4): 131–164.

Dennett, D. C. (1996). Kinds of Minds: towards an understanding of consciousness. Weidenfield and Nicholson, London.

Dick, P. K. (1978). Do Androids Dream of Electric Sheep? Gollancz, New York.

Dretske, F. I. (1981). Knowledge and the Flow of Information. Blackwell, Oxford.

Maturana, H. R. and F. J. Varela (1987). The Tree of Knowledge: the biological roots of human understanding. Shambhala, Boston, Mass.

Rose, J. and J. G. Gamble, Eds. (1994). Human Walking. Baltimore, Williams and Wilkins.

Ryave, A. L. and J. N. Schenkein (1974). Notes on the art of walking. Ethnomethodology: selected readings. R. Turner. Harmondsworth, Middx, England, Penguin.

Stonier, T. (1994). Information and the Internal Structure of the Universe: an exploration into information physics. Springer Verlag, Berlin.

Stonier, T. (1997). Information and Meaning: an evolutionary perspective. Springer-Verlag, Berlin.

Tomasello, M. and M. Carpenter (2007). Shared intentionality. Developmental Science 10(1): 121–125.

Tomasello, M., M. Carpenter, et al. (2005). Understanding and sharing intentions: the origins of cultural cognition. Behavioral and Brain Sciences 28: 675–735.

Vygotsky, L. (1986). Thought and Language. MIT Press, Cambridge, Mass.

Wiener, N. (1948). Cybernetics. Wiley, New York.

Wiener, N. (1950). The Human Use of Human Beings: cybernetics and society. Discuss books, Boston, Mass.

Wilson, B. (1990). Systems: concepts, methodologies and applications. John Wiley, Chichester, UK.

6
Data: Form to inform

Introduction

In much popular usage, the terms data and information are not only bandied about a lot; they are frequently used interchangeably. For example, people speak of both data and information transmission, of data stores and information stores, and of data manipulation and information processing. In this chapter we elaborate upon the nature of what we referred to in Chapter 2 as forma. Forma relates to the physical and empirics levels of signs upon the semiotics ladder. Part of the reason for considering the nature of forma is that doing so helps us to better understand and to provide greater precision to the concept of data as well as highlighting the many differences between data and information.

In Ronald Stamper's original conception (Stamper, 1973), empirics equates with the precepts of information or communication theory as represented in the Shannon and Weaver model of communication described in Chapter 4. In this sense, empirics, refers to the physical characteristics of the medium of communication, particularly the study of the signals used to code and carry the signs of a message, as well as to communication channels and their characteristics. We prefer to define empirics in a broader sense as concerned with the physical characteristics of signs. This allows us to include a concern with how signs are represented or stored using various different media as well as the traditional concern with how signs are coded as signals which travel along various communication channels or sensory modalities.

There is evidence of symbolic manipulation by humans for at least 50,000 years. Some suggest that data representation inherent in symbolism emerged with our species: Homo Sapiens (Marshack, 2003). Homo sapiens (wise man) is also Homo habilis (man the toolmaker). But man is not unique amongst species as a user of tools. Many species of monkey and ape, for instance, have been shown to use simple tools to transform aspects of their world, such as in the use of sticks to dig for termites by chimpanzees. Nevertheless, as a species we do appear unique in the complex ways in which we manipulate signs as 'tools'.

Some have argued that clay tokens as described in Chapter 1 are not actually the earliest evidence of human symbolism. Alexander Marshack (Marshack, 2003), for instance, suggests that symbolism such as scratches on antler horn from the Upper Palaeolithic (35,000–10,000 B.C.) period may constitute some of the earliest use of a tally, related perhaps to calendar events such as the gestation period of a horse or the phases of the moon. More recently Genevieve Von Petsinger (Ravilious, 2010) has identified 26 signs painted on cave walls with a Worldwide distribution and dating to the same Upper Palaeolithic period. Figure 6.1 illustrates these signs and plots them in terms of their frequency of

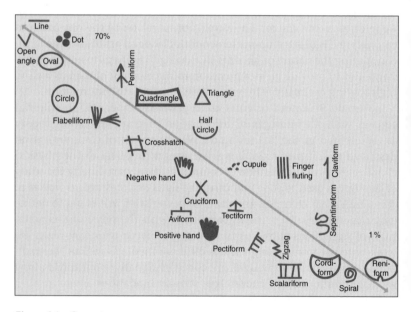

Figure 6.1   Cave signs

occurrence in various cave settings from the top left to the bottom right of the figure.

We shall argue that symbols from prehistory and symbols within our modern world all have particular characteristics in common. A symbol is any facet of the world that can be modulated and which is regarded as significant by some group of actors. The question of what is significant depends on both the cognitive and social background of this group of actors. In other words, symbols are both individual (perceptual/ cognitive) and group (social) constructs. Whereas perception and cognition, forming key functions of the human psyche (Chapter 5), determines what can be used as symbols, what is actually regarded as symbolic will be largely determined by culture.

In the process of defining forma we shall start to distinguish between signals, symbols and signs. Signals relate to patterns of energy or matter in the environment and as such are physical constructs. In contrast, symbols relate to sensation and as such are perceptual and cognitive constructs. Signs, as an encompassing concept, relate symbols to meaning and to eventual action and as such are also social constructs.

The cave signs illustrated in Figure 6.1 are in at least one sense familiar to modern man – they all consist of graphical symbols. But data or more precisely forma is not limited to graphical representation. To help ground our discussion of the nature of forma and to help us make the concept 'strange' we consider symbols from a different age and extinct culture that used a distinctive 'technology' for the representation of symbols. During the time of the Inka Empire in South America, collections of knotted strings known as khipu were used for symbolic representation (Beynon-Davies, 2009g). For the Inka, khipu were used to represent key data of significance. The forma of khipu were used to inform performance in many aspects of this society's life.

Inka Khipu

The Inka people made up a sophisticated and wealthy society existing in a comparatively hostile environment – the high Andes in South America. The civilisation was highly successful although it survived for a comparatively short time (c.1200–1475 AD). The success of Inka society is remarkable in that it operated effectively without the benefits of a 'written' language or any mode of transportation based on the wheel (D'altroy, 2002).

Such success is generally attributed to the ability of the Inka 'bureaucracy' to record details of the empire's activities, and to use this information efficiently to administer the far reaches of the empire. This control was also clearly reliant on effective information flow between parts of the empire, in that the creation, storage and transmission of records was essential for maintaining institutional structures such as agriculture and defence.

Not surprisingly, the Inka bureaucracy sent and received many messages daily. Typically such messages contained details of resources such as items required or available in store houses, taxes owed or collected, census data, the output of mines or the composition of particular workforces.

Messages had to be clear, compact and portable, and for this purpose a form of data representation known as the khipu was used. This was an assemblage of coloured, knotted, cotton or camelid (llama or alpaca wool) cords. In the language of the Inka the word khipu means to knot and hence specialist personnel known as the khipucamayuq (the keeper of the khipus) were responsible for encoding and decoding messages contained in the khipus. Encoding or 'writing' a khipu involved tying together a complex network of cords of different materials and colours, and tying into them a series of different forms of knot. Decoding or 'reading' a khipu involved a khipucamayaq both in visual inspection and running his fingers rapidly over the knots, rather like a Braille reader.

Several hundred examples of khipu survive and typically vary from having a few cords to, in the largest case, being over 3 meters long and having over 2000 cords (Urton, 2003). There is much argument as to whether khipu were merely used as mnemonic devices or acted as true signifying artefacts. As mnemonic devices they would merely be used to trigger the memory of an individual khipucamayuq. As a signifying artefact, they would need to encode signs from some mutually agreed sign-system used collectively by khipucamayuq as a distinct group of communicants.

Andean scholars believe that there is sufficient evidence to suggest that khipu were true significant artefacts. This inference is based upon the historical record which suggests that khipu were rolled up and transported by chains of specialist runners over long distances. The creator and 'sender' of the khipu must therefore have been different from the reader or 'receiver' of khipu. This implies some form of encoding of data in such artefacts using what we shall refer to as a mutually understood ontology: a shared set of representations of the world.

This interpretation suggests that khipu were used by the Inka as a three-dimensional sign-system in which data was recorded by tracing figures in space with pieces of cord. At the technical level and at the level of empirics, khipu can be considered purely as physical artefacts and analysed solely in terms of their methods of construction. A number of facets have been identified within khipu for encoding the variety demanded of the construction of messages with a significant meaningful content (Figure 6.1). William Conklin (Conklin, 2002) and Gary Urton (Urton, 2003) suggest that these elements were used by a khipucamayuq in a sequence of decision-making related closely to the natural order of construction of khipu. This construction is regarded as being equivalent to 'writing' or encoding a message in a khipu. First, the maker of khipu would consider the construction of cords. Then he would consider the placement of cords upon other cords. This would be followed by choices concerning the construction of knots as well as the placement of knots upon cords. We shall consider these constructional elements in the sequence indicated in Figure 6.2 and shall refer to them as facets: as distinct categories of difference evident in khipu.

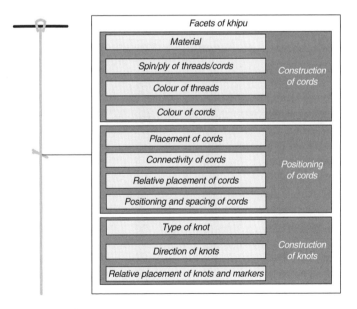

Figure 6.2   Khipu facets

The construction of cords within khipu varies in terms of the type of material used, the spin and ply of threads/cords, the colour of threads and the overall colour of cords.

Facet 1: Type of material

Normally a single khipu cord was produced from fibres of camelid (alpaca or llama) wool. Sometimes cotton is used and when used is usually dyed.

Facet 2: Spin and ply of threads and cords

Cotton or camelid fibres were spun using a drop spindle to produce a thread and such threads could be spun in either of two ways. A clockwise or rightward spinning motion produces an 'S' thread – this is so-called because the fibres in the thread run obliquely from upper left to lower right. An anti-clockwise or leftward spinning motion produces a 'Z' thread – so-called because the fibres run obliquely from upper right to lower left (Figure 6.3).

A single khipu cord consists of one or more threads which are doubled, twisted or plied together in a particular way, and finished with an

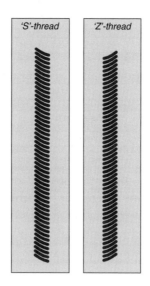

Figure 6.3   S and Z threads

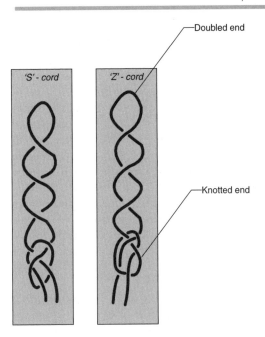

Figure 6.4   S and Z cords

end knot. Hence, each khipu cord has a doubled end and a knotted end. Spinning of threads and plying of cords are inevitably performed in opposite directions to produce greater tensile strength in the finished cord. Hence, Z-threads will be plied in an S arrangement within a cord and vice versa. This is illustrated in Figure 6.4.

Facet 3: Colour of threads

Many cords in khipu are left with their natural cotton or camelid hues. Some cords, particularly those of cotton, are dyed a particular colour. Hence, a khipu thread has a particular colour. Maria and Robert Ascher (Ascher and Ascher, 1978) identify different shades of red, reddish orange, reddish brown, brown, greyish brown, yellowish brown, yellow, olive green, greyish green, greenish blue, blue and black. They use the Inter-Society Colour Council-National Bureau of Standards (ISCC-NBS) method of designating and naming colours to record the colours of the khipu. This system consists of 120 colours and shades or hues which, added together, produce 267 colour blocks. Within this classification system given hues are described using adjectives such as light, moderate, deep, vivid/strong, and dark. On this basis, the Ascher's utilise a set of 59 colours, including white (neutral) and black, from the ISCC-NBS palette, to describe the cords of extant khipu.

In contrast, on the basis of an analysis of colour naming used by native Quechua (the lingua franca of the Inka empire) speakers, Gary Urton (Urton, 2003) proposes a more restricted 'palette' of 24 distinct colours for cords or threads within khipu. This palette consists of two main colour groupings or 'rainbows'. One, the *Creator Rainbow*, includes the colours yellow, violet, green and rose. The other, the *Mourning Rainbow*, consists of the colours violet, green, blue and plum. Since there is overlap between these two groupings he proposes an overall palette consisting of six main colour classes: yellow, violet, green, rose, blue and plum. Each of these colour classes also has four to five main hues: light/pale, moderate, deep/strong, dark and black. Black is composed of essentially a very dark hue of any colour class.

As mentioned above, William Conklin (Conklin, 2002) suggests that the dominant material used in the construction of khipu is undyed cotton. He describes this as coming in eight distinct and natural colours: white, beige, light brown, dark brown, chocolate, reddish-orange brown and mauve. Therefore, it is possible that there are at least two distinct colour groupings evident in khipu: natural undyed colours and dyed colours. Inspection of the palette suggested by the Aschers suggests that approximately 30 or so of their 59 colours might fall roughly into those that occur naturally in unrefined cotton or camelid fibre. This leaves some 30 or so colours that would demand some dying process. In this manner, Urton's proposed 26–30 distinct colours seem to correspond with the group of dyed colours.

Facet 4: Colour of cords

A cord is typically made up of a number of threads. This means that a cord is either of a single colour and hue or contains threads of more than one colour and hue (multi-coloured). The Aschers suggest three ways in which threads of different colours can be combined in a given cord (Ascher and Ascher, 1997). First, a cord could be produced from threads of two colours plied in an S-direction to form a 'barber-pole' or 'peppermint stick' effect. Second, two threads of different colours can be plied in a Z direction to produce a 'mottled' effect. Third, in some cases cords of different colours are joined so that one coloured cord begins where the other one ends. Conklin (Conklin, 2002) suggests a fourth method where a few threads of dyed alpaca wool were added as an accessory to a cord for a few centimetres somewhere along its length (Figure 6.5).

The overall structure of a typical khipu is illustrated in stylised form within Figure 6.6. All extant khipu follow this pattern, suggesting the existence of a number of conventional practices used by the khipu-camayuq in the construction of these artefacts. A central main cord formed the 'horizontal' dimension of the khipu with a diameter typically between one half a centimetre and two thirds of a centimetre.

The construction of the khipu main cord was the same as for any cord, as described above. This means that the two ends of a main cord are typically different. One end was closed in the sense that the cord forms an end knot: the other end of the main cord was open in the sense that it consists of a loop. Occasionally, this open end of the main cord may have an additional 'dangle' cord attached, so-called because

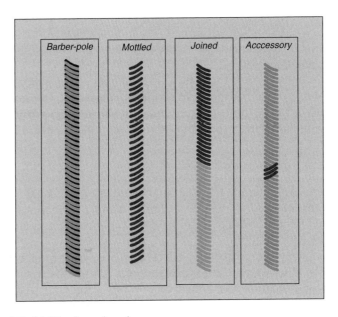

Figure 6.5   Multi-coloured cords

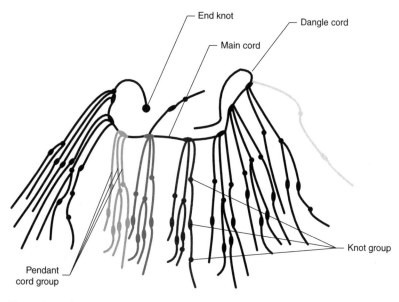

Figure 6.6   The structure of khipu

its method of attachment (see Figure 6.7) causes it to dangle from the end of the main cord.

To the central axis of the main cord a number of pendant cords are attached in the manner shown in Figure 6.8. This involved passing the pendant cord over the main cord and through its own twisted end. After being placed in its correct position it was pulled taut and fixed in place.

Pendant cords can hence be considered to form the 'vertical' dimension of the khipu. Subsidiary cords are frequently knotted to the pendant cord via similar hitch knots. Such subsidiary cords could, in turn, have cords attached to them in a similar manner to form a tree-like structure. Hence, cords appear to have a level or position in a distinct hierarchy within khipu.

Pendant cords are frequently collected together on the main cord in groups. In other words, there is evidence of a distinct spacing between clusters of pendant cords. When this occurs, a top cord is typically attached to the group, but falling in an opposite direction to the direction of pendants within the group. Such special cords are attached to

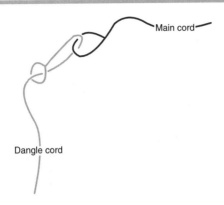

Figure 6.7 Attachment of a dangle cord

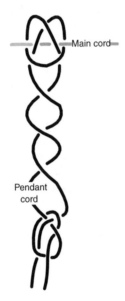

Figure 6.8 Attaching a pendant cord

the main cord in a manner which suggests that they bear a particular relationship to a group of pendant cords.

Top cords are attached to their pendant group in one of three ways (figure 6.9). They can be attached to the main cord adjacent to their

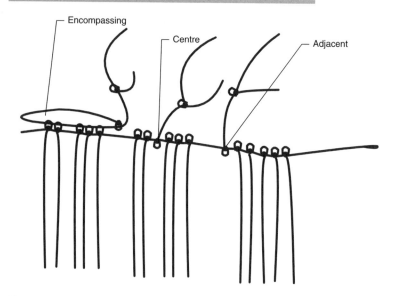

Figure 6.9 Attaching top cords to a pendant group

group, or attached from the centre of the pendant group. They may also encompass a group in the sense that the top cord is passed through the hitch knots of each of the pendant cords in the pendant group.

Khipu can hence be considered a three-dimensional network of cords in which the connectivity, relative placement and spacing of cords may all represent distinct facets of difference.

Facet 5: Connectivity of cords

The way cords were connected together is likely to indicate linkages between component elements of a message. For instance, as mentioned, top cords are sometimes attached to a pendant group, presumably indicating some relationship with the pendant group. Dangle cords are also sometimes attached to one end of the main cord.

Facet 6: Relative placement of cords

The relative placement of cords on other cords, particularly the placing of pendant cords on the main cord, is likely to signify some meaning. For example, subsidiary cords are frequently added as 'modifiers' to pendant cords.

Facet 7: Positioning and spacing of cords

The positioning of cords and as a consequence the spaces between cords was probably used to indicate the presence or absence of key elements of a message. For instance, pendant cords frequently are organised into groups of cords followed by a distinct space on the main cord.

Both Conklin and Urton consider the knot as the fundamental signifying unit of Khipu. In terms of construction, knots vary both in type and direction of main axis.

Facet 8: Type of knot

Knots are normally tied at various positions along pendant or subsidiary cords. Four main types of knots are used within khipu: loop hitch knots, single knots, 'long' knots and figure-eight knots. The Aschers also identify an extended variant of the figure-eight consisting of an extra turn. The five types of knots are illustrated in Figure 6.10. Loop hitch knots are used to attach cords to another cord as described above. The other types of knots are tied on to the main cord, pendant, dangle or subsidiary cords. Within Figure 6.10 a short-hand is included for each type of knot which we use in diagramming Khipus, in terms of what we shall refer to as data structures, in Chapter 7.

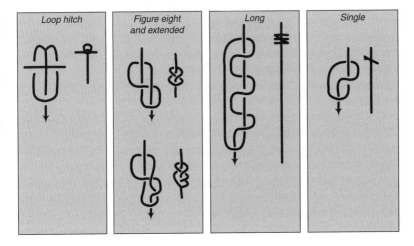

Figure 6.10   Knot types

Facet 9: Direction of knots

Urton notes that each type of knot may be tied in one of two ways (Urton, 2003). In terms of a hitch knot, the holding element of the knot may be either in front of the knot or behind the knot. The former Urton calls a recto hitch knot and the latter a verso hitch knot (Figure 6.11).

In terms of single, long and figure-eight knots the orientation of the dominant diagonal axis of these knots is used to distinguish between what Urton calls 'S' knots and 'Z' knots (Figure 6.12).

Facet 10: Relative placement of knots and markers

The relative placement of knots on individual cords is generally seen to signify meaning in some way. For instance, particular types of knots typically appear at particular points on a string, such as a figure of eight knot close to the end of a pendant or subsidiary cord. The Aschers also mention that markers such as tassels are sometimes attached to the main cord at particular points.

Signals

The main reason for spending such time in detailing the way in which khipu were constructed is to demonstrate how we can focus upon the

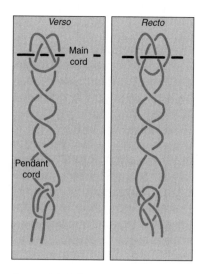

Figure 6.11   Recto and verso hitch knots

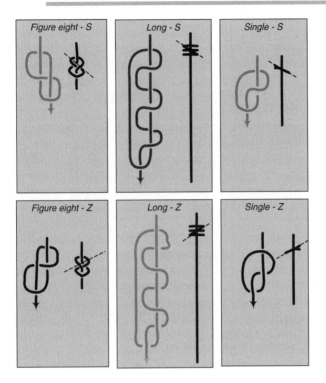

Figure 6.12 S and Z knots

forma of some artefact of communication independently of its use within communication and performance more generally. At the level of forma we are primarily concerned with how matter or energy is used to signal symbols.

Following Sebeok (Sebeok, 1976) we can classify forma in terms of the form of matter or energy used to signal something (Figure 6.13). Theoretically, any form of matter, whether it be solid, gas or liquid, can be used as forma. Likewise any form of chemical or physical energy can be used to provide a signal for communication.

Organisms exist in a surrounding environment of energy and matter. Hence, ambient energy in this environment could be said to be continually signalling. Maturana and Varela (Maturana and Varela, 1987) argue that organisms are 'structurally coupled' to their environment.

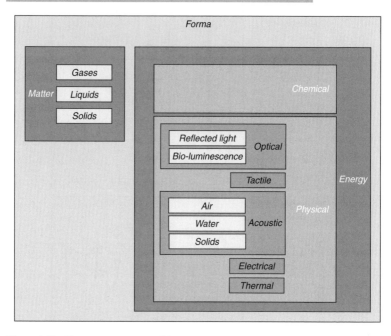

Figure 6.13   Forma as matter and energy

Organisms perturb this environment through their effector apparatus and the environment perturbs the organism through the organisms' sensory apparatus.

As discussed in Chapter 4, any form of energy propagation can be used to form a signal. A signal therefore consists of the patterned modulation of energy or matter along some communication channel. For instance, human speech travels as a signal consisting of a pattern of sound waves (acoustic energy through air), while facial expressions rely upon the reflectance and transmission of light (optical, reflected, physical energy). In contrast, honeybees can communicate through the transmission of particular odours (gases diffusing through air) and through vibrating honeycomb within the hive (manipulation of a solid).

As we have seen, to transmit a signal along a communication channel the signal must be subject to some modulation. Modulation is the process by which variety (Chapter 4) is introduced into a signal. If we are unable to modulate the pattern of a signal then no information can be communicated between transmitter (sender) and receiver along a communication channel. Once we can vary the signal then it becomes possible to code certain messages using variations or differences in the signal.

Consider two communication problems which can be understood solely from the perspective of forma. In the search for extra-terrestrial intelligence (SETI) you need some means of identifying whether an alien civilisation is trying to communicate with you using a particular signal. In zoology scientists need to prove that the clicks and whistles used by dolphins are a form of communication (McGowan, Hanser et al., 1999).

George Kingsley Zipf (Zipf, 1965) was an American linguist and phi-lologist who studied statistical occurrences in different languages. He noticed that a small collection of elements (such as letters and words) in natural human languages are used very frequently by users of the language but that the vast majority of elements are used infrequently. This insight provides hints of an appropriate method for determining whether a signal is utilising a sign-system for coding. For instance, if you count the number of times particular letters of English appear in written extracts of the language and plot the logarithm of their fre-quency of occurrence a –1 (negative) slope is achieved. This holds true when you plot the elements of most human written languages against their frequency of occurrence. Interestingly, a random string of letters (not conveying any evidence of a sign-system) appears as a flat slope on the graph (Figure 6.14).

More interestingly if we plot all the elements of radio signals received by SETI to date they approximate to the random or flat slope. This indi-cates that to the present day no alien life form appears to be attempting to communicate with the human race.

However, in contrast, if we plot the patterns of squeeks and whistles produced by adult dolphins on this graph the line approaches the –1 slope (–0.95). This is evidence that something is being communicated between individuals of this non-human species. But to know what is being communicated we need to interpret the signal or decode the mes-sage. For this we need to know the syntax and semantics of the sign-system used by dolphins.

The same is true for khipu. The close study of the empirics of this artefact as described above suggests its use as a sign-system amongst the

121

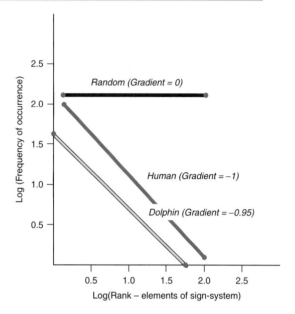

Figure 6.14   A Zipf plot of Human and Dolphin sign-systems

Inka. If we were to plot the constructional elements from extant khipu in terms of their frequency of occurrence a negative slope would result. This suggests that khipu have a key and basic property associated with significance. However, as we shall see in Chapter 7, we only have appropriate syntax and semantics for certain types of this artefact. Much of the syntax and semantics of this aspect of forma remains to be discovered.

Discrimination

One of the key problems with the standard model of communication as outlined in Chapter 4 is that it assumes an inherent relationship between some actor which effects or sends a message using some signal or receives or senses some message embedded in a signal. This ignores the fact that we as organisms are continually in communication with our environment. In this sense, the environment is the continual basis for what we might refer to as natural signs, as well of course as signs created by other organisms.

To reiterate the case of a person walking along a pavement or sidewalk discussed in Chapter 5. That person needs to be continuously aware of the signalling from the environment to enable her to navigate from where she is now to where she would like to be. Using her senses she is continuously interpreting natural signs.

Perception – the process by which an actor uses its sensory apparatus in this way – relies on an actor's ability to discriminate; to discern differences in the world. Such differences relate to the modulation of signals. This is essentially what we mean by patterning in the world: a pattern being a regular or repeated set of differences.

The essence of discrimination or difference is being able to 'draw' a boundary around some thing. In doing so an actor distinguishes that which is inside the boundary and hence part of the thing from that which is outside the boundary and not part of the thing. Spencer-Brown (Spencer-Brown, 1969) symbolises this as O, where the circle represents the boundary and the act of 'drawing' the boundary amounts to the base act of discrimination; which, it is further argued, may be the base operation of the process of perception itself. This is why we used the symbol O as the logo for the prologue and why a circle forms a key component of the logos used in further chapters, including the current one.

Generally speaking there are two types of signals: digital and analogue. A digital signal has a small number of possible values, two for a binary digital signal. An analogue signal has values drawn from a continuous range. The value of the signal varies over this range.

Fred Dretske (Dretske, 1981) argues that physical signals of ambient energy are necessarily analogue, or continuous in nature. Hence, both light and sound can be considered a waveform emanating from some source. Sound, for instance, can be considered a pressure wave which travels through a solid, liquid or gas and can be represented as a sinusoidal wave as in Figure 6.15. The figure also illustrates how such a signal can be digitised, in this case by sampling the frequencies of sound at specific time intervals.

Dretske argues that a primary function of the nervous system is to convert analogue signals from the environment into some form of digital representation. It does so by chunking up the digital signal and applying categories (having a limited number of states) to the analogue signal through some process of discrimination. This is a necessary part of what Gregory Bateson (Bateson, 1972) refers to as the making of

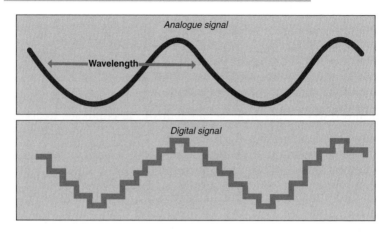

Figure 6.15   Analogue and digital signals

differences. This also has much similarity with Stafford Beer's (Beer, 1972) idea of the way in which some system, in this case an organism, attenuates the variety in its environment in order to deal with it effectively.

Take the example of colour. In Fred Dretske's terms, as humans we all perceive, more or less, the visual colour spectrum as a series of analogue signals. In terms of human sight, human beings can perceive light (see) in a spectrum of wavelengths between 380 nanometres and 740 nanometres. However, as we shall describe later, humans appear to agree upon and recognise a coherent set of colour differences based upon a discrete chunking of the visible spectrum. Six mono-chromatic colours in this so-called visible spectrum correspond to light of a single wavelength: red (700–630 nm), orange (630–590 nm), yellow (590–560 nm), green (560–490 nm), blue (490–450 nm) and violet (450–400 nm). This digitisation hence forms part of the background for colour perception and determines the range of colour discrimination that can be used to code forma on this sensory modality.

Depending upon our sign-system we also assign a coherent set of digital labels to chunks of the human visual spectrum. Take the facets described in the khipu case such as the 60 or so colours from which khipu cords were constructed. These represent a typified set of differences observable amongst extant khipu. Clearly, the way in which such

124

differences were produced and the ways in which such differences were perceived is likely to have been significant to a particular community of actors: the khipucamayuq.

Symbols, perception and cognition

Therefore, signals have an existence independent of any sensing agent. They are objective. However, to become symbols we must have some sensing actor that is able first to sense or perceive the signal, second to interpret the signal and third to use this interpretation as a stimulus to behaviour. This assumes that a critical process of perception is involved in perceiving a signal and that a process of cognition is involved in turning a signal into a symbol. It also assumes that a critical process of interpretation is involved in turning a symbol into a sign.

Since a symbol is any aspect of the world that can be modulated as a signal and hence used in communication, symbols are both individual/cognitive constructs and group/social constructs.

Within the human sphere, symbols as cognitive constructs consist of modulated aspects of the world dependent on the five human senses: sight, touch, smell, taste and hearing. The physical makeup of Homo Sapiens determines what humans are capable of sensing: the range of phenomena that can be discriminated using a particular sense. This sets the perceptual and cognitive background for what humans can use as symbols. There is thus a close relationship between symbols, signals and sensing. A symbol is an aspect of the world that can be modulated in a signal and hence can be communicated and sensed by actors in some communication.

Human sight and hearing are the most developed in terms of having the largest range of perceptual discrimination. We would therefore expect a greater range of symbolic expression using these perceptual dimensions amongst human actors. Colour is clearly a critical part of human visual perception, as described above. In terms of hearing, humans can produce a wide variety of sounds using the vocal tract, known as *phones* or *features* in linguistics. These form the possible background for the use of sounds as symbols in speech. The frequency of a sinusoidal wave such as a sound wave refers to the number of times the sine pattern repeats in a given period of time. Human hearing is generally considered to be able to sense sounds in the frequency range 20 Hz and 20,000 Hz. Phonemes are the smallest units of sound used to make differences and are formed as composites of frequencies from this range. Phonemes are 'written' to the auditory or sensory modality by use of the vocal tract to form distinct morphemes – meaningful utterances.

However, the act of 'reading' some aspect of forma should not be regarded as a passive process. We do not as actors passively receive data from our environment; we are actively monitoring our environment for it or paying attention to it. Peter Checkland and Sue Holwell (Holwell and Checkland, 1998a) make this point by distinguishing between capta and data. Data may be continually signalled from our environment but only a small part of it is focused upon by any given actor with a sufficiently complex form of psyche. Capta therefore represents that data to which a particular actor has focused attention.

Hence, we know that the colour of cords is a specific facet of difference within khipu. We also know that in many instances the makers of khipu undertook some effort in producing certain coloured threads. Hence, it is reasonable to assume that colour constituted an important part of the forma of this artefact. We can presume that certain colours were capta for the khipucamyuq and that decoding the meaning of khipu involved associating aspects of colour perception with particular concepts or categories. We shall discuss some aspects of such interpretation in Chapter 7.

Symbols and culture

The range of features in the world that can be modulated (that make differences) is potentially infinite. Different cultures choose different aspects, features or facets of the world as significant. A finite set of facets or differences derived from the infinite variety in the world is used to code a conventionally organised set of symbols necessary for communication. We refer to the collection of such symbolic patterns as an ontology.

The term ontology derives from the Greek *ontos* for being and *logos* for study of. Within philosophy generally the term ontology refers to that branch of philosophy that deals with the nature of being or reality. More recently, the term has been used within Computer Science and Cognitive Science to refer to a model for representing the world. In its most general sense then, an ontology can be considered an organised and symbolic representation of the world.

Whereas human cognition determines what can be used as symbols, what is actually regarded as symbolic will be culturally determined. Symbols as social constructs rely on a shared ontology amongst a group: the context within which a group of signs is used in continuous communication by a social group or groups. Hence, a shared ontology is a necessary pre-condition for joint communication and effectively frames or controls such communication.

Some have taken the next logical step and argued that culture acts as a constraint on cognition in that people from different cultures frame and perceive the world differently. This is known as the Sapir-Whorf hypothesis; sometimes referred to as the linguistic relativity hypothesis. It proposes that the structure of a language, or more generally a sign-system, in large measure affects the way we perceive the world.

The idea was first developed by the German-American linguist Edward Sapir and taken further by his student Benjamin Lee Whorf (Carroll, 1956). Whorf came to linguistics from a background as a fire insurance inspector. What first attracted him to the issues of language was the way in which workmen he inspected acted in relation to petrol drums. Normally, workmen were extremely careful with full drums of petrol. However, they tended to take a very casual attitude towards empty petrol drums. Empty petrol drums are a natural fire hazard because petrol vapours remaining in the drum are extremely inflammable. Whorf therefore concluded there was something about the very word *empty* that was triggering what might be conceived as irrational behaviour amongst the workmen.

Whorf took up the study of North American languages such as Hopi, Nootka and Shawnee. What fascinated him was that Hopi, for example, has a distinct future tense but no distinction between present and past tense. However, Hopi is very rich in other ways. For instance, verbs are inflected for such unfamiliar notions as duration and repetition. This means that concepts which in English might be expressed by totally different verbs are expressed in Hopi by different forms of a single verb:

- róya = it makes a turn; royáyata = it is rotating
- tíri = he gives a start; tirírita = he is trembling
- wíwa = he stumbles; wiwáwata = he is hobbling along

Whorf therefore makes the suggestion that whereas English speakers perceive stumbling and hobbling along as two distinct activities, Hopi speakers perceive them as aspects of the same activity.

Navaho also has a rich vocabulary for describing lines of various shapes, colours and configurations. For example:

- Dzígai = a white line running off into the distance
- Adziisgai = a group of parallel with lines running off into the distance
- Hadziisgai = a white line running vertically upward from the bottom to the top of the object
- Adhééhesgai = more than two white lines forming concentric circles

This large vocabulary allows Navaho speakers to speak effortlessly about all kinds of geometrical arrangement which would require lengthy descriptions in English. The suggestion is that Navaho speakers perceive the world in geometrical terms differently than English speakers. In support of this, it is noteworthy that Navaho place names are overwhelmingly geometrical in nature. For instance, a certain rock formation in Arizona is named in Navaho Tsé Áhé'ii áhá = two rocks standing vertically parallel in a reciprocal relationship to each other. In English the same rocks are called Elephants feet.

The assumption that different languages divide up the world differently is not in doubt as the examples above illustrate. The leap to the assumption that this means that different people using different languages perceive the signals inherent in the world differently remains controversial.

One of the most famous tests of this hypothesis lies in an investigation of the way in which colour terms are formed in different languages. Every language has a set of basic colour terms. English, for example, is usually seen to have eleven = black, white, red, green, blue, yellow, orange, purple, grey, brown and pink. Other languages have a different number. As we have seen Quechua has six, Nez Percé (North America) has seven, Ibo (Nigeria) has four and Jalé (New Guinea) has just two. The complete visual colour spectrum is then chunked up amongst the terms. Hence in Hanunóo (Phillipines) the four colour terms work as follows:

- (ma)biru = black and the darker shades of brown, blue and purple
- (ma)lagti? = white and the paler shades of pink, blue and yellow
- (ma)rara? = red, orange and maroon
- (ma)latuy = yellow and the lighter shades of green and brown.

The anthropologists Brent Berlin and Paul Kay (Berlin and Kay, 1969) tested the use of colour terms by people speaking dozens of different languages with different numbers of basic number terms. They found that the boundaries of colour terms are extremely fuzzy. Speakers of English, for instance, are uncertain as to where red fades into pink, orange or purple. However, when subjects were asked to select from a colour chart the most typical example of a colour term the results were not fuzzy at all. English speakers generally agree very closely about what shade of red constitutes the most typical example of red. They further found that all languages show similar agreement about what they referred to as the central foci of colours. For instance, in Hanunoo the four foci correspond to black, white, red and green. While languages have a different number of colour terms then the foci appear to be universal. Languages seem to select terms from a maximum of about 11 foci: distinct and coherent sets of differences associated with this sensory modality.

Hence, evidence seems to suggest that we all as members of the same species perceive the physical world in a similar manner but that language is used to signify this world in different ways in different cultures. For instance, certain sounds and colours will have significance in particular cultures. Only certain of the sounds that a given human is capable of making will be used to form the phonemes of a given spoken language. In a similar manner, every natural language has a set of basic colour terms.

Therefore, whereas symbols are formed by humans through human perception and cognition, what is regarded as the meaning of the symbol will be culturally determined. By this we mean that cultures develop <u>conventional</u> expectations of patterning in the world. For example, as identified above, there are sixty or so perceivable colour differences used in the construction of khipu cords. Each colour could be used to code some significant meaning. In practice, it is likely that combinations of coloured threads tied within pendant cords were used to convey conventional meanings.

Natural, embodied and disembodied forma

Inherently, we have referred to three distinct types of forma within this chapter in terms of the source of some signalling: what we shall refer to as natural, embodied and disembodied forma.

Forma produced from the natural environment signal natural signs. Hence, objects in the external environment of some actor are continuously signalling their properties and can be picked up by sensors within the sensory apparatus of the actor. Many modern farming methods rely on such natural signs. Mushrooms, or more precisely the vegetative part of the organism known as its mycelium, are 'tricked' into a reaction when a damp layer of soil is placed above it. The organism senses it is under attack and responds by producing fruit, the mushroom itself, which is potentially capable of reproducing itself through spores. Salmon are also 'tricked' into hatching at appropriate times for convenient transportation to fish-beds by carefully controlling the amount of heat and light in their ambient environment.

Changes enacted by the actor using its effector apparatus will signal to other actors and hence also act as forma. Hence, a prairie dog might move its vocal chords to produce a specific set of sounds or a honeybee might move its body in various ways or a human might make particular facial expressions. This is what we mean by embodied forma in the sense that the forma is reliant on some form of bodily action on the part of the actor.

Figure 6.16 illustrates the sonogram for one of the distinct vocalisations made by prairie dogs (Placer and Slobodchikoff, 2004). This particular warning bark is used when a dog predator approaches. Such calls are repeated within larger units known as bouts. Two dominant frequencies are evident in the sonogram which is divided into 45 segments of short barks of about one tenth of a second in duration. Since frequency corresponds to the 'pitch' of sounds, higher frequencies mean higher pitch.

Contrast this pattern with the one represented in Figure 6.17. This is a sonogram which stands for *coyote* in the sign-system employed by prairie dogs. This sound pattern, which lasts only of the order of a few seconds, is clearly distinguishable as an element of forma by prairie dog actors.

Finally, actors may produce artefacts which are given existence beyond the body. Such artefacts can hence persist beyond any one communication and can signal to multiple actors sometimes remote in time and space. This is what we mean by disembodied or persistent forma. Khipu are key examples of such disembodied forma. Although the bodily acts of some human actor, a khipucamayuq, was necessary to produce a given khipu, this artefact then achieved an independent

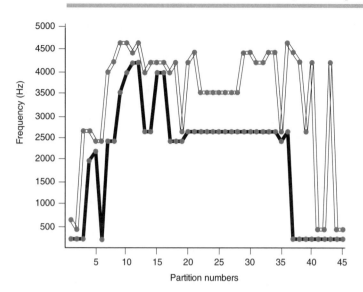

Figure 6.16   The call for 'Dog' articulated by prairie dogs (adapted from Placer and Slobodchikoff, 2004)

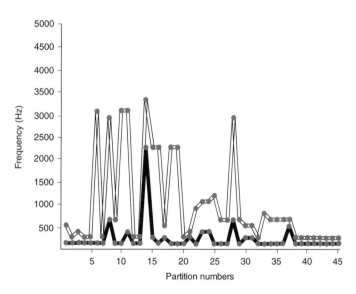

Figure 6.17   The call for 'Coyote' articulated by prairie dogs (adapted from Placer and Slobodchikoff, 2004)

existence of the actor who created it. Also, this artefact could persist in the sense that it could be transported through time and space by other actors and indeed 'read' by remote actors.

Khipu like the clay tokens described in Chapter 1 therefore represent craft or *techne* used in fulfilment of communication and it is to the invention of such techne that we owe more complex developments in the representation of significance such as the invention of writing and digital computers.

Persistent forma

Hence, the idea of disembodied forma bears a clear relationship to the idea of persistent forma. By persistence we mean that symbols exist for some duration over and above the communication within which the symbols were used. This means that symbols are physical constructs that can be 'stored' using some medium.

Not all forma demonstrates persistence. For instance, within human speech, spoken words as sound symbols decay rapidly in air. Spoken words have no life over and above the act of communication within which they take place. In contrast, a clay token can act as a durable representation of the type and quantity of goods stored in warehouses (Beynon-Davies, 2009f). Also, a khipu persists beyond the act of communication it is attempting to represent. As such, persistent symbols become artefacts capable of independent consideration and manipulation by different people, situated in different spaces and at different times. It also, as we shall see in the next chapter, opens up the possibility of automating aspects of processing of symbols.

Peter Gardenfors (Gardenfors, 1995) unpacks this notion in terms of the distinction between cued and detached representations. Cued representations are symbols that stand for something that is present in the current situation – what we referred to above as natural signs. In contrast, detached representations *'stand for objects or events that are neither present in the present situation nor triggered by some recent situation'*. Gardenfors posits that animal communication, such as the honeybee dances described in Chapter 4 and the barks of the prairie dogs discussed in this chapter, relies primarily upon cued representations. Within higher organisms the use of detached representations within both internal and external communication is characteristic of a higher level of psyche consisting of more elaborate cognitive functions such as the ability to plan and self-awareness.

There is also a link to the embodiment of communication as discussed above – the way in which organisms communicate by manipulating aspects of their physical makeup directly, whether this be in terms of movement or manipulating internal organs such as the larynx in the case of humans or wings in the case of the honeybee. Such embodied forma involves 'writing' to a particular sensory modality such as the auditory channel and 'reading' from this channel. However, forma also includes consideration of 'techne' in sign-systems – the activities involved in producing signs using 'tools' which persist beyond the body and beyond any one communication. Such 'technical' activity involves manipulation of a persistent rather than non-persistent forma.

European honeybees clearly utilise non-persistent forma for communication in support of food foraging, as do most animal species (Crist, 2004). In other words, the symbols used are highly coupled both to immediate physical performance and to the immediate physical environment of the actor. The symbols are 'written upon' and 'read from' certain sensory modalities which by definition are tightly coupled to the sensory and effector apparatus embodied in the organism. Hence, a honeybee may vibrate its wings to indicate its presence to other bees and bees may signal that they are aware of its presence by vibrating the honeycomb with their legs. These symbols are hence reliant on physical performance and decay rapidly, meaning that they do not persist beyond immediate communication. They are what Gardenfors calls cued representations.

Many forms of detached representation are also embodied as in the case of the signs of human spoken language. Detached representations break the immediacy and locality constraints of cued representations. Persistent forma take detached representations and give them external or disembodied form. Persistent forma involve the manipulation of technology – the transformation of some physical objects using tools. Hence, Homo Sapiens is unique amongst animal species in building substantial sign-systems around persistent systems of data.

Variety of forma

Since a symbol is any aspect of the world that can be modulated and used in communication, the degree of modulation possible determines the variety or complexity of a sign-system. To refresh, the variety of a system refers to the number of states the system may take (Chapter 2).

In a sign-system the variety of this system is related to the degree with which signals composed from the sign-system can be modulated. Using communication theory as described in Chapter 4, this can be used to describe the amount of information that can be conveyed by the sign-system in communication.

Take the example of the khipu. Gary Urton proposes a method for calculating the variety or 'information' capacity of khipu as a sign-system (Urton, 2003). If we assume that the knot is the primary discriminatory element of khipu then seven levels of decision-making are proposed by Urton to account for the significance of such a knot (Figure 6.18). First, the decision is made as to the material to be used for the pendant cord. Second, a decision is made as to the colour of the cord. Third, the spin of threads and the ply of cords are established. Fourth, the method of

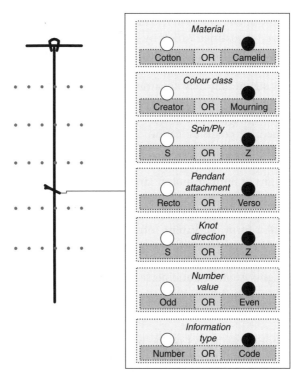

Figure 6.18   'Signature' of a khipu knot

attaching the pendant cord to the main cord is decided upon. Sixth, the number value associated with the knot is determined. Seventh, and finally, the method of interpreting the knot as a decimal value or a code is determined. This last facet determines whether a knot should be read as a number or some other signifying unit (Chapter 8).

Within Figure 6.18, the binary contrast between Urton's facets is represented by the presence of a white stone or a black stone. There is evidence that such stones were used as an aid by khipucamayuq in 'reading' khipu. Hence, the 'signature' of any particular knot could be represented as a sequence of stones and the complete set of knots on a pendant cord as a binary array. For instance, the knot in Figure 6.18 might have been coded with the 'signature' ○○●○○●●○.

If Urton's assumptions are correct, then the variety of the khipu as a sign-system would be $2^7 = 128$. In other words, there would be 128 ways in which a particular knot could be tied, given use of different materials, colours, spins and so on. However, there are some difficulties with the elegant simplicity of this scheme. Six of the facets (material, spin/ply, pendant attachment, number value and information type) are binary in nature. Hence, the variety for these six facets is 64 (2^6). However, the colour class is not strictly binary except in the sense that in Urton's classification of colour, the major colour grouping or rainbow could be determined. In coding the actual colour a possible range of 24 colours/hues is proposed. Hence, each knot of a khipu could have 64×24 variations = 1536 (Beynon-Davies, 2009g).

If Urton's interpretation of a khipu knot as forma with seven facets is correct, then a variety of 1536 for this particular sign-system is somewhat more than the 1000 to 1500 Sumerian cuneiform signs identified and more than twice the 600 to 800 Egyptian and Mayan hieroglyphic symbols. This leads him to suggest that considered purely as forma, khipu are capable of representing complex things such as narrative.

However, given that Urton uses only five of the ten possible facets identified earlier in this chapter, it is theoretically possible for the variety of this particular sign-system to be much larger than that proposed. For instance, as we have seen, there is some dispute as to the actual number of distinct colours evident in khipu. The Aschers, for instance argue for 59 distinct colours rather than Urton's 24. We suggested a compromise is possible between this disparity; that a palette of natural cotton colours and hues can be added to Urton's apparent palette of dyed colours and hues. This revised palette of roughly sixty distinct colours would suggest a maximum variety of 60 × 64 = 3840 – that a knot could be created out of various materials in 3840 different ways.

The variety of a sign-system gives a clue as to the amount of significance that can be coded and communicated using particular forma. As we have seen, the most basic unit of discrimination is binary in nature. Not surprisingly then, Shannon's 'information' theory is a theory of forma measured in terms of binary decisions. Logarithms to the base 2 are used as a measure of the entropy or negentropy of a message. It is therefore no surprise to find that most tele-communication channels nowadays use a form of binary coding (conceived as 0s or 1s similar to the dots and dashes of Morse code) and hence are binary communication channels.

Claude Shannon was particularly interested in the question of how you measure the 'information' content of a given signal emitted along some defined communication channel. Putting aside some of the difficulties with this concept of 'information' raised previously, at the level of forma, such a measure is related to the degree of variety in a signal. A statistical measure of the variety in a signal provides an indication of the level of communication being conveyed by a signal. To calculate this first translate the message into a binary code, then count the binary digits in the message string. This gives you a measure of the communication content of the message.

Take an example. During the time of the Napoleonic Wars a communication system was set up by the Royal Navy consisting of a series of flags hoisted on the rigging of warships. The use of a particular sequence of flags was used to code a particular message such as the famous message *'England expects...'* at the battle of Trafalgar. Suppose a sailor wanted to signal a number between 0 and 127 by means of flags. Using a single flag for each number he needs 128 flags to achieve this. If he decides to use a decimal system to code the numbers being transmitted he needs 21 flags – 10 for the units, 10 for the tens and 1 for the hundreds. Using a binary system he would requires just 14 flags – seven ones and seven zeros.

The capacity of some communication channel refers to the amount of data that can be transmitted along the channel in some given period of time. The bandwidth of a channel refers to the minimum and maximum frequencies allowed along a channel, which in a digital communication channel corresponds to bit rate: the number of binary digits (bits) that can be transferred per second between sender and receiver.

In persistent forma data have to be represented in some way for storage and manipulation. From the discussion above it is evident why most data can be ultimately coded in terms of binary digital (bit) representation. However, within modern digital computing, the measure of the quantity of data stored is typically expressed in terms of the number of bytes rather than bits. A *byte* consists of 8 bits – the word being a contraction of 'by eight'. The capacity of some particular form of storage can then be described in terms of kilo-bytes (Kbytes: 1 thousand bytes – 10^3), mega-bytes (Mbytes: 1 million bytes – 10^6), giga-bytes (Gbytes: 1 billion bytes – 10^9), or tera-bytes (Tbytes: 1 trillion bytes – 10^{12}).

Persistent forma are an inherent feature of and a key problem for the modern world. New measures of the volume of data are becoming required as ICT becomes more and more embedded in modern-day life. For instance, Google's whole data storage was estimated as being 5 peta-bytes (10^{15} bytes) in 2004. It was also estimated that print, magnetic and optical storage media produced about 5 exa-bytes (10^{18} bytes) of data in 2002. Ninety two per cent of this data was stored on magnetic media, mostly in hard disks. Five exa-bytes is equivalent to the size of data contained in 37,000 new libraries the size of the Library of Congress book collection. More recently, it has been estimated that 1,200 exa-bytes of digital data will be generated in 2010.

Conclusion

The logo at the beginning of this chapter is meant to stand for a signal. It is meant to remind us that each sign has a physical or material form independent of the user. We use the term forma as a term to stand for this physical or material aspect of a sign. Charles Pierce (Pierce, 1931) and Charles Morris (Morris, 1946) tend to use the term *sign-vehicle* for this concept, implying it is the means by which significance is transported between actors.

Forma then is concerned with the way in which symbols are formed from signals. Signals relate to patterns of energy or matter in the environment and as such are objective, physical constructs. In contrast, symbols relate to sensation and as such are subjective, perceptual and cognitive constructs. Signs relate symbols to meaning and to eventual action and as such are inter-subjective or social constructs.

In our conception, symbols as sensory constructs are equivalent to data: a datum being a single item of data is equivalent to a symbol. Data is concerned primarily with the physical characteristics of signs. It is concerned with how signs are represented or stored using various different media as well as the traditional concern with how signs are coded as signals which travel along various communication or sensory channels. A symbol therefore is any aspect of the world that can be modulated as a signal and hence used in communication. Symbols are both individual/cognitive constructs and group/social constructs.

Organisms exist in a surrounding environment of energy and matter. Ambient energy in this environment is continually signalling. Any form of energy propagation or the manipulation of matter can thus be used for signalling. A signal consists of the patterned modulation of energy or matter along a particular communication channel. Signals therefore have an existence independent of any sensing agent. They are objective. However, to become symbols we must have some sensing actor that is able first to sense the signal, second to interpret the signal and third use this interpretation as a stimulus to action. This assumes that a critical process of perception is involved in turning a signal into a symbol and a critical process of cognition is involved in transforming a symbol into a sign.

The world has potentially an infinite range of features that can be modulated (that make differences). Different features or facets from this infinite variety are chosen to be significant by different cultures. Such cultures use a finite set of facets to code a conventionally organised set of symbols and use such symbols within communication and performance. Therefore, whereas symbols are perceived and interpreted by humans through human perception and cognition, what is regarded as the meaning of the symbol will be culturally determined. By this we mean that cultures develop <u>conventional</u> expectations of the patterning of significance in the world.

Analysing signs as data involves considering them as symbol structures. A number of facets of difference within Khipu have been described in some detail within this chapter. These include the construction of cords, the placement of cords, the construction of knots and the placement of knots. The use of each facet in isolation within the construction of khipu has the potential to be symbolic. In combination it is likely that they form a symbolic system with a high variety or complexity. The actual meaning associated with such forma is still a matter of some debate and will be considered in more detail in Chapter 8.

In terms of its physical form, each sign generates 'costs' for its storage, transmission and processing. For instance, when a person utters a word she has to expend energy with her body to vibrate air molecules. When a person in ancient Sumeria created a clay token or an Inka tied a knot upon a khipu they did so through physical effort: the manipulation of matter. The costs of forma are hence associated with notions of embodiment and the use of tools.

The concept of embodiment is potentially useful in defining the special class of forma we refer to as techne or technology. Anything produced solely and directly by the body is not techne but may be artefactual. Human speech is an artefact, a creation, reliant on the innovation of human spoken language. However, speech requires the body for its production, and solely the body. Writing or written language is however techne. To produce writing one typically uses the body but one augments this use through tools, whether such tools be clay and stylus, threads of llama or alpaca wool, or keyboard and computer screen. In other words, embodied communication relies on human gesture, including the use of the human vocal tract. Disembodied, augmented or technical communication relies on the use of tools for its production.

Disembodied forma or techne normally has the key advantage of being persistent forma. By persistence we mean that symbols exist for some duration over and above the communication within which the symbols were used. Hence, khipu could be produced by one actor, packed up, and transported many thousands of kilometres to be read and understood by some other actor.

Signals, as forms of energy transmission, tend by their very nature to be non-persistent. Persistent data is stored data: the representation of data in some persistent medium; typically some form of matter. The key advantage of persistent forma such as khipu is that they become artefacts capable of independent consideration and manipulation by different people, situated in different spaces and at different times.

Symbols of course have little value in isolation. Symbols are normally combined in systems or larger recurring patterns of forma. We refer to such organised patterns of data as a data system. This is the topic of the next chapter.

References

Ascher, M. and R. Ascher (1978). Code of the Quipu: Data Book. University of Michigan Press, Ann Arbor.
Ascher, M. and R. Ascher (1997). Mathematics of the Incas: Code of the quipu. Dover Publications, New York.

Bateson, G. (1972). Steps to An Ecology of Mind. Balantine books, New York.

Beer, S. (1972). Brain of the Firm: the managerial cybernetics of organisation. Allen Lane, London.

Berlin, B. and P. Kay (1969). Basic Color Terms: their universality and evolution. University of California Press, Berkeley and Los Angeles, California.

Beynon-Davies, P. (2009f). Neolithic Informatics: the nature of information. International Journal of Information Management 29(1).

Beynon-Davies, P. (2009g). Significant threads: the nature of data. International Journal of Information Management 29(3): 170–188.

Carroll, J. B. (1956). Language Thought and Reality: Selected writings of Benjamin Lee Whorf. MIT Press, Boston, Massachusetts.

Conklin, W. J. (2002). A Khipu Information String Theory. Narrative Threads: accounting and recounting in Andean Khipu. J. Quilter and G. Urton. Austin, Texas, University of Texas Press: 53–86.

Crist, E. (2004). Can an insect speak?: The case of the honeybee dance language. Social studies of science 34(7): 7–43.

D'altroy, T. N. (2002). The Incas. Basil Blackwell, Oxford.

Dretske, F. I. (1981). Knowledge and the Flow of Information. Blackwell, Oxford.

Gardenfors, P. (1995). Cued and detached representations in animal cognition. Behavioural processes 35: 263–273.

Holwell, S. and P. Checkland (1998a). Information, Systems and Information Systems. John Wiley, Chichester, UK.

Marshack, A. (2003). The Art and Symbols of Ice Age Man. Communication in History: technology, culture and society. Boston, Pearson Education.

Maturana, H. R. and F. J. Varela (1987). The Tree of Knowledge: the biological roots of human understanding. Shambhala, Boston, Mass.

McGowan, B., S. F. Hanser, et al. (1999). Quantitative tools for comparing animal communication systems: information theory applied to bottlenose dolphin whistle repertoires. Animal Behaviour 57(3): 409–419.

Morris, C. W. (1946). Signs, Language and Behavior. Prentice-Hall, New York.

Ravilious, K. (2010). The writing on the cave wall. New Scientist. 2748: 12–14.

Pierce, C. S. (1931). Collected Papers. Harvard University Press, Cambridge, Mass.

Placer, J. and C. N. Slobodchikoff (2004). A method for identifying sounds used in the classification of alarm calls. Behavioural Processes 67(1): 87–98.

Sebeok, T. A. (1976). Contributions to the Doctrine of Signs. Indiana University Press, Bloomington, Indiana.

Spencer-Brown, G. (1969). Laws of Form. Allen and Unwin, London.

Stamper, R. K. (1973). Information in Business and Administrative Systems. Batsford, London.

Urton, G. (2003). Signs of the Inka Khipu: binary coding in the Andean Knotted-String Records. University of Texas Press, Austin, Texas.

Zipf, G. F. (1965). The Psycho-Biology of Language: an introduction to dynamic philology. MIT Press, Cambridge, Mass.

7
Data systems: Patterns of forma

Introduction

In the previous chapter we elevated the idea of data to that of forma: the physical nature of signs. In this chapter we focus upon systems of such forma. Symbols relate together and are operated upon in data systems. A data system is a physical symbol system consisting of physical patterns (symbols) which can be combined into structures and manipulated to produce new structures. We suggest a particular interest in those data systems in which the symbols have some persistence. By persistence we mean that symbols exist for some duration over and above the communication within which the symbols were used.

Not all symbol or data systems demonstrate persistence. However, this key characteristic offers sign users a key advantage: persistent symbol systems open up the possibility of becoming collective 'tools'. Hence, a system of artefacts used for representing and processing persistent symbols, is what we mean or should mean by the term 'information technology'. The advantage of defining 'information technology' in terms of primitives associated with some persistent data system is that this concept can be applied to a vast array of historical and cultural artefacts that are and have been used within human activity for the purposes of group communication.

The case described in this chapter provides further material to help ground and validate our attempt to systematically define the concepts of data, information, information system and information technology. It is particularly interesting because it marks a key transition point in the development of the technology of forma. During the last years of the 19th century, Herman Hollerith (Austrian, 1982) developed an electro-mechanical system using punched cards for tabulating data collected by the US census. This innovation stimulated the development of punched card technologies that were used worldwide in both the public and private sector for over fifty years. Such technologies provided the bedrock for the rise of the computing industry following World War II.

The Hollerith electric tabulating system

The notion of a census as an accounting of people or things seems to be pretty much universal across human cultures in which states have formed. Indeed, as we have seen in Chapter 1, there seems some suggestion that a listing of things is inherently associated with the rise of the state in the sense that human innovations such as cities, the rise of agriculture and the keeping of records seemed to have emerged in tandem.

Hence, there is evidence of the collection of census data in the system of clay tokens studied by Schmandt-Bessarat and dating between 8,000–3,000 B.C (Beynon-Davies, 2009e). However, the first documented census was undertaken by the Babylonians over 5000 years ago. Records suggest that such a census was undertaken every six or seven years and counted the number of people and livestock, as well as quantities of butter, honey, milk, wool and vegetables.

In the previous chapter we have seen that among the Inka in the high Andes assemblages of knotted string were significant artefacts (Beynon-Davies, 2007). At the provincial level, the Inka used khipu within annual censuses of the population. Census data included records of births, deaths, marriages and other changes of a person's status. Individuals of each sex were assigned to one of ten categories corresponding not with their chronological age but to their stage in life and ability to perform useful work. Separate khipu were apparently kept for this purpose by each province.

Hence, censuses and state-istics have always been used in association with particular concerns of the state (Beynon-Davies, 2009c). The founding fathers of the United States of America wrote into the constitution that a census of the population should be conducted every ten years and the US Census Bureau was established for this purpose. The first US census was undertaken in 1790 when the population was a little under four million and continued to be conducted by assistant federal marshals up until 1890. During this century, all processing of census data was conducted by hand. For the 1880 census the Census Bureau received an increase in funding and was able to employ its own 'enumerators'. Also, formal enumeration districts were defined for the first time. Over the period, an increasing range of characteristics about the US population were collected (age, gender, race, place of birth, occupation and so on).

In the 1850 census, analysis or tabulation was performed for the first time by the method of 'tallying'. This involved examining each census questionnaire or schedule returned from a census district and recording a mark within a square box on a tally sheet for each characteristic or combination of characteristics to be tabulated. Totals for segments of the population were then calculated by adding counts from particular tally sheets.

Not surprisingly, with population increase, it took almost ten years to complete this processing of data by hand. For the 1890 census an army of 50,000 census takers were expected to pose 235 questions. Using the tallying approach and the expected need to cover an estimated 63 million Americans it was predicted that this census would take over ten years to complete. Hence, it was feared that the completion of the 1890 census would overlap with the start of the 1900 census.

Figure 7.1 illustrates the major activities undertaken within the system of census-taking as evident in the 1890 US census. The precedence of activities is indicated with dotted arrows.

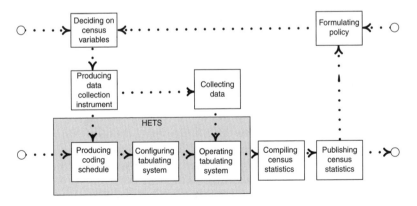

Figure 7.1   The 1890 census as an activity system

The place of data systems throughout history can be traced to what James Beniger refers to as 'crises of control' in particular societies. Beniger implicitly adopts a view of society as a system and he builds upon classic notions of control, feedback and the place of information within systems. He argues that *'because both the activities of information processing and communication are inseparable components of the control function, a society's ability to maintain control – at all levels from inter-personal to international relations – will be directly proportional to the development of its information technologies'*. In other words, he sees a positive feedback loop between technological innovation which sustains human life in a society and innovations in the technology of control. *'Each new technological innovation extends the processes that sustain life, thereby increasing the need for control and hence for improved control technology. This explains why technology appears autonomously to beget technology ... and why ... innovations in matter and energy processing create the need for further innovations in information processing and communication technologies'* (Beniger, 1986).

Consider, for instance, the process of industrialisation in the 19th Century which introduced innovation in transportation and communication. This innovation in turn tended to break down barriers isolating local markets and extended the distribution of goods and services to national and even global markets. This meant that the market equilibrium under which production is regulated by means of direct communication between producer and consumer became disrupted. This constituted a control crisis that needed resolution in new forms of communication technology such as the telegraph.

Similarly, technological innovation supplied the solution to the 'crisis in control' evident in the US census. In 1890, the first automated census was conducted successfully due to an invention introduced by Herman Hollerith, known as the Hollerith Electric Tabulating System (HETS). The position of HETS within the overall activity system of census-taking is plotted on Figure 7.1.

Herman Hollerith was born in 1860 of German immigrant parentage and graduated from Columbia University School of Mines with a mining engineering degree in 1879 at the age of 19 (Biles, Bolton et al., 1989). That year, one of his former professors requested that he come work for the US Census Bureau. After three years there, Hollerith moved to Boston to teach mechanical engineering at MIT, followed by a brief stint of employment at the US Patent Office. In 1884 he made his first patent application for an early form of automatic tabulating system based on the use of punched paper tape. In 1887 he filed a patent for a revised system based upon the use of punched cards. This underwent a number of trials such as in Baltimore's Department of Health, the Surgeon General's office of the War department and by the US Navy.

Before being adopted by the US Census however, HETS had to prove its value. In 1889 a committee of statisticians was therefore appointed by the Secretary of the Interior to investigate three main proposals for improving the speed with which analysis of census data might take place. The first consisted of hand transcription onto slips of paper using different coloured inks for each characteristic of the population. Analysis using this 'slip system' involved sorting slips by colour and counting them by hand. The second consisted of transcription onto colour-coded cards or 'chips'. Analysis using this 'chip system' also involved sorting the cards by colour and counting by hand. The third proposal considered was the use of HETS.

A test was devised using census schedules from 10,491 people resident in four districts of St. Louis. The test consisted of two parts: recording the data and analysis (sorting and counting) of data. It took operators 72 hours and 27 minutes to punch this data onto punched cards as compared to 110 hours and 56 minutes to transfer this data onto the chip system and some 144 hours and 25 minutes onto the slip system. In tabulating the data the Hollerith system took 5 hours and 28 minutes in comparison with 44 hours and 41 minutes for the chip system and 55 hours and 22 minutes for the slip system. Hollerith was awarded the contract.

HETS comprised an integrated manual and electro-mechanical system consisting of the following technology: an approach for coding data on punched cards and two associated mechanisms for punching such cards known as a gang punch and a pantograph punch; a mechanism for 'reading' the data on punched cards known as a circuit-closing press; a mechanism for sorting cards known as a sorting box and a mechanism for tabulating results known as a tabulator. The way in which these technologies interacted within HETS is illustrated in Figure 7.2. On July 1st 1890, 2000 clerks began processing the US census assisted by Herman Hollerith himself. Ninety-six tabulators were employed with associated punches, presses and sorters.

The use of Hollerith machines for this census brought the timescale for the analysis and tabulation of data down to two and one half years,

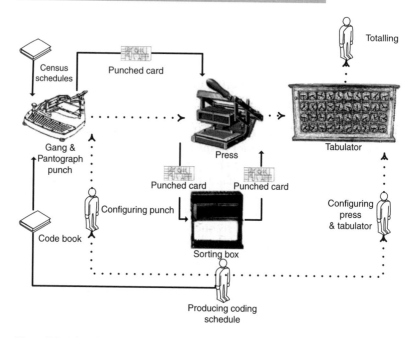

Totalling

Census schedules

Punched card

Gang & Pantograph punch

Press

Tabulator

Punched card   Punched card

Configuring punch

Configuring press & tabulator

Code book

Sorting box

Producing coding schedule

Figure 7.2 The flow of work through the Hollerith Electric Tabulating System

saving tax-payers five million dollars, which at the time was a third of the census department's budget.

HETS was an integrated system in the sense that production of a coding scheme for the punched card initiated configuration of various other elements of the system. This meant that the punching of cards, the reading of cards and the tabulation of data all had to be designed before the systems could be put into operation. A template was produced for the pantograph punch to help staff code data appropriately onto punched cards. Then connections between a card reading press and a tabulator mechanism had to be hardwired. A sorting box had also to be configured to work with the card reading press.

Operating the system involved coding the data onto punched cards, reading data, sorting data and tabulating data. A number of these activities were performed in cycles. For example, once cards had been punched they were put through the reading, sorting and tabulating process seven times in the 1890 census.

Coding data onto punched cards

The first element that needed to be configured in HETS was the production of a scheme for coding data from census returns onto punched cards; referred to as the code book on Figure 7.2 (Beynon-Davies, 2009c). Each census schedule was completed for a household and one punched card was produced using this code book for each person in the household.

The 1890 census recorded for each individual characteristics such as the name, enumeration district, race, gender, age, occupation, relationship to head of household, month of birth if born within the year, marital status, number of years married, place of birth, father's birthplace, mother's birthplace, (for married women) number of children and level of citizenship.

As mentioned, Hollerith originally experimented with the use of paper tape for coding data. However, cards offered a number of advantages over paper tape. They could be easily filed away and once prepared could be used over and over. Also, they were easier to correct or replace and the recording of data could be performed by relatively unskilled individuals.

The use of punched cards for control purposes was originally pioneered in the Jacquard loom, a machine that automated the task of weaving complex patterns. In this loom, pasteboard cards with punched holes were used. Holes in the cards determined the passage of rods that controlled the operation of the loom. Despite this history, Hollerith himself claimed that the idea of using punched cards was suggested to him when taking a train journey. He observed conductors using their punches to quickly code data about the characteristics (such as height, hair colour, size of nose and so on) of an individual onto a ticket. These codes, which were known to other railway conductors, were used to detect fraudulent use of tickets.

Cards within HETS were designed to be the size of a dollar bill of the time. This enabled Hollerith to re-use containers from the US treasury department as storage. After initial problems with their design, Hollerith eventually insisted that cards be made from heavy stock Manila paper of an appropriate quality. He was also to insist that customers such as the US Census use cards produced by his own company.

The structure of a punched card used in the 1890 census is illustrated in Figure 7.3. A reference grid has been added to the illustration to allow us to refer to areas used for coding. The card was made up of

	1	2	3	4	5	6	7	8	9	10	11	12	13	14	15	16	17	18	19	20	21	22	23	24
A	1	2	3	4	GM	UM	Jp	Ch	Oo	In	20	50	80	Dv	Un	3	4	3	4	A	E	L	a	g
B	5	6	7	8	CL	UL	O	Mu	Qd	Mo	25	55	85	Wd	Cy	1	2	1	2	B	P	M	b	h
C	1	2	3	4	CS	US	Mb	B	M	O	30	60	O	2	Mr	O	15	O	15	C	G	N	c	i
D	5	6	7	8	No	Hd	Wr	W	F	5	35	65	1	3	Sg	5	10	5	10	D	H	O	d	x
E	1	2	3	4	Fh	Ff	Fm	7	1	10	40	70	90	4	O	1	3	O	2	St	I	P	e	l
F	5	6	7	8	Hh	Hf	Hm	8	2	15	45	75	95	100	Un	2	4	1	3	4	K	Un	f	m
G	1	2	3	4	X	Un	Ft	9	3	i	e	X	R	L	E	A	6	O	US	Ir	So	US	Ir	So
H	5	6	7	8	Ot	En	Mt	10	4	k	d	Y	S	M	F	B	10	1	Gr	En	Va	Gr	En	Va
I	1	2	3	4	W	R	CK	11	5	l	o	Z	T	N	G	C	15	2	Sv	FC	EC	Sv	FC	EC
J	5	6	7	8	7	4	1	12	6	m	f	NO	U	O	R	D	Un	3	Nv	Bo	Hu	Nv	Bo	Hu
K	1	2	3	4	8	5	2	Oo	O	n	g	a	V	P	I	A1	Na	4	Dk	Fr	It	Dk	Fr	It
L	5	6	7	8	9	6	3	O	p	o	h	b	v	Q	K	Un	Pa	5	Ru	Ot	Un	Ru	Ot	Un

Figure 7.3   Structure of a punched card used in the 1890 census

24 columns and 12 rows, allowing 288 distinct holes to be punched. The lower right corner of the card was clipped to ensure correct orientation of the card in the punch and reader. Irregularly shaped regions or 'fields' (so-called because they reminded Hollerith of strips of field on a farm) were used to code facets or characteristics of the individual. Fields were ordered in sequence on the card corresponding to data organised about the individual on the census schedule. The twenty-one fields started at the top left of the card and moved roughly in a clockwise fashion around the card.

For instance, the third field on the card (A7-A10, B8-C8 and D8) was used to code a person's race, the fourth field (C9, D9) recorded gender, and the seventh field (A14-B14, A15-D15) recorded marital status. Some characteristics were coded across more than one field. Hence, the fifth field (B10-F10, A11-F11, A12-F12, A13-B13, E13-F13, F14) recorded the age-band of the individual (0–4, 5–9, 10–15 and so on) and the sixth field (C13-D13, C14-E14) the unit within the age band. Place of birth was recorded as a two-letter code in fields 10 (A20-E20, A21-F21, A22-F22) and 11 (A23-F23, A24-F24).

Therefore, holes punched through cells on the card would code data about that individual. For example, one hole for race might be punched in D8 to denote that the individual was white. Also a hole would be punched in B12 plus C14 to indicate that the individual was 57. In terms of place of birth, holes punched in (F21, A23) coded KA which stood for Germany; holes punched in (A20, A24) coded AG for Connecticut.

A punch known as a gang punch was used to code a set of cards by the district in which an enumerator worked. A complete batch of schedules for a district was therefore punched together. The gang punch was a lever-operated device which could punch through five or six cards at once. The 48 hole positions on the left end of the card (A4 to L8 in Figure 7.3) were used for this coding. Each of the 40,000 enumeration districts was given a unique code. Each card was also printed with a serial number allowing it to be compared against the original census return if needed.

Hollerith also invented a pantograph punch to code attribute data in predetermined positions on the standardised cards and designed to reduce the strain on operators in the production of punched cards. Basically, this device consisted of a metal plate containing 240 holes. Over this plate swung an extension with a sharp end. This was directed into the cells on the punched card appropriate for the individual determined from the census schedule. Each operator was able with this pantograph punch to produce approximately 500 cards per day. This eventually rose to a peak of 700 cards per day per individual on average.

Sorting data

Tabulation is the process of ordering and presenting data in tabular form. Seven counts or tabulations were required of the analysis for the 1890 census. For instance, in the first tabulation data was organised by gender, race, place of birth and residential (farm/house) ownership. In the second run, tabulation was done by gender, race, marital status and age.

Tabulation required multiple sorting of cards by the characteristics specified in the tabulation. To improve the efficiency of this process, Hollerith designed a semi-automatic sorting device or 'sorting box'. This mechanism enabled the operator to pre-sort cards for the next run with one hand while operating the reading press (see below) with the other.

The census card used in the 1889 census had a maximum of 24 classifications in any one field. Hence the sorting box was designed with 24 compartments. A compartment cover on the box was unlatched when 'read' by the circuit press. The operator would then remove the card from the press and insert it by hand into the compartment. This process could be run a number of times. Hence, the operator might first sort by gender. Then he might sort by race, then by place of birth and finally by residential ownership.

Reading data

For the 1890 census the HETS system contained a reading mechanism known as the circuit press. This consisted of an upper part comprising an array of 288 spring-loaded pins and a lower part comprising an array of mercury pans. The operator placed a punched card in the press and closed it. Pins passing through holes made contact with the collection of mercury pans and established electrical circuits with an array of 40 counters in a tabulator.

Tabulating data

Counters in the tabulator were driven by electromagnets and incremented the relevant clock for each connection made. Each clock could register up to 9,999. After a number of cards in a batch were processed in this manner the operator took readings off the dials and entered them as batch totals on a form. The clocks were then set back to zero.

Given that there were 40 counters in the tabulator, if configuration was restricted to the implementation of direct circuits between pins in the press and counters in the tabulator then only 40 categories of data might have been analysed by HETS at one time. However, Hollerith included a series of relays in the configuration which allowed seventy categories of data to be processed during the first run through the system. For example, in the first tabulation one counter registered the total number of native white persons aged 45+. Hence, the counter was wired into a relay circuit that passed a current if one of the holes (F11, A12-F12, A13-B13 and E13-F13) was punched, the citizen was white (D8) and both parents were born in the United States (G19 and G22).

Forma and physical symbol systems

Data systems work at the level of forma: patterns of data representation and use. In the 1970s two computer scientists Alan Newell and Herbert Simon (Newell and Simon, 1976) proposed the concept of a physical symbol system. This idea was originally developed as a means of providing background theory to what Newell and Simon referred to as the *Sciences of the Artificial*. It was also critical in formulating the so-called physical symbol system hypothesis: that a physical symbol system has the necessary and sufficient means for generating intelligent action.

The concept of a physical symbol system bears a marked similarity with our conception of a data system. A physical symbol system consists of physical patterns (symbols) which can be combined into structures and manipulated to produce new structures. However, we make no claims that a data system can generate intelligence; instead, a data system takes its place within a wider set of systems generating significance, some of which are concerned with issues of mind, thought and meaning (Chapters 5 and 8).

As we argued in Chapter 6, anything which has a physical form and can be modulated can be used as forma. Any matter of energy within the physical environment can be manipulated as patterns to act as a sign vehicle. Hence, a human being may make movements with their larynx, tongue and mouth to create sound waves. Distinct differences in such uttered sounds are used to code *phonemes*. In a spoken language a phoneme is the smallest unit of sound employed to form meaningful contrasts between utterances. Thus a phoneme is a group of slightly different sounds which are all perceived to have the same function by speakers of a particular language. An example of a phoneme is the /k/ sound in the word skill.

The transformation of physical matter to create physical items as forms of data representation seems characteristic of many human cultures. Hence, in terms of the example described in the previous chapter it makes sense to refer to khipu as forma (Beynon-Davies, 2009g). Khipu consist of the structured manipulation of matter – threads of cotton and camelid wool. The manipulation of threads into cords and then into knots can be seen to be a consistent set of formative action. As we shall discuss below, there is evidence to suggest the knot group – an identifiable set of knots tied upon a pendant cord – as being the base significant element within this data system.

A Hollerith card, as discussed in the current chapter, is another key example of forma. Data representation in the Hollerith case followed historical practice of using physical tokens to represent data. Within HETS, punched cards served a similar function to pendant cords on a khipu, clay tokens within Sumerian 'accounting' and, as we shall see, wooden blocks within the operations rooms of the World War II Warning Network. A configuration of holes punched on a particular card served to code data as a record of characteristics appropriate to a particular individual. Hence, punching a hole at grid point C9 on a card coded the individual as male while punching a hole at grid point D9 coded the individual as female. The process of 'writing' such data involved the use of specific tools, namely the pantograph and gang punch. The process of 'reading' such data involved use of another tool: the circuit-closing press.

The spoken word, the khipu and the Hollerith punched card are hence all examples of a physical symbol system. They all consist of physical patterns that are used to code symbols. Such physical patterns can also be combined into or manipulated into larger and more complex structures. Hence, a pendant cord can be added to a larger structure of a pendant group and the phoneme can act as a constituent element of a word, which in turn can act as a constituent of a phrase, sentence and conversation. A Hollerith card was also a constituent part of a larger set of cards used to represent characteristics of a particular population.

Data model

Syntax expresses the structure of some sign-system: the relations between one sign and another. At a very high level of abstraction, the syntax of some data system can be expressed in terms of a data model: a formal 'meta-language' for representing, organising and manipulating data (Tsitchizris and Lochovsky, 1982). Any data model can be seen to consist of two sets of primitives: representors and operators. Representors are primitives of data representation or organisation. Operators are primitives of data manipulation or processing.

In terms of data representation, a data model can be described at a high level of abstraction in terms of a hierarchy of data items, data elements and data structures. A data item is the lowest-level of data organisation. A data element is a logical collection of data items and a data structure is a logical collection of data elements.

Let us consider some examples of data representation. As we have argued above, it is possible to consider khipu as a data system: a system for encoding and decoding symbols. Urton and Conklin argue for the knot as the fundamental symbolic element within khipu. In this view, the construction and positioning of knots relative to each other upon a pendant cord constituted a datum (Beynon-Davies, 2009g). A related collection of knots upon a cord – what we have referred to as a knot group – constituted a data item. The collection of knots within a knot

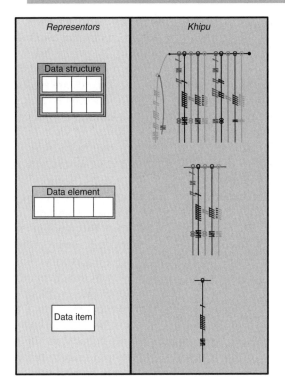

Representors	Khipu
Data structure	
Data element	
Data item	

Figure 7.4   Khipu as a data system

group serves to value the data item. Similarly, a group of pendant cords would constitute a data element and the entire assemblage of cords within a khipu constituted a data structure (Figure 7.4).

The Khipu and the Hollerith punched card are actually examples of a particularly prevalent data model which began life as a 'technology' to enable the control of the state but particularly started to flower during the rise of the industrial revolution and the development of the modern office, as described in Chapter 2. This data model uses the inter-related constructs of fields, records and files. Fields are data items, records are data elements and files are data structures within this data model. Although this data model assumed some significance with the rise of the modern office and bureaucracy, we would argue that the file-based, sometimes referred to as the records-based, data model has existed for many thousands of years in numerous distinct human civilisations. In a sense, records by their very nature involve the use of signs to act as a persistent signification of something. By persistence we mean that a communication is encoded in some reified form which allows it to be transported through time and space. Records are typically collected together in the data structure of a file. Collecting records together in a particular file normally implies some meaningful association between these data elements.

One can clearly argue, for instance, that 'accountants' in Ancient Sumeria used an inherently file-based data model based around the creation and manipulation of physical tokens (Beynon-Davies, 2009e). Clay tokens of various types constituted the data items in this data model. The analysis conducted by Schmandt-Bessarat indicates that the variety in this sign-system is 492 since this amounts to the sum of the number of token sub-types she identified. Hence, there are roughly 500 different things that could be represented as data items within this data model. Sometimes, a collection of such data items were collected together and enclosed in a clay envelope. This envelope was fixed in baking as a data element or record of an economic transaction. It could also be argued that the co-location of tokens and clay envelopes within some location such as a temple precinct equated to the creation of a data structure or file which served perhaps to record information such as the surplus of a particular harvest stored for later use.

The Hollerith card is much more familiar as forma since its fundamental elements, as we shall see underlies the fundamentals of data representation as employed in modern digital computing technology. Clearly, each card acted as a record of one individual. The fields (a term, as we have seen, invented by Hollerith) defined on the card were used to code properties of the individual using a defined set of alphanumeric codes. Hence, holes punched in a particular field valued this data item.

Representors amount to the static side of a data system. Operators amount to the dynamic side of a data system, exercised through data processing. In terms of such data processing it is useful to define a number of core types or classes of formative act from which all forms of such processing can theoretically be built: create, read, update and delete (Figure 7.5). A formative act consists of the operation of one or more operators on one or more representors. Create or 'write' actions involve creating new data structures or representing new data elements

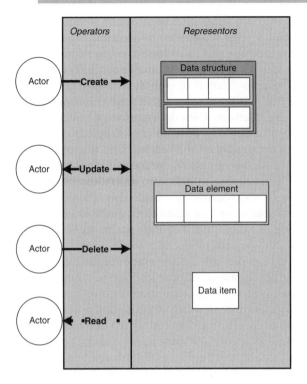

Figure 7.5   Operators and representors

within data structures. Update actions involve changing the value of data items in the sense that the symbols appropriate to the data item are changed. Delete actions involve removing entire data structures or data elements from within data structures. Retrieval or 'read' actions involve accessing data from data items, data elements and data structures.

We can represent a *create* formative act using the symbol ⌐ – the opposite of the mathematical symbol for 'not' – ¬ – which we use to represent a *delete* formative act. Hence, ⌐<d> represents the bringing into existence of the named data representor *d* enclosed in angled brackets, while ¬<d> represents the removal from existence of a named data representor. Likewise, we represent an *update* formative act as (↓<d>) and a *retrieval* or read formative act as (↑<d>). An update amounts to changing

155

some properties of a representor while a read amounts to the sensing of the properties of some representor by an actor.

Khipucamayuq engaged in all these types of formative act in relation to khipu. For instance, a create formative act in this case might consist of constructing a pendant cord with its associated knot group and tying this cord to the main cord (⊢<pendant cord>). In contrast, an update act might involve changing the configuration of a particular knot group upon the pendant cord (↓<pendant cord>), perhaps by deleting a given data item or knot group on the pendant cord (Figure 7.6).

Within the Hollerith case the process of tabulating can be decomposed into its base forms of formative act. Tabulation involved a repetitive process in which cards were read. This actually amounted to the circuit press reading up to 40 data items at the same time off one card. Each reading of a particular data item would cause an update to a particular counter upon the tabulator.

Therefore, from our base or core classes of formative acts more complex patterns of formative acts can be built. For instance, the transmission of data over some communication channel can be seen to consist of a combination of both a 'write' (send) and a 'read' (receive) action. Hence, human speech, could be considered in terms of both writing to and reading from a vocal-auditory sensory modality.

Similarly, sorting can be seen to consist of a process of reading data elements from one data structure and creating their occurrence in an

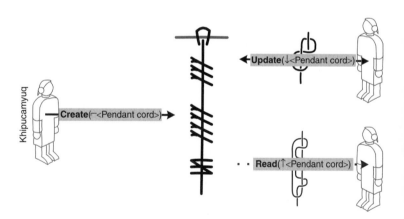

Figure 7.6 Khipu formative acts

ordered sequence according to set criteria in some other data structure. This is fundamentally the function that the Hollerith sorting box performed.

Facial expressions as forma

Facial expressions, just like human speech, which we considered first in Chapter 3, can be considered a data system. The forma of facial expression relies on the embodied experience of two types of actors: the actor making the facial expression and the actor observing the facial expression. The actor making the facial expression relies on the effector apparatus of the human body. In the case of facial expressions such effector apparatus consists primarily of the musculature of the face. Facial expressions rely on the ability of a person to manipulate this musculature. Contraction of muscles, either singly or in combination with other muscles, changes a person's facial expression. A given facial expression can therefore be analysed in terms of the combination of muscles activated and how they are activated. The forma of facial expressions also relies on the sensory apparatus of observers. Perception of facial expressions relies on the human eye and its ability to sense certain defined wavelengths of light reflecting off of some human face.

In the 1970s, Ekman and Friesen (Ekman and Friesen, 1978) invented a coding system for facial expressions based upon an understanding of the musculature of the face. The aim of this Facial Action Coding System (FACS) was to provide professionals such as clinical psychologists with a systematic way of identifying the emotional intent of some facial expression. Using FACS, human observers manually code a given facial expression into specific Action Units (AU). FACS defines thirty to forty AUs, each of which constitutes a contraction or relaxation of one or more muscles in the face. For example, FACS can be used to code a sincere or involuntary 'Duchenne' smile which, as we have seen, involves contraction of the zygomatic major muscle (lip corner puller) and the inferior part of orbicularis oculi muscle (cheek raiser).

The use of coding schemes for facial expressions such as FACS validates treating human facial expressions as a data system. A particular facial expression has symbolic value. Within this data system a given facial expression may be considered a data structure in that it can be

157

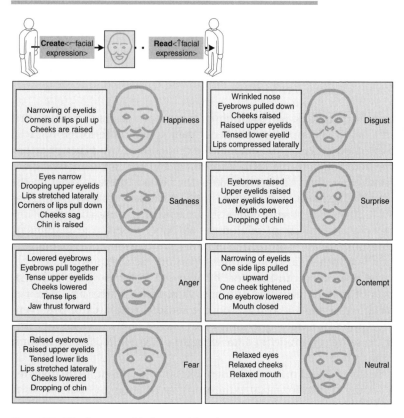

Figure 7.7   The forma and informa of facial expressions

seen to be made up of a number of symbolic elements, comprising movements of facial musculature. However, facial expressions comprise a non-persistent data system. It is non-persistent in the sense that a given facial expression can be created by an actor and 'read' by some other actor. However, it makes no sense to speak of updating or deleting a facial expression. This is because the facial expression is normally fleeting – it typically lasts only for a few seconds. Figure 7.7 illustrates a number of data elements associated with particular facial expressions and how such data elements aggregate into the data structure of a typical emotive facial expression as coded by schemes such as FACS.

Persistent data systems

There is hence one critical difference between data structures such as the Hollerith punched card and facial expressions as types of physical symbol system or data system. One is non-persistent while the other is persistent.

A persistent data system has the key advantage that external objects can be manipulated by multiple actors, at different places and at different times. Such persistent data systems achieve particular usefulness as systems of 'record'-keeping. There are thus particular advantages to the use of persistent data systems within communication. First, the number of actors involved in communication is no longer limited to those immediately present within the communication situation. As a consequence, a persistent data system turns one-to-one or one-to-many communication into many-to-many communication. Second, the senders of a communication can be physically dis-located in time and space from the receivers of a communication. This extends the innate cognitive capacity for memory within the organism but it also has the potential for turning individual memory into collective or social memory.

This can be summed up by saying that within a persistent data system, symbols can not only be written and read from such a data system; they can also be updated and deleted from this data system. Hence, multiple actors, perhaps distributed both temporally and spatially, can participate in the manipulation of a system of external objects. This opens up the further possibility that formative acts of both representation and operation can be performed by external 'tools': by machine.

From records to writing

Schmandt-Besserat paraphrases the eminent anthropologist Claude Levi-Strauss as stating that writing was invented for the exploitation of man by man. In other words, tokens were used within early accounting systems in Mesopotamia as a means of power. Tokens were used primarily as a means to control the amount of goods delivered to the temple and their re-distribution. The development of the token system therefore reflects the development of authority. They were a bureaucratic tool used to control the production of goods and their pooling for state benefit. This has much synergy with Beniger's conception of the place of information and information technologies in society as tools for control. He states that, '...*a society's ability to maintain control – at all levels from inter-personal to international relations – will be directly proportional to the development of its information technologies*' (Beniger, 1986).

The cycles of influence characteristic of Beniger's crises of control can take thousands of years or just a few years to enact. For example, the invention of Sumerian plain tokens seems to have been an innovation stimulated by human settlement and agriculture and the need to 'account' for an economic surplus. In turn, the use of such tokens contributed to the rise of a hierarchical social order and division of labour. This more complex social order demanded more complex ways of accounting which led to the development of complex tokens, clay envelopes and eventually cuneiform writing. This cycle occurred over a number of millennia.

In contrast, elements from the case of the Hollerith Electric Tabulating System document a crisis of control which occurred over a matter of a few decades. The state requirement to run a decennial census in the face of rising population and problems of manual data-handling caused a particular crisis in tabulation. This led to innovations in automatic data processing – the invention of new 'information technology' as a solution to this crisis of control.

As we argued in Chapter 1, the rise of such techne can be seen to compensate for limitations in human capacity, particularly human cognition. In support of cooperative and simple activities between individuals in small communities human memory is sufficient. However, as communities grow in size the complexity of activities also increase. In particular, activities of economic exchange typically take place between strangers and generally are reliant typically on some division of labour.

In such circumstances humans invented the externalisation of memory in records. Records compensate for the limitations of individual human memory and extend it into social memory. Records of economic transactions, for instance, institutionalise memory of past economic exchanges and the obligations placed upon individuals engaged in such exchange. Accurate record-keeping is also critical in establishing and sustaining trust between strangers engaging in economic exchange and for supporting social relationships such as ownership and debt.

Michael Hobart and Zachary Schiffman (Hobart and Schiffman, 1998) offer a useful historical perspective on the long-term nature of information and information 'technology'. Although both writing and speech constitute communication and therefore impart information, they limit their definition of the first information age to the invention of writing. In their eyes, writing is seen as the first information technology: *'Both writing and speech constitute communication, but of the two only writing extracts the sounds of speech from their oral flow by giving them visual representation'*.

However, following Schmandt-Besserat we would argue that writing is actually not the first information technology. Marcia and Robert Ascher (Ascher and Ascher, 1997), for instance, emphasise that writing is actually not a necessary condition for civilisation. Instead, some medium for record-keeping is required. In the pre-literate societies of Ancient Sumeria and the Andean peoples of the Inca, information was recorded through physical artefacts consisting of clay tokens and knotted strings. This suggests a much broader definition for information technology. Technology is any organised collection of artefacts created by humans to extend their capabilities or to compensate for their limitations. Information technology is any such collection of artefacts used to extend human information processing and communication capabilities or compensate for inherent cognitive and social limitations in this area.

Having said this, the development of writing was undoubtedly a significant leap forward in the sophistication of information technology. For instance, it has been proposed in relation to Sumerian clay tokens that the impressions made on the outside of clay envelopes were the first step in the development of writing. The two-dimensional impressions made on the outside of clay envelopes may have begun as a way of making doubly sure that an accounting of things was accurate. Richard Mattesich interprets this practice as the earliest example of double-entry accounting (Mattesich, 2000). Also, checks could be made of the contents of an envelope without breaking the envelope itself.

At a certain stage the Sumerian 'accountants' realised that the notation used on the outside of the envelope made both the envelope itself and the tokens contained inside redundant. Hence, during the period 3,500–3,100 B.C. the clay envelope gave way to the clay tablet. Accounting now took place merely by impressing symbols for the things recorded directly onto a tablet. With the rise of such pictography around 3,100 B.C. a further recognition occurred that quantities which previously had been expressed by direct or concrete correspondence between the sign and the commodity could be abstracted and represented by explicit symbols, used to represent a cardinal number such as 'three'.

Hence, Roy Harris (Harris, 1986) portrays the decisive step from the use of tokens to the use of written script as the movement from a 'token-iterative' sign-system to an 'emblem-slotting' sign-system. The clay tokens initially described in Chapter 1 used a token-iterative system. Within a token-iterative sign-system the concept of <three sheep> would be represented as <sheep, sheep, sheep>. In an emblem-slotting sign-system the same concept would be represented by two signs or emblems: one representing <sheep>, the other the cardinal number <three>.

From records to information technology

There is also clear resonance between the idea of a data system and that of an abstract machine known as a Turing machine, so-called because it was proposed by Alan Turing in the 1930s (Copeland, 2004). Turing, a mathematician by trade, is generally seen to be one of the founding fathers of modern Computer Science. In a famous paper published while he was a Cambridge Don, Turing discusses a thought experiment in which he describes the properties of an abstract machine which supplies the core principles of modern computation.

In this paper he conjectured that his Turing machine possesses the power to solve any problem that is solvable by computational means. Hence, Turing machines are generally described as being 'universal' machines. Such an abstract machine defines the key properties of modern digital computers because it proposed the automation of certain of the manipulations exercised upon persistent forma and the storage of such sequences of operations as 'programs'. We shall first consider this machine as it was originally described. Then we shall consider the relationship of this machine to our concept of a data system.

In his original conception, a Turing machine is made up of a number of theoretical parts: a control mechanism, an instructions table, a state register, an input medium (tape) and a read/write mechanism (tape head). Although Turing never pictured this computational engine, a possible visualisation of this 'machine' is provided in Figure 7.8.

Fundamentally, the Turing machine can be considered a system. The input into the system is conceived as an infinitely long piece of paper tape. This tape is divided into a sequence of discrete cells with each cell containing a symbol from some finite set of symbols, which includes a

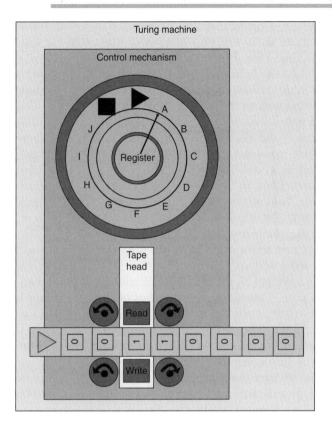

Figure 7.8 A Turing machine

blank symbol. Cells are assumed to contain the blank symbol until they are written to. A special symbol is also sometimes included as part of this set of symbols and is used to indicate the start of the tape.

The Turing machine is equipped with a tape head through which the tape passes. The transformation of the system involves manipulating the tape in the sense that this tape head is used either to write a symbol to a cell of the tape or to read a symbol from a cell of the tape. Once a cell is read from or written to the tape head, this mechanism can also advance the tape by one cell or move the tape backwards by one cell. Hence, two sets of rollers are represented in Figure 7.8 to indicate these operations.

As a system, a Turing machine is controlled by a control mechanism which can be set in one of a number of finite states at any discrete instant in time. One of these states is deemed to be the initial state and another state the halt state of the machine. A state register acts as a memory in this system and stores the current state of something known as the Turing table or instructions table which we discuss below. A special start state is declared with which the state register is initialised.

In terms of our description of a control process in Chapter 4, the Turing table represents a set of control inputs to the control mechanism which defines its decision strategy. The Turing table thus stores a finite set of instructions, in which each instruction can be considered an IF THEN rule. Thus one example of an instruction might be: *IF state of the machine is Q AND the symbol currently read is S THEN perform action A AND put machine in new state Q1.*

As indicated above, the Turing machine can perform two types of actions: write actions and move actions. A write action consists of replacing a symbol on the tape with another symbol and then shifting to a new state. A move operation consists of moving the tape head one cell to the right or one cell to the left and then shifting to a new state. Which action will be performed at a particular time depends upon the current symbol in the cell visible to the tape head as well as the current state of the Turing machine's control mechanism.

Suppose we have ten possible states that the machine can be in, corresponding to the first ten letters of the alphabet, plus a start (►) and a halt (■) state. Suppose also that we have three symbols in the alphabet that can be read from or written to the tape: □ (start), 0 (blank) and 1. Table 1 represents part of a possible instructions table for a Turing machine.

In his thought experiment Turing originally conceived of his 'machine' as a human acting in a rule-governed way with pencil and

Table 1   A sample instructions table

| Tape symbol | Current state A | | | Current state B | | | Current state C | | |
	Write symbol	Move tape	Next state	Write symbol	Move tape	Next state	Write symbol	Move tape	Next state
0	1	R	B	1	L	A	1	L	B
1	1	L	C	1	R	B	1	R	■

paper. It was only with the advent of electronic equipment that the idea of Turing machines could be practically realised. However, the important point is that the theoretical computational abilities of the system remain the same, regardless of the technology. In fact, Turing's abstract machine, by its very nature, is more versatile than the modern digital computer since the Turing machine is never restricted by a lack of storage space. It uses a tape of infinite length, whereas an actual computer must employ finite storage, however great.

Within the Turing machine we have all the elements of a data system. In terms of representors, the tape represents a data structure in which each cell consists of a data element. Symbols can be written to and read from this tape. The key advance is that the set of data operations as well as the set of data representors are disembodied within the idea of a Turing machine. Data operations are performed in terms of a set of stored instructions. This key characteristic makes it possible to automate data processing.

This characteristic makes it possible not only to represent data in an external form but also a decision strategy as a set of operations to be performed against some data-set under the control of some 'mechanism'. This is the fundamental idea of an *algorithm* – a defined set of instructions for achieving some goal.

The Hollerith electrical tabulating system has some but not all of the elements of a Turing machine. As we have seen, Hollerith actually experimented initially with paper tape but eventually decided upon a form of data representation which was disembodied in the form of punched cards. These cards are subject to a series of disembodied data operations. However, in the early versions of the Hollerith tabulator the operations themselves and the sequence in which they were performed were set by the physical makeup of the machine. However, the key innovation in this formative technology was the implementation of a device that could perform a series of formative acts in sequence: this is essentially what an algorithm comprises and is the essential principle underlying the operation of the modern digital computer.

There are hence two sides to any information technology. Formative acts comprise not only acts of representation: they also include acts of manipulation or processing. The key innovation in the Hollerith case comprised the introduction of automatic data processing. This allowed more complex data processing operations to be built upon the base operations of writing and reading data. The process of tabulation involves sorting data into sets with similar properties and counting such sets. Within the HETS such sorting relied on the operation of the card sorter followed by counting using the tabulator.

The technology underlying the HETS can therefore be seen as an attempt to address limitations in human cognitive ability. Through automation, the speed of sorting and 'tallying' or counting data was much improved. Also, automation of these processes reduced errors characteristic of the manual reading, sorting and counting of data using the previous information technology of tally sheets.

Census-taking is a particularly interesting activity system from the point of view of information technology. As mentioned above, census-taking is almost as old as the concepts of information technology itself. This is because of the inherent link between information and statistics. Statistics is fundamentally information collected about the attributes of some given population. Originally, such 'state-istics' were collected solely by governments to aid in policy-making relevant to the state. However, it did not take long for business organisations to recognise the value of collating statistics on 'populations' of relevance to their activities such as worker productivity, inventory and sales.

Early automatic data processing technology such as that used within HETS had a massive impact upon government activities such as conducting a census. Within a year of completing the 1890 census, Hollerith machines were being applied in the national censuses of Austria, Canada and Norway. This is because HETS caused significant improvement in the efficiency of conducting the data-handling activities characteristic of its activity system.

The advantages of such an approach quickly promulgated more widely, particularly into the private sector. In the early 1900s, improvements in and adaptations of HETS enabled its use in the commercial arena within applications such as railway freight management, cost accounting, sales analysis and inventory control. It is no accident that the successful introduction of automatic data processing into business organisations for these purposes accompanied the rationalisation of work processes innovated by Frederick Taylor and the standardisation of goods required by the new wave of industrialisation. Taylorism itself, which we shall discuss in Chapter 10, would not have flourished without accurate information supplied by the automation of data processing and such information technology in turn stimulated greater standardisation of goods and services.

Data systems, lists and databases

The idea of a data system then allows us to plot a clear historical path from embodied forma such as human speech through persistent forma such as khipu to forma which is processed automatically by machines. The core of many modern ICT systems can be considered as a collection of business rules which implements some form of decision strategy. The key input into this decision strategy is data read from certain data structures. The key output from this decision strategy is a series of writes, updates or deletes to data structures. In abstract terms this describes the operation of two fundamental technologies embedded in modern ICT systems: databases and business rules. We discuss the former within the current chapter and defer discussion of business rules to Chapter 11.

Many of the examples of persistent forma described in our cases actually comprise lists of things. As we have seen, Denise Schmandt-Besserat (Schmandt-Bessarat, 1996) has proposed that clay tokens dating back to 8,000 B.C. are some of the earliest examples of lists of commodities. Mahmoud Ezzamel (Ezzamel, 2009) has argued that the construction and dissemination of lists were performative rituals critical to the maintenance of the ideological order of ancient Egypt. Gary Urton (Urton, 2003) has argued for the place of assemblages of knotted strings, known as khipu, as unique artefacts for the making of lists amongst the Inka. More recently, Atal Gawande (Gawande, 2010) has argued that procedural lists such as checklists are critically important to the effective coordination of action in areas such as surgery.

Modern Information and Communication Technology (ICT) has made the making of and use of lists much easier. Larger lists can be built and such lists can be manipulated far more quickly than in the past. Hence, it is comparatively easy to search a list containing millions of items in many varied and complex ways in a matter of a few seconds. The practical ease with which modern list-making can occur, linked to the increasing rationalisation of action in modern life, has meant that we rely more upon lists than at any time in human history.

167

In such terms a list is a key example of persistent forma. Fundamentally, it amounts to a set of symbols, each of which serves to stand for some thing. The symbols persist in the act of representation beyond that which they represent. The making of a list constitutes a collection of formative acts – at its most extreme one formative act for each item in the list.

At its most basic a list corresponds to a *set* of elements. A set is a collection of distinct objects, considered as an object in its own right. There are two ways of describing, or specifying the members of, a set. One way is by intensional definition, using a rule or semantic description such as *A is the set whose members are the first four positive integers* or *B is the set of colours of the French flag*. The second way is by extension – that is, listing each member of the set. An extensional definition is denoted by enclosing the list of members in brackets such as C = (4, 2, 1, 3) or D = (blue, white, red). Most lists are actually ordered sets known as sequences or tuples, implying that both the elements of the list and the position of the elements in a list are significant – hence the tuple <1,2,3,4> is different from the tuple <2,4,3,1>.

The mathematician and computer scientist Ted Codd (Codd, 1970) had the key insight of mapping aspects of set theory – particularly the idea of tuples – onto a data structure that had been around for many thousands of years. The most common data model that has been employed for representation of persistent forma as we have seen has been referred to as a file-based data model and this data model uses the inter-related constructs of fields, records and files. Codd proposed mapping the data structure of a file onto that of a mathematical relation, being a set of tuples. This data structure fundamentally underlies the data systems used within modern digital computing systems.

Codd's so-called relational data model underlies most modern databases which are referred to as relational databases. Within this data model there is one data structure: the relation. Each relation is made up of a number of data elements called tuples and each tuple is made of a number of data items known as attributes. Most now tend to use the terms table, row and column as synonyms for relations, tuples and attributes.

Consider how a modern relational database might store data used by clerks within the Mileage and Demurrage department of the Railway Clearing house, as described in Chapter 2. Within this case we described how account clerks would create a movement record upon waste sheets to signify distinct events within the railway network. A possible structure for such movements records expressed as a relation is provided below:

Movements

Serial no.	Outbound	Inbound	Tarpaulin	Loading	Mileage	Demurrage
2463	3	1	Yes	Yes	No	No
4120	2	2	No	No	Yes	Yes
5643	1	3	Yes	No	No	Yes
5644	3	1	Yes	Yes	No	No

The column headed serial number identifies each train journey. The columns inbound and outbound record the number of days taken in the inbound and outbound journey of a particular train. The columns tarpaulin and loading indicate whether the particular train was lightly loaded and had a tarpaulin during its journey. Finally, the column headed demurrage flags whether such charges were assigned to a particular train journey.

Conclusion

Alan Turing was no ivory tower theorist. Throughout his short life he had an abiding interest in mechanisms of various sorts. It should therefore come as no surprise to expect to find that Turing was very much aware of the dominant use of descendants of Herman Hollerith's tabulating machinery within the modern office during the first four decades of the 20th century. Such technology of forma was used to support repugnant as well as munificent human activity systems. Black (Black, 2002), for instance, documents the way in which later generations of tabulating machinery based on Hollerith's original design were used by the Nazis to compile two censuses of the German population in 1933 and 1939. These censuses, which effectively could not have taken place without the use of Hollerith technology, allowed the Nazi regime to identify Jews and other nominated groups in the population for eventual transmission to the death camps. Tabulating machines were even used in the death camps themselves to process data about the efficiency of the extermination effort.

169

Turing and others, working at Bletchley park during World War II, were to refine many of the principles evident within tabulating machines and apply them in the design of electronic data processing equipment in support of code-breaking German radio traffic. These machines became the forerunners of the modern digital computer. The intelligence provided by this operation, known as Station X, was critical to the effective deployment of military operations both on land, on the sea and in the sky. For instance, it contributed to the successful protection of Allied ship convoys during the Battle of the Atlantic, defeat of Field Marshall Rommel's army in the North African desert, victory against the Italian navy at the Battle of Matapan and the successful planning of the invasion of Europe by the Allies in 1944 (Smith, 1998).

The logo at the start of this chapter is meant to stand for the patterning of forma. Data systems are systems of forma. As such they cross over from empirics into syntactics upon the semiotics ladder. Within a data system we are interested not only in the formation of symbols from matter and energy but also in how such symbols relate in larger structures. Symbols relate together and are operated upon in data systems. A data system is a physical symbol system consisting of physical patterns (symbols) which can be combined into structures and manipulated to produce new structures.

The syntax of some data system is expressed in terms of some data model: a formal 'meta-language' for representing, organising and manipulating data. A data model can be seen to consist of two sets of primitives: representors and operators. Representors are primitives of data representation or organisation. Operators are primitives of data manipulation or processing.

As far as data representation is concerned, a data model can be described at a high level of abstraction in terms of a hierarchy of data items, data elements and data structures. A data item is the lowest-level of data organisation. A data element is a logical collection of data items and a data structure is a logical collection of data elements.

The use of physical items as forms of data representation seems characteristic of many human cultures. Data representation in the Hollerith case followed historical practice of using physical tokens to represent data. Punched cards served a similar function to pendant cords on a khipu, clay tokens within Sumerian 'accounting' and as we shall see wooden blocks within the operations rooms of the Warning Network (Beynon-Davies, 2009d). A configuration of holes punched within a particular field within a particular card acted as a data item in that it served to code a particular characteristic associated with a particular individual.

As for data processing, we defined a number of core types or classes of formative act from which all forms of such processing can theoretically be built: create, read, update and delete. A formative act consists of the operation of one or more operators on one or more representors. Within the Hollerith case, the process of 'writing' data upon punched cards involved the use of the pantograph and gang punch. The process of 'reading' such data involved use of the circuit-closing press.

The HETS is a particularly good example of a persistent data system which opens up the possibility that formative acts of representation and operation can be performed by machine. The concept of a persistent data system thus provides greater clarity to the essence of information technology. James Beniger provides a useful conceptualisation of the purpose of technology: '...*the term technology is intended not in the narrow sense of practical or applied science but in the more general sense of any intentional extension of a natural process'. 'Technology may therefore be considered as roughly equivalent to that which can be done, excluding only those capabilities that occur naturally in living systems*' (Beniger, 1986). Technology is hence not natural; it is artificial or created either to extend human capability in some way or address human limitations in some way.

A persistent data system is an example of techne or craft. Such a system consists of crafting external representations of things which could stand independently of the body; detaching such representations not only from immediate situated experience but also from the immediate communication of such experience. There is evidence to support the idea that this first intellectual leap was taken because of the importance of recording things. Hence, within this conception, even though khipu would not traditionally be considered a form of 'writing', there is substantial evidence to suggest the use of this artefact as a form of data system.

We believe that our framework supplies a more historically encompassing and less culturally-centric conception of 'information technology'. Basing the essence of such technology in the concept of a data system allows us to make sense of a vast array of artefacts used across time, space and human cultures for physical symbol representation and manipulation. It also allows us to see the genesis of such artefacts in non-persistent forma as well as the key advantages accrued in the movement to persistent forma.

It should be apparent from this discussion that the term *information technology* is a rather unsatisfactory one. This is because information is subtly different from data and information systems are subtly different from data systems. The precise nature of these distinctions will become apparent within the next two chapters.

References

Ascher, M. and R. Ascher (1997). Mathematics of the Incas: Code of the quipu. Dover Publications, New York.

Austrian, G. (1982). Herman Hollerith: forgotten giant of information processing. Columbia University press, New York.

Beniger, J. R. (1986). The Control Revolution: technological and economic origins of the information society. Harvard University Press, Cambridge, Massachusetts.

Beynon-Davies, P. (2007). Informatics and the Inca. International Journal of Information Management 27(5): 306–318.

Beynon-Davies, P. (2009c). Formated Technology and Informated Action: the nature of information technology. International Journal of Information Management 29(4): 272–292.

Beynon-Davies, P. (2009d). The 'Language' of Informatics: the nature of information systems. International Journal of Information Management 29(2): 92–103.

Beynon-Davies, P. (2009e). Neolithic Informatics: the nature of information. International Journal of Information Management 29(1): 3–14.

Beynon-Davies, P. (2009g). Significant threads: the nature of data. International Journal of Information Management 29(3): 170–188.

Biles, G., A. A. Bolton, et al. (1989). Herman Hollerith: inventor, manager, entrepreneur – a centennial remembrance. Journal of Management 15(4): 603–615.

Black, E. (2002). IBM and the Holocaust. Time Warner.

Codd, E. F. (1970). A Relational Model for Large Shared Data Banks. Comm. of ACM 13(1): 377–387.

Copeland, J. B. (2004). The Essential Turing. Oxford University Press, Oxford.

Ekman, P. and W. V. Friesen (1978). Facial action coding system. Consulting psychologists press, Palo alto, Calif.

Ezzamel, M. (2009). Order and accounting as a performative ritual: evidence from Ancient Egypt. Accounting, Organizations and Society 34: 348–380.

Gawande, A. (2010). The Checklist Manifesto: how to get things right. Profile books, New York.

Harris, R. (1986). The Origin of Writing. Duckworth, London.

Hobart, M. E. and Z. S. Schiffman (1998). Information Ages: literacy, numeracy and the computer revolution. John Hopkins University Press, London.

Mattesich, R. (2000). The Beginnings of Accounting and Accounting Thought. Routledge, London.

Newell, A. and H. A. Simon (1976). Computer Science as Empirical Inquiry: Symbols and Search. Comm of ACM 19(3): 113–126.

Schmandt-Bessarat, D. (1996). How Writing Came About. The University of Texas Press, Austin, Texas.

Smith, M. (1998). Station X: the code breakers of Bletchley Park. Channel 4 books, London.

Tsitchizris, D. C. and F. H. Lochovsky (1982). Data Models. Prentice-Hall, Englewood-Cliffs.

Urton, G. (2003). Signs of the Inka Khipu: binary coding in the Andean Knotted-String Records. University of Texas Press, Austin, Texas.

8
Information: In-form to perform

Introduction

Gregory Bateson (Bateson, 1972) in his *Ecology of Mind* Defines information tantalisingly as any difference that makes a difference. By this he means that an environment with no evidence of, what we referred to in Chapter 4 as modulation, conveys no information. In other words, if the environment is entirely uniform in nature then it will have no effects upon organisms. Fortunately, differences are endlessly transmitted around the physical environment. Differences in the surface of an object become differences in the wavelengths of light. Differences in light signals become differences in stimulation on the sensory cells making up the eye of some organism such as a human. These differences stimulate in turn differences in patterns of activity in the nervous system of the organism which in turn stimulate differences in bodily movement such as posture and locomotion.

Bateson thus argues that differences are continuously being made in the world. However, only those differences that can be perceived and interpreted by an organism can be considered signs. Hence, differences may have an objective existence over and above perceiving actors in the sense that differences are evident in the signalling of things. But only when such signals become *capta* (Holwell and Checkland, 1998a) – are perceived as symbols – and assigned some meaning by actors should we speak of the presence of signs.

This highlights an important point about symbols: a symbol points in two directions. On the one hand, it points to the physical world and relates to signals emanating from the ambient environment. On the other hand, a symbol points to the social world: it relates to effects such as individual and social actions. Interposing between these two is the realm of psyche – of perception and cognition – the motors for the generation of meaning. In Chapter 2 we introduced the term *informa* to refer to this latter pattern of organisation; which is the focus of the current chapter.

Informa underlies our response to the world in numerous areas of our lives. Take the area of consumption and our response to advertising. We might argue over the issue of whether advertising conveys information but we probably would not argue that we normally have some response to it. What marketing people attempt to do is to manipulate our responses in subtle ways. They attempt to affect not only our perceptions of products and services but how we think about such products and services; this is in the hope that they can influence our reaction to such products and services. This is the realm of informa.

Informa therefore relates symbols to meaning. Semantics is concerned with the content or meaning of signs used within the message conveyed in a communicative act. As we shall see, a simple model of meaning is one in which a sign is broken down into three component parts which are frequently referred to collectively as the meaning triangle (Ogden and Richards, 1923). The meaning triangle helps distinguish systematically between data and information. As we have seen in Chapter 6, a datum, a single item of data, corresponds to a symbol or a set of symbols in the meaning triangle. Information concerns intentionality (with-a-t) and intensionality (with-an-s). Information conveys the aboutness of thoughts. Information also occurs in the 'stands-for' relations between the symbol (designation) and its concept (intension) as well as in the imputed relation between the symbol and its referent (extension). However, the association between information and meaning is not an immutable one. Information is both a noun and a verb. Meaning is an accomplishment, is ever-changing and is reliant on actors using sign-systems.

We bring together and expand upon a number of previous examples to help illustrate the nature of information within this chapter: clay tokens, khipu and human facial expressions. However, to set the scene, let us first consider some of the difficulties of defining the precise nature of information.

Problems with information

Information is commonly seen to be a critical concept for the 21st century because of its importance to the competitiveness of the private sector globally and even as an important 'commodity' in modern economies. Information is even developing as an important element of concern within the natural sciences, particularly within physics and biology, causing some to refer to information as the new *language of science* (Von Baeyer, 2003).

However, the concept of information is generally treated in one of two ways. It is either defined quite narrowly, as we have seen in Chapter 4, such as in terms of the transmission of binary digits (bits), or it is taken-for-granted in the sense that it is used as an important term but its meaning is very poorly defined and understood. Hence, for instance, the recent natural science definition for information only considers certain aspects of what we shall consider information. Whereas within general management information is seen as important to management but the term is largely left undefined by writers on this subject, such as Michael Porter (Porter and Millar, 1985). Therefore, although information is critical 'stuff' it is extremely difficult 'stuff' to pin down; it is probably not even 'stuff' at all.

The following examples demonstrate some of the difficulties in defining information.

If information is a commodity it is a very strange commodity. As Ronald Stamper states, '*Information is a paradoxical resource: you can't eat it, you can't live in it, you can't travel about in it, but a lot of people want it*' (Stamper, 1985). If somebody sells information the commodity does not pass from seller to buyer like a traditional commodity such as food; the seller still retains the information. The 'consumption' of information is therefore radically different from the consumption of physical commodities such as food, wine and electronic goods.

Much modern communication occurs through use of technology. However, technologically mediated communication may actually suffer from loss of information. As previously mentioned, within a telephone conversation, because the persons in the conversation are not co-present, significant information is lost in the communication. This is not solely because the electronic signal travelling down the telephone line conveys only a certain percentage of the frequencies of normal face-to-face human speech. It is also because people cannot see each other and hence a great deal of the information conveyed in bodily gestures and expression is lost to the participants in the telephone conversation.

A person α looks across at a fellow person β situated at the opposite end of some room. He holds up one hand and points one finger upwards clenching the remaining fingers in a fist. How is person β to interpret what person α is trying to tell him? Is it to be interpreted as an *insult*, as a *command* to get him one more of something or is the finger merely being used as a *pointer* to something perhaps stuck on the ceiling of the room?

These examples highlight a number of issues which need to be considered in any truly accurate consideration of what is information. They highlight that information is particularly associated with communication, that communication involves signs and that the use of such signs involves interpretation. The examples also demonstrate that information is inherently bound closely with numerous phenomena – language, action, logic and technology; to name but a few. Hence, an understanding of the place of information in human organisation demands the multi-layered or multi-levelled perspective we take in this book.

Our specific aim in the current chapter is to unpack the issue of human interpretation in terms of the concepts of intentionality and intensionality and consider how these relate to our conceptual framework and the nature of informa. We maintain that these concepts, gleaned from philosophy on the one hand and linguistics on the other, which we have referred to at a number of points in previous chapters, are important to the essence of what we mean by signs and how signs are used in processes of signification within systems of significance.

Aboutness

The term intentionality is often simplistically summarised as 'aboutness' or the relationship between mental acts/states and the external world. According to the *Oxford English Dictionary* it is *'the distinguishing property of mental phenomena of being necessarily directed upon an object, whether real or imaginary'*. The philosopher John Searle (Searle, 1983) defines intentionality as the special way the psyche has of relating to the world.

For philosophers, such as Searle, intentionality encompasses a vast range of mental phenomena such as believing, desiring, wishing, knowing, guessing, forgetting and intending. Idioms such as these are referred to as *propositional attitudes*, since what they have in common is that they are all attitudes towards or about something. Hence, believing is always believing that something is the case and wishing is always wishing for something.

However, a major problem with the discussion about the nature of intentionality is that philosophers often fail to make explicit whether or not they use the term to imply concepts such as agency or desire. Such concepts are purposeful or teleological. Daniel Dennett (Dennett, 1987), as we shall see, explicitly invokes teleological concepts in his 'intentional stance' which we consider below. However, most philosophers use intentionality to mean something with no teleological import. Thus, a thought can be *about* a chair without any implication of a purposeful intention relating to the chair.

Dennett: Intentionality and control

The eminent American philosopher Daniel Dennett (Dennett, 1987) maintains that when an actor attempts to explain and predict the behaviour of some object, they can choose to view it on at least three different levels of abstraction which he refers to as the physical stance, the design stance and the intentional stance.

The most concrete level is the physical stance. This demands an understanding of the workings of the physical world: the level of the physical sciences. Therefore, at this level, the actor is concerned with the composition of matter and energy. For instance, in looking at a strip made up of two types of metal bonded together she can predict how it will bend as the temperature changes, based on the physical properties of the two metals.

A more abstract level is adopted in the design stance, which works with an understanding of the purpose, function and design of things. Hence, in terms of the design stance an actor can understand the bimetallic strip as a particular type of thermometer, not concerning herself with the details of how this type of thermometer happens to work. The actor can also recognise the purpose that this thermometer serves inside a thermostat and even generalise to other kinds of thermostats that might use a different sort of thermometer.

The most abstract level is the intentional stance, which works at the level of 'minds': of psyche. At this level, an actor is concerned with things such as belief, thinking and intent. When an actor predicts that a honeybee will fly from the hive in a particular direction based upon an understanding of elements of the dance of a related bee, she is taking an intentional stance towards this animal. Likewise, when some human actor correctly predicts the emotional state of some other human actor on the basis of that actor's facial expression then they are taking an intentional stance towards that actor.

When we take the intentional stance towards something we are naturally awarding the status of an *intentional system* towards that object. Dennett describes this as an entity *'whose behaviour can be predicted by the method of attributing belief, desires and rational acumen'* (Dennett, 1987). This means that we attribute a number of things to an intentional system: a. the ability to possess mental states such as beliefs and desires; b. The expectation that the behaviour of the system is directed towards the attainment of such beliefs and desires; c. The expectation that the system will behave in a rational manner in terms of such attainment.

Therefore, as we have seen, Dennett proposes an account of psyche as a control system (Chapter 4) for behaviour and the evolution of psyche in terms of the sedimentation of increasingly complex control systems within organisms (Dennett, 1996). He sees the purpose of psyche is to produce future – the ability to generate 'moves' and to test these moves against some environment. More complex psyche produces more and better future, as an attempt to reduce uncertainty in decision-making (Chapter 5).

The idea of an intentional system and the stance taken towards it is a critical part of the psyche of what Dennett refers to as *Gregorian creatures*. Such organisms utilise control systems that are able to select better moves in terms of some external environment because they are able to build and exploit an internal environment. This internal environment enables them to test out moves before actually undertaking them in practice. This allows them to weed out probable unsuccessful moves before undertaking them. Such organisms find it useful to adopt an intentional stance because it enables them to make predictions as to the likely behaviour of other intentional systems within their environment. The organism can then plan and execute its behaviour in terms of such predicted intentions.

Searle: Intentionality and communication

Another North American philosopher, John Searle uses the concept of intentionality in his attempt to link the concept of mental states with communicative behaviour (Searle, 1983). He maintains that intentionality is expressed through *illocutionary acts*: acts of communication in which actors create and send messages in an appropriate context with certain intentions (Searle, 1970). The communication of such intentions is important for joint action – coordinated and collaborative action. In such terms, a communicative act is some aspect of performance designed by one actor, A, to influence the performance of some other actor, B.

Searle identifies a number of different forms of informative or communicative act in terms of what he refers to as *illocutionary force*. This concept is further defined in terms of the ideas of *direction of fit* and *conditions of satisfaction*.

Illocutionary force relates to the idea of a propositional attitude described above and refers to the kind of attitude a speaker has when he says something and the direction of fit between the world and the propositional content of the communicative act (the word). Consider three communicative acts: [Please take the customer order], [Will you take the order?], [You will take the order]. The propositional content of these three messages is the same – [that you will process the customer order]. The illocutionary force differs: the first is a request, the second a question and the third a prediction.

Hence, Searle formulates five key types of illocutionary or communicative act in terms of illocutionary force: assertives, directives, commissives, expressives and declaratives (Searle, 1975).

Assertives are communicative acts that explain how things are in the world, such as reports and assertions. Such acts commit the speaker to the truth of the expressed proposition, as in, '*Our orders have fallen by 10% this month*'.

Directives are communicative acts that represent the senders' attempt to get a receiver to perform an action, such as requests, questions, commands and advice. As such, they are meant to cause the receiver to take a particular action. Hence, an actor might ask of another actor: '*Please ensure that our production target is met next quarter*'.

Commissives are communicative acts that commit a speaker to some future course of action such as promises, oaths and threats. They are communicative acts that represent a speaker's intention to perform an action, as in, '*I promise to write a letter*' or '*I refuse to pay a bill*'.

Expressives are communicative acts that represent the speakers' psychological state, feelings or emotions such as apologies, criticisms and congratulations. They express a speaker's attitudes and emotions towards some proposition. Hence, an actor might state, '*I am unhappy with Joe's overall performance this month*'.

Declaratives are communicative acts that aim to change the world through the communication itself, such as baptism, pronouncing someone husband and wife and sentencing a prisoner. Hence, they are usually communicated against a normative background and are frequently institutionalised, such as '*This order has been fulfilled*'.

The term direction of fit was invented by John Austin (Austin, 1971) to refer to the relationship between mental states (perhaps rather confusingly called the *word*) and reality (or what philosophers refer to as the *world*). Three directions of fit are proposed: word-to-world, world-to-word and null. A word-to-world direction of fit is intended to describe the world. A world-to-word direction of fit is intended to change the world. A null direction of fit occurs when having some mental state implies that some fitting to the world has already taken place (Figure 8.1).

The semiotician Umberto Eco (Eco, 2009) has recently published a fascinating book on the use of lists and catalogues of things throughout history. He believes that society makes lists as part of its attempt to impose order or control on the world. The surgeon Atal Gawande (Gawande, 2010) concurs with this viewpoint and has recently argued for the importance of checklists as key aids in the control or coordination of behaviour in critical areas such as engineering and surgery.

However, a close analysis of these two texts demonstrates that lists of things actually serve a number of different functions as artefacts of communication. Eco primarily documents lists as assertions about how the World is ordered – this person owns this land while this person owns this land. In contrast, Gawande documents the importance of lists as directives to action – do this, then this, then this....

It is therefore possible to unpack the key function as well as limitations of lists in terms of the notion of direction of fit. Consider the following example (Searle, 1995). A woman gives her husband a shopping list on which are written the words: beer, butter and bacon. The man takes the list to the supermarket and puts things in the cart to match the items on the list. Hence, the list functions like an order or a desire and it has the world-to-word (list) direction of fit. It is the responsibility of the man to make the world, in terms of his purchases, match the items on the list (the word).

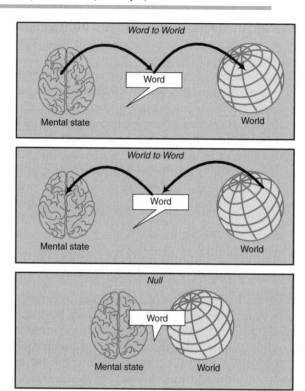

Figure 8.1   Direction of fit

Suppose the man is followed by a detective. The detective writes down everything that the man places in his shopping trolley. He thus writes down beer, butter and bacon on his list. Hence, when both the detective and the man reach the checkout they have identical lists. However, the function or direction of fit of the two lists is different. In contrast to the man's world-to-word direction of fit, the detective's list has a word-to-world direction of fit.

The differences between these two functions become apparent when we examine what happens when an error is made. Suppose the husband fails to bring home bacon, but instead brings home gammon. In terms of the detective's list the error is easily corrected. He crosses out bacon and substitutes gammon. However, in the case of the man the situation is not so easily corrected. Correcting his list does not change the state of the world.

The direction of fit of a communicative act therefore relates to its conditions of satisfaction. As Searle states, '*An intentional state is satisfied if the world is the way it is represented by the intentional state as being. Beliefs can be true or false, desires can be fulfilled or frustrated, intentions can be carried out or not carried out … It is a general feature of intentional states that they have conditions of satisfaction … if one wanted a slogan for analysing intentionality, I believe it should be this: By their conditions of satisfaction shall ye know them.*' (Searle, 1995)

Not surprisingly, Searle's types of communicative act described above each have an associated direction of fit. Assertives have a word-to-world direction of fit. It is the function of the detective's list to match reality – it functions as an assertion of what happened. Directives have a world-to-word direction of fit. The husband's shopping list is a directive. It is the responsibility of the husband to make the world match the items on the list (the word). Commissives also have a world-to-word direction of fit. Hence, a promise is taken as a commitment by some actor to change the world at some future time to match the promise. Expressives have a null direction of fit in that the act of communicating an apology is an apology. Declaratives have both a world-to-word and word-to-world direction of fit. Declaring someone husband and wife creates the event declared; the state of the word and the world are unified.

Now let us consider an example from a previous chapter in this light. As discussed in Chapter 3, human facial expressions are particularly associated with human emotions and as such can be typically seen to be 'about' such emotions as experienced by a person. But what is an emotion? Paul Ekman (Ekman, 2003) believes that an emotion '*is a feeling, a set of sensations that we experience and often are aware of*'. This feeling can be brief, lasting only a few seconds or minutes. If the experience lasts hours, Ekman describes it as a mood not an emotion.

As well as the expression being about some emotion, the feeling itself is typically about something in the 'world' that matters to the person. We also typically experience emotions as happening to us and not being chosen by us. Hence, an emotion can be considered a mental state and it is a conscious mental state that has some limited duration. Further, the mental state is involuntary and is *about* something in the world that matters to us.

Hence, in terms of informa, facial expressions are best seen as expressive communicative acts, as illustrated in Figure 8.2. Being examples of such acts, emotions have a null direction of fit in the sense that having the emotion is already evidence of a change to the world. Producing the facial expression is itself evidence of having a particular emotional state.

Hence, at the level of informa a given symbol (facial expression) produced by one actor communicates some mental content to another actor. The other actor 'reads' the facial expression by matching the symbolic elements of the facial expression with aspects of his or her internal environment. But how are such intentions communicated between one actor and another? This is where intensions (with-an-s) have a role to play.

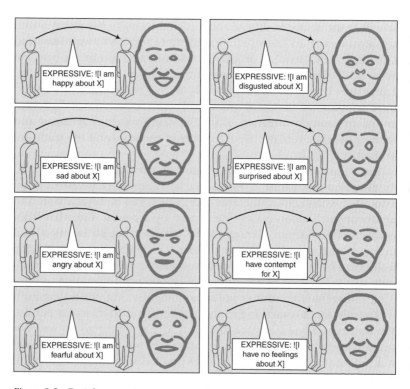

Figure 8.2   Facial expressions as expressives

First, however, since we have made links between animal and human communication in previous chapters, let us examine the question of whether certain animals display evidence of intentionality.

Intentionality and animal Psyche

Intentionality, as we have seen, is a key characteristic of psyche. However, following Dennett (Dennett, 1996), psyche, conceived of as a control system, can be seen not as a fixed concept but as a dimension or continuum of varying complexity. This approach offers a partial solution to the contentious issue of animal psyche: whether animals have 'minds'.

Consider again the case of communication amongst vervet monkeys. The ethologist Richard Seyfarth (Cheney and Seyfarth, 1985) describes the way in which vervet monkeys use several different alarm calls when predators are spotted. Three of these calls act as very precise signs signifying the presence of a particular type of predator. These communicative acts are therefore quite simple, signifying intentions such as: ⊢[I have seen a snake], ⊢[I have seen a leopard], ⊢[I have seen an eagle] – the symbol '⊢' being used to signify an assertion. Other monkeys respond to the snake call by looking downwards or approaching and examining the snake. In response to the eagle call they look up and seek cover in the undergrowth. In response to the leopard call the monkeys climb hurriedly into the trees. More recently, Constantine Slobodchikoff (Slobodchikoff, Perla et al., 2009), as described in Chapters 3 and 6, identifies similar types of communicative behaviour amongst Gunnison prairie dogs.

The philosopher Ruth Millikan (Millikan, 2005) argues that such examples are clearly evidence of animal intentionality. However, she argues that the intentionality implicit in much animal behaviour relies upon what she refers to as *pushmi-pullyu* representations; after the two-headed Llama-like animal described in the Doctor Doolittle novels. Such representations have three characteristics. First, they are both indicative (assertive) and imperative (directive): they indicate not only what is the case but also what to do about it. Second, they relate the animal itself to whatever else they represent. Third, they are highly inarticulate, meaning that they are designed for a very specific purpose and find difficulty in being used for any other purpose. Following Millikan, it is possible to interpret the communicative acts of the European honeybee, of vervet monkeys and of Gunnison prairie dogs as prime examples of such pushmi-pullyu representations.

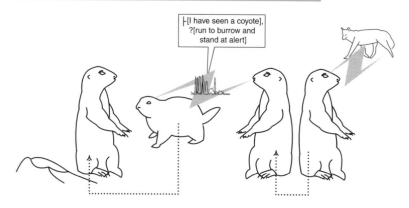

Figure 8.3   Pushmi-Pullyu representations

Take as another example, the proposed 'language' of prairie dogs. Alarm calls are by far the most well-studied forms of prairie dog communication, particularly amongst Gunnison prairie dogs. As we have seen, the alarm calls comprise loud and often repetitive vocalisations that sound similar to certain forms of bird call. Such calls are given by one or more prairie dogs within a colony when a predator is detected (Figure 8.3). A particular type of call produces a distinct escape response on the part of other prairie dogs on hearing the call. For example, when a red-tailed hawk is detected a single prairie dog usually gives a single sharp bark. All the other prairie dogs in the immediate flight path of the hawk then immediately run to their burrows. Those outside the flight path stand upright and watch the path of the hawk. In contrast, when a coyote approaches the colony, many animals start to produce an alarm call. Upon hearing this call prairie dogs run to the lip of their burrows and stand upright on their hind legs, watching the progress of the coyote. Animals that were below ground also emerge and stand at the lips of their burrows.

This suggests that such alarm calls in-form within the reactive psyche of a prairie dog through clear patterns of stimulus and response. Such a decision strategy has even been represented as a decision tree or as a series of decision rules as below:

- IF predator-call is 'human' THEN run to burrow AND perform a colony dive (all animals within a colony dive into their burrows)

- IF predator-call is 'hawk' THEN run to burrow AND perform a limited dive (only those dogs within flight path dive into burrows)
- IF predator-call is 'coyote' THEN run to burrow AND stand at alert
- IF predator-call is 'dog' THEN stand at alert at your current position

This proposal of cued and pushmi-pullyu representations also seems to have a resonance with recent thinking in the study of our human ancestors. The cognitive palaeontologist Steven Mithen (Mithen, 2006) has proposed that modern human language evolved from earlier forms of proto-language, in which the units of the language were what he refers to as manipulative rather than referential and composed of an entire message rather than the units of a language. He gathers a vast range of evidence to support his argument that this proto-language was holistic, manipulative, multi-modal, musical and mimetic. It was multi-modal because it was used not only in vocal mode but also in bodily gestures. It was musical because it used elements such as rhythm and mimetic because it was likely to have used iconic signs – symbols that bear a resemblance to that which they represent. He therefore refers to such a proto-language by the acronym HMMM and argues for it being the form of communication system used by the immediate ancestors of Homo Sapiens and by the Neanderthals in Europe.

The stands for relation

In very broad terms it is useful to see Daniel Dennett as primarily a philosopher of mind, interested in the biological underpinnings of psyche as a control system for behaviour. John Searle, in contrast, is both a philosopher of mind and a philosopher of language. He is interested in how the stuff of thought is given representation in acts of communication and how such communicative acts influence behaviour.

For philosophers of language, intentionality is largely an issue of how symbols can have meaning and therefore overlaps somewhat with the linguistic notion of intensionality. However, intentionality (with-a-t) should not be confused with intensionality (with-an-s), although the two are related upon the semiotics ladder. In terms of semiotics, intentionality is largely a concept of relevance to pragmatics: communicative purpose. In contrast, intensionality is largely a concept relevant to semantics: communicative meaning.

Illocutionary or communicative acts presuppose the existence of a sign-system in which the signs used for the expression of propositions and attitudes (illocutionary forces) have an established meaning amongst a group of communicants. Semantics is concerned with the content or meaning of signs used within the message conveyed in a communicative act. It is here that intensionality has its place.

Intensionality can be best understood by applying a simple model of meaning in which a sign is broken down into three component parts, frequently referred to collectively as the *meaning triangle* (Ogden and Richards, 1923). The *designation* of a sign refers to the symbol (or collection of symbols) by which some concept is known. The *extension* of a sign refers to the range of phenomena that the concept in some way covers. The *intension* of a sign is the collection of properties that in some ways characterise the phenomena in the extension, and is the idea or concept of significance (Figure 8.4).

Intensionality is particularly used to refer to the stands-for relation between a symbol (designation) and its concept (intension). The relation between a symbol and its referent is normally regarded as an imputed relation. In other words, it relies on the transitive relation between symbol

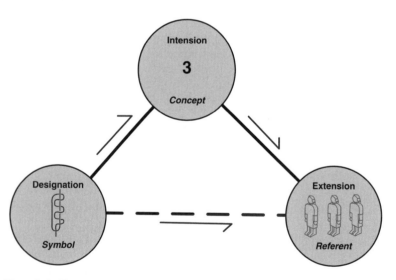

Figure 8.4   The meaning triangle

and concept and concept and referent. This assumes that one cannot symbolise *some thing* without having a concept to which this thing refers and which contributes to the thinking of some particular actor.

Implicitly, we have used the meaning triangle in previous chapters to distinguish systematically between data and information. A datum corresponds to a symbol or a set of symbols in the meaning triangle. Information particularly occurs in the 'stands-for' relations between the symbol (designation) and its concept (intension) and the symbol and its referent (extension).

Let us apply this idea to one of our cases. At the level of semantics, the meaning of symbolic elements within khipu (Beynon-Davies, 2009g), as discussed in Chapters 6 and 7, remains to be established, since the way in which data was encoded in khipu is still very much a matter of debate and investigation. Leland Locke (Locke, 1923) in the 1920s established that 100 or so of the remaining khipu were used to store the results

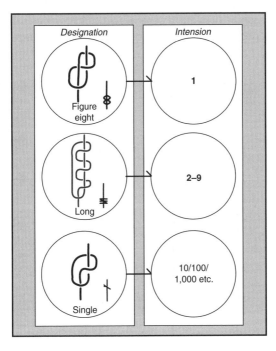

Figure 8.5   Aspects of Khipu semantics

of record-keeping possibly in support of Inka imperial administration. Gary Urton (Urton and Brezine, 2005) has recently shown how khipu acted as a complex accounting system which enabled census and tribute data collected in the empire to be synthesised, manipulated and transferred between different accounting levels within this administration.

Evidence suggests that knot groups tied on pendant cords within certain types of khipu studied by Locke and Urton represent numbers to the base 10 (decimal). Particular knot types such as single, figure-eight and long knots and their positioning upon pendant cords signify distinct numbers. The closer the knot to the top of a cord: the higher the number. At the very top a single knot represented multiples of 10,000, then 1,000, then 100, then 10 (Figure 8.5).

A long knot was used to signify units between 2 and 9: the number of wrappings in the long knot signifying the actual number. Hence, the long knot illustrated in Figure 8.5 represents the number 3. A figure-eight knot was used to signify 1. The number 0 was represented by absence of a knot at an appropriate position in the knot group on a pendant, dangle or subsidiary cord. Figure 8.6 provides some examples of number representation using knots upon pendant cords.

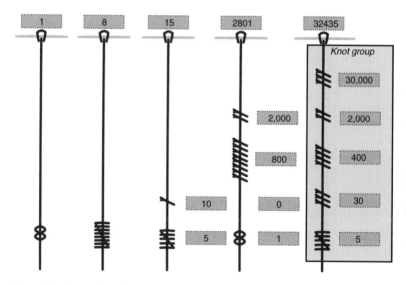

Figure 8.6   Examples of number representation in khipu

Maria and Robert Ascher (Ascher, 2002) agree with Locke that knots tied to pendant, subsidiary or tertiary cords are likely to have been used to signify numerals or magnitudes of things. However, they also propose that numbers could be used as 'labels' denoting other referents. In this sense, they propose the use of knot groups as a more extensive form of coding. In this perspective, a given knot group on a khipu can be considered similar in nature to a modern bar code, with individual knots substituting for the bars of the code.

The Aschers also suggest the usefulness of engaging in thought experiments in order to understand the potential capacity of khipu for the purposes of signification. For instance, consider such an experiment in which a khipu is used as a record of the tribute supplied to the Inka state in a particular year by a particular provincial area of the Empire. A schematic of the data structure for such a khipu is illustrated in Figure 8.7.

Within this khipu, the dangle cord and its subsidiary cord identify the particular tributary unit to which the records apply. The main body of this khipu is made up of four groups of five pendant cords each, in which a common pattern of knots is tied to these groups of pendant cords. The first pendant cord in a group (coloured moderate red) identifies a particular tributary unit of 100 people. The second pendant (coloured deep plum) signifies the amount of maize supplied to the Inka state by the tributary unit. The third pendant (coloured deep red) represents the number of llamas supplied as tribute. The fourth pendant

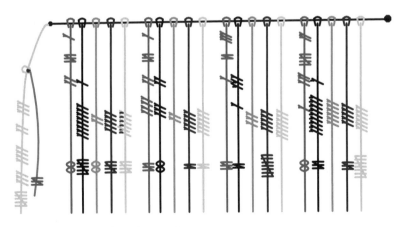

Figure 8.7   A khipu thought experiment

(coloured deep green) records the labour tax paid. The final and fifth cord (coloured light green) in the group records the number of units of coca supplied to the state. Hence, the leftmost pendant group begins with a cord identifying the tributary unit = 13201. This is followed by a pendant group recording specific elements of tribute: 185 units of maize, 21 llamas, 54 units of labour and 64 units of coca.

As we mentioned in Chapter 1, the semantics of Sumerian clay tokens is also subject to much interpretation. It has been proposed that a clay token was used to stand for two concepts through its existence and shape: the quantity of some commodity and the type of commodity. Hence, there was meant to be a one-to-one correspondence between the designation, intension and extension within this sign-system. Schmandt-Besserat (Schmandt-Besserat, 1992) believes that there is sufficient evidence for the range of intensions and extensions for particular types of plain and complex token. Hence, a particular form of incised disk stood for an item of cloth or garment while another form of incised disk stood for a sheep.

However, a key criticism of the meaning triangle as a model of semantics is that it tends to suggest that the assignment of meaning is fixed or immutable. In practice, the association between sign and meaning is typically reliant on context; it is a cultural accomplishment. This means, as we have argued in some detail in earlier chapters, that the intensionality associated with most signs is arbitrary in nature. The same sign may mean different things in different social contexts; or different signs may mean the same thing depending on context.

Hence, in Dennett's (Dennett, 1996) terms, Homo Sapiens is a species of organism with a highly evolved control system that exploits the significance of 'tools'. What he refers to as *Gregorian creatures* are those whose inner environments are informed by designed portions of the external environment. Such creatures are able to create 'tools' which imbue other users with the 'intelligence' built into the tool. One of the most powerful of such tools is a sign-system such as spoken language. The presence of words from such a language imbues the Gregorian creature with the ability to construct a rich internal environment and use this to produce ever more subtle move generators and move testers.

However, one should not assume that Homo Sapiens is an organism solely possessed of a Gregorian psyche. Such a psyche co-exists within the human organism with examples of Popperian, Skinnerian and Darwinian psyche. As we have suggested in Chapter 5, Popperian psyche maintain internal environments. At a lower level, Skinnerian psyche are able to perform simple forms of associative learning. At the lowest level, Darwinian psyche perform on the basis of hardwired relations between stimuli and response. This suggests that the behaviour of a complex organism such as a human actually relies on what the computer scientist Marvin Minsky (Minsky, 1988) refers to as a complex *Society of Minds*.

Semiosis as in-forming

Our purpose in examining intentionality and intensionality in such detail is to help illuminate the nature of informa. In a classic paper published in the 1980s, Richard Boland (Boland, 1987) criticised a number of taken-for-granted assumptions associated with the concept of information and proposed a richer account of this concept. For Boland, conventional ways in which information is treated solely as a noun commit what the philosopher Gilbert Ryle (Ryle, 1949) refers to as a *category mistake*. It is because of such a category mistake that some of the problems we have with understanding the nature of information described in an earlier section occur.

Information relies on the patterning of the world in symbols through forma; but information is not a given in the presence of such symbols. Instead, information is a process of sense-making within acts of communication. As such, it should be rewritten as a verb – in-formation – because '*Information is an inward-forming. It is the change in a person from an encounter with data*'.

Boland argues that, '*... our images of information without in-formation lead to an ignorance of language and our human search for meaning which together deny the very possibility of human communication. The process of constructing the social world is a process of language and communication.*' He further argues that, '*language is symbolic action, through which we search for meaning in the world.*' and that, '*the search for meaning is a continuous search that is never completely or finally realised*' (Boland, 1987).

Hence, meaning is a continuing accomplishment through dialogue. '*It is through dialogue that we accomplish and re-accomplish meaning, and thus bring order to the social world. Through dialogue we name objects and give them significance... It is through dialogue that the symbolic order of our shared world is made real. Through dialogue we tell each*

other what is important and why. We search for the purpose, significance and meaning of our institutions and ourselves that is the social order' (Boland, 1987).

Although Boland never debates with the terms intentionality and intensionality directly in his paper, we would propose that the *in* within the term in-formation actually refers to two things. On the one hand, *in* refers to intentionality and intentions. On the other hand, *in* refers to intensionality and intensions. In-formation is therefore a process in which intentions and intensions merge. In-formation is an entangled accomplishment consisting of the merging of individual (internal) and social (external) representations of the 'world'.

In this view, information is a change in an actor experienced from an encounter with data or forma. Data as symbols signify intensions. Such intensions are used to communicate the intentions of one actor to another actor. As such, in-formation relies both on a collective intentionality and a collective intensionality amongst a particular group of actors.

Tomasello et al. (Tomasello and Carpenter, 2007) propose that what they refer to as shared intentionality is a defining difference between ourselves and our nearest evolutionary relatives – the great apes. *'Shared intentionality ... [r]efers to collaborative interactions in which participants have a shared goal (shared commitment) and coordinated action roles for pursuing that shared goal'* (Tomasello and Carpenter, 2007). The notion of shared intentionality is based upon a model of intentional action founded in the idea of a control system or process, which we introduced in Chapter 5 (Figure 8.8). Such a control process is composed of a goal to which the system is directed, the ability to act to change aspects of the environment, the ability to perceive the environment so as to know when the state of the environment matches the goal. But shared intentionality can only emerge at the level of what we referred to in Chapter 5 as a Gregorian psyche: the level at which a complex inner environment is able to 'model' the external environment sufficiently well for the actor to take intentional action.

Tomasello et al. (Tomasello, Carpenter et al., 2005) likewise propose three developmental levels of shared intentionality. Within what they refer to as dyadic engagement, behaviour and emotions are shared between two actors. An individual is capable of interacting with some other actor through the expression of emotions and behavioural

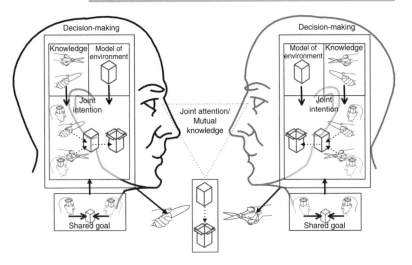

Figure 8.8   Collective intentionality

turn-taking. Within triadic engagement goals and aspects of perception are shared between two actors. An individual interacts with some other actor in pursuit of a shared goal. Both inter-actants monitor each others' behaviour in achievement of such a goal. Within collaborative engagement two actors hold joint intentions and joint attention. Actors not only share goals, but they also share action plans – joint intentions and mutual knowledge. They behave in terms of complementary roles shaped by such intentions.

It is therefore through the stance that we take that the 'aboutness' of our mental states is similar to the 'aboutness' of the mental states of other actors that social interaction becomes possible. This notion of collective intentionality bears a resemblance to what Peter Checkland (Checkland, 1987) refers to as Weltanschaung, translated into English as World view. This concept borrowed from German philosophy originally referred to the framework of ideas and beliefs through which an individual interprets the world and interacts with it. Checkland and others tend to use it to refer to a shared interpretative accomplishment of some human group. Hence, shared intentionality becomes collective intentionality when aspects of such intentionality are enacted between actors within a coherent group.

Tomasello et al. propose that the cognitive ability underlying shared intentionality is a necessary precursor to the creation and use of sign-tools and to the development of complex sign-systems such as human language. He utilises ape studies to demonstrate that there is evidence of dyadic and sometimes triadic engagement amongst the great apes, but little evidence of collaborative engagement. Hence, he proposes that collaborative behaviour reliant upon shared intentionality developed with the emergence of the modern human species and that this provided an advantage to our species in its survival. He further proposes that an 'ontogenetic pathway' is evident in the development of human infants – before three months they show evidence of dyadic engagement. At 9 months they understand goal-directed behaviour (triadic engagement) and at 14 months they understand other persons as intentional systems (collaborative engagement).

We have deliberately referred to a world view as an accomplishment of collective intentionality to emphasise that our world views are not fixed and immutable. We create, re-affirm and change this collective 'aboutness' through dialogue. We use signs (and more particularly their intensions) to help communicate and coordinate our intentions. Such communication relies on the presence of collective intensionality or a common ontology amongst a group of communicants.

As such, an ontology provides a shared vocabulary, which can be used to 'model' a domain in terms of the type of objects or concepts that exist, as well as their properties and relations. We can use the term to denote a common set of representations used by a group of communicants by which they transfer intent from one actor to another. Like world views, ontologies are not fixed; they are continuing and communicative accomplishments and in effect can be seen as an emergent effect of any system of communication.

As a key example, the khipucamayuq were a specialist class of information workers amongst the Inka and as such formed a group of communicants with a shared world view and ontology based in part around the use of key forma: the khipu. To encode and decode data within khipu, khipucamayuq had to draw upon interdependent resources of collective intentionality and intensionality. To create a khipu, such as the one illustrated in Figure 8.6, a given khipucamayuq had to have an understanding of the organisation of Inka society, particularly the role of the fundamental agricultural unit, known as ayllu, and the commitments such a unit would make on an annual basis in supplying a proportion of its production as tribute to the state. The khipucamayuq needed to also have a close practical understanding of the construction of khipu and how to use particular constructional elements to stand for or record aspects of collective intention such as commitments, directives, assertives or declaratives between various individuals and groups.

Conclusion

As we have seen, the keeping of records is a Worldwide and historical phenomenon which appears particularly associated with the rise of the state. The Mexica civilisation of central America, better known as the Aztecs, kept records of things using a complex sign-system based upon pictograms (Smith, 2003). Within many such records a common glyph or sign was used to indicate the transfer of information from one actor to another as in Figure 8.9. The logo for this chapter is based upon this speech glyph and is used to stand for informa.

To reiterate, a symbol, such as this speech glyph, points in two directions. On the one hand, it points to the physical world and relates to signals travelling within the ambient environment – in this case, sound waves travelling through air. On the other hand, a symbol points to the social world: it relates to effects such as individual and social action – such as the planting of crops. Interposing between these two is the realm of psyche: the generator of meaning. Informa refers to this latter

Figure 8.9 The Mexica speech glyph

pattern of organisation and is concerned with the content or meaning of signs used within the message conveyed in a communicative act.

Within this chapter we have made the case for considering meaning as not a given but as a continuing accomplishment of intentionality and intensionality as exercised by actors. Intentionality is aboutness – the relationship between mental acts/states and the external world and in terms of semiotics is largely a concept of relevance to pragmatics. But intentionality overlaps somewhat with the notion of intensionality. Intensionality is defined by the stands for relation between the symbol (designation) and its concept (intension) and is largely of relevance to semantics.

In this chapter we have used a number of cases of sign-systems to ground our discussion. For instance, we considered 'making faces' or the limited set of human emotive facial expressions. This case demonstrates the explanatory usefulness of the concepts of intentionality and intensionality in understanding what information is. An emotion is a mental state. But one rarely has an emotional experience in and of itself. Emotions are typically about something in the world. They are also embodied experiences. Part of such embodiment involves the production of some facial expression. A particular mental state (emotion) is therefore an intention in the sense of being about some aspect of the world. We are not normally sad, happy or angry in isolation. We are typically sad, happy or angry about something.

Facial expressions act as symbols for the intensions of the human emotions. Each facial expression, taken as a whole, is a symbol which relates to some intension: the idea or concept of a particular emotion. In this mode, facial expressions serve as expressive communicative acts. The creation of a particular facial expression serves to signify to other actors the emotion called out in the actor.

This means that information relies on the patterning of the world in symbols; but information is not a given in the presence of such symbols. Instead, information is a process of sense-making within acts of communication. As such, it should be rewritten as a verb – in-formation – because it is an inward-forming. We may also say that the *in* within in-formation actually refers to two things. On the one hand, *in* refers to intentionality and intentions. On the other hand, *in* refers to intensionality and intensions. In-formation is therefore a process in which intentions and intensions merge. In-formation is an entangled accomplishment involving the mix of individual (internal) and social (external) representations of the 'world'. <u>In</u>-formation therefore can be seen to rely upon <u>ex</u>-formation – the expression of symbols in forma. Informa relies upon data or forma but is directed towards <u>per</u>-formation, performa or activity.

The necessary complexity underlying this process of in-formation helps to distinguish between action and agency. Action or activity implies some actor, a term we have used at many points within previous chapters. However, the relationship between actor and psyche is a matter of much debate. The philosopher Fred Dretske (Dretske, 1999), for instance, makes a clear distinction between an actor and an agent. A machine, such as a thermostat, can be considered an actor. It 'senses' some change in its environment and effects some change in another actor – probably a boiler or furnace. Likewise a plant such as a flower can be considered an actor. It might change its colour at a particular time of the year and through this action obtain an ecological advantage in attracting a wider range of pollinators.

However, neither a thermostat nor a plant displays agency. In the case of a thermostat its behaviour or action is designed; in the case of the plant its behaviour or action has evolved. But in neither case does a psyche which is self-aware interpose between a sensory apparatus and an effector apparatus. Only when such a level of psyche mediates between sensation and action should we speak of agency.

For both Dretske and Dennett psyche is conceptualised as a control system. Dretske, however, maintains a narrower conception of psyche than Dennett. For Dretske psyche must involve meaning, learning and the manipulation of internal representations. For our purposes, the evolutionary nature of psyche as expressed in the work of Maturana, Varela and Dennett has more utility. On the one hand, the notion of a hierarchy of psyche helps explain the complexity of control in humans as compared to much of the animal kingdom. On the other hand, it does not deny an inevitable similarity between the operation of certain aspects of animal psyche and layers within the human psyche. It also does not exclude the idea of a limited concept of machine psyche. Hence, it is likely that the concept of agency is a relative one which depends on the degree of complexity associated with processes of control embedded in particular forms of psyche.

Sign-systems co-exist with and are produced by lower as well as higher levels of psyche. Within the human sphere, facial expressions, for instance, are clearly produced by some lower, unconscious level of mind. In contrast, speech is clearly produced within the higher levels of the conscious human psyche. Both such sign-systems rely upon the notion of collective intensionality, which we examine in greater detail within the next chapter.

References

Ascher, R. (2002). Inka Writing. Narrative Threads: accounting and recounting in Andean Khipu. J. Quilter and G. Urton. Austin, Texas, University of Texas Press: 103–118.

Austin, J. L. (1971). How to Do Things with Words. Oxford university press, Oxford.

Bateson, G. (1972). Steps to An Ecology of Mind. Balantine books, New York.

Beynon-Davies, P. (2009g). Significant threads: the nature of data. International Journal of Information Management 29(3): 170–188.

Boland, R. J. (1987). The In-formation of Information Systems. Critical Issues in Information Systems Research. R. J. Boland and R. A. Hirschheim. New York, John Wiley.

Checkland, P. (1987). Systems Thinking, Systems Practice. John Wiley, Chichester.

Cheney, D. L. and R. M. Seyfarth (1985). Vervet monkeys alarm calls: manipulation through shared information. Behaviour 1/2.

Dennett, D. C. (1987). The Intentional Stance. MIT Press, Cambridge, Mass.

Dennett, D. C. (1996). Kinds of Minds: towards an understanding of consciousness. Weidenfield and Nicholson, London.

Dretske, F. I. (1999). Machines, plants and animals: the origins of agency. Erkenntnis 51: 19–31.

Eco, U. (2009). The Infinity of Lists. Maclehase Press, New York.

Ekman, P. (2003). Emotions Revealed: understanding faces and feelings. Weidenfield and Nicholson, London.

Gawande, A. (2010). The Checklist Manifesto: how to get things right. Profile books, New York.

Holwell, S. and P. Checkland (1998a). Information, Systems and Information Systems. John Wiley, Chichester, UK.

Locke, L. (1923). The Ancient Quipu or Peruvian Knot Record. The American Museum of Natural History, New York.

Millikan, R. G. (2005). Language: a biological model. Clarendon Press, Oxford.

Minsky, M. (1988). The Society of Mind. Simon and Schuster, New York.

Mithen, S. J. (2006). The Singing Neanderthals: the Origins of music, language, mind and body. Weidenfeld & Nicolson, London.

Ogden, C. K. and I. A. Richards (1923). The Meaning of Meaning. Routledge and Kegan Paul, London.

Porter, M. E. and V. E. Millar (1985). How Information Gives you Competitive Advantage. Harvard Business Review 63(4): 149–160.

Ryle, G. (1949). The Concept of Mind. Hutchinson, London.

Schmandt-Bessarat, D. (1992). Before Writing. The University of Texas Press, Austin, Texas.

Searle, B. J. R. (1970). Speech Acts: An essay in the philosophy of language. Cambridge University Press, Cambridge.

Searle, J. R. (1975). A Taxonomy of Illocutionary Acts. Language, Mind and Knowledge. K. Gunderson. Minneapolis. Volume 7.

Searle, J. R. (1983). Intentionality: an essay in the philosophy of mind. Cambridge University Press, Cambridge, UK.

Searle, J. R. (1995). The Construction of Social Reality. Penguin, London.

Slobodchikoff, C. N., B. S. Perla, et al. (2009). Prairie Dogs: communication and community in animal society. Harvard University Press, Cambridge, Mass.

Smith, M. E. (2003). The Aztecs. Blackwell, Oxford.

Stamper, R. K. (1985). Information: mystical fluid or a subject for scientific enquiry? The Computer Journal 28(3).

Tomasello, M. and M. Carpenter (2007). Shared intentionality. Developmental Science 10(1): 121–125.

Tomasello, M., M. Carpenter, et al. (2005). Understanding and sharing intentions: the origins of cultural cognition. Behavioral and Brain Sciences 28: 675–735.

Urton, G. and C. J. Brezine (2005). Khipu accounting in ancient Peru. Science: 1065–1068.

Von Baeyer, H. C. (2003). Information: The new language of science. Weidenfeld & Nicolson.

9
Information systems:
Patterns of informa

Introduction

Grace Hooper, the creator of the business programming language COBOL, once said that *'Life was simple before World War II. After that, we had systems.'* The Second World War was noteworthy not only for the scale of this conflict; it was also an incubator for a whole range of innovations in 'systems' that have affected human societies across the world up to the present day.

A key example of such a system was the one created by the Royal Air Force's Fighter Command during the summers of the late 1930s and known as the Warning Network (Beynon-Davies, 2009d). It claimed to have played a critical role in a decisive battle against the German Luftwaffe – the Battle of Britain – in 1940. Since control of the skies was an essential pre-condition of a successful sea-borne invasion, this victory contributed, in part, to the decision of German High Command to abandon the planned invasion of Britain and turn its attention eastwards towards the Soviet Union. This, in turn, created space for the invasion of continental Europe by the Allies in 1944.

The Warning Network is a classic example of what we should mean by an information system. Information systems consist of patterns of informa: of in-forming. Information systems are systems for using signs in the sense that they act as a communication medium between different people, sometimes spatially and temporally distant. Therefore, the sign-systems of relevance to information systems are best described as semi-formal sign-systems: some of their features are designed; some of their features emerge in continuous human interaction. Using this conceptual lens, information systems can be seen to consist of patterns of communicative or informative acts using semi-formal sign-systems to make decisions and as a consequence to create, control and maintain social action.

On the one hand, an information system is tied to action. On the other hand, an information system is tied to a system of artefacts. The 'language' of some information system includes formal messages that create, control and maintain social interactions in an organisational context. Such messages not only serve to make statements about the world. They are also used to give orders, make promises or commitments, classify things and so on.

The Warning Network

Air Marshall Huw Dowding established RAF fighter command in 1935 (Holwell and Checkland, 1998b). At that time, he was extremely aware of the limitations of the British Air ministry in meeting the minimum target levels set for fighter aircraft production. Dowding therefore looked for other ways of providing an advantage to his fighter aircraft in an air battle. He therefore set up an organisational structure within fighter command which would enable it to sense enemy aircraft quickly and respond and intercept such aircraft within minutes.

During the early 1930s accepted military strategy for air defence was to fly so-called 'standing patrols' on flight paths likely to intercept bombing raids by an enemy. This constituted an extremely expensive military strategy in that fighter aircraft had to be kept permanently in the skies. Not surprisingly, this strategy was eventually replaced with the use of interceptor flights that could take-off quickly and attack incoming bomber raids. However, the key question remained, how was an air force to determine the precise position of incoming enemy aircraft in sufficient time to enable effective interception?

The key solution to this problem involved the utilisation of radio technology to detect aircraft – a technology that became known as *radar*. This technology developed out of an observation in 1934 that an aircraft flying through radio beams across Kiel harbour reflected them to produce an image of a battleship. This insight stimulated research and development both in Germany and Britain to attempt to exploit this technology for military purposes. By 1935, both the Germans and British had access to this technology and indeed German radar was technically superior to its British equivalent at the time. The crucial difference was that the British were better able to utilise the technology within systems of air defence. The British were able to gain what would become known in modern management jargon as *competitive advantage* (Porter, 1985) from this technology.

In June of 1940, Air Marshall Huw Dowding's fighter command faced a number of major challenges. The RAF had lost 500 operational fighter aircraft and 300 pilots in the air battle over Flanders and France. Having 620 operational fighters remaining, Fighter Command was therefore 50% below the 1200 target established in 1939 as that needed to win an air battle with the Luftwaffe over the UK. Dowding therefore had to find ways of utilising his limited resources to maximum effect.

The first step in the process was the establishment of an effective organisation for command and control. A headquarters for fighter command was established at Bentley Priory in Stanmore just north of London. This had overall strategic control of operations. The organisa-tion of Fighter Command was divided into four geographical groups covering major parts of the country, each group being controlled by a Group station. Number 10 group covered South West England and South Wales with its HQ at Box in Wiltshire, number 11 group cov-ered London and South East England and was based at Uxbridge in West London, number 12 group covered the Midlands and was centred on Watnall in Nottinghamshire, while number 13 group covered the remainder of England to the North and was based at Kenton Bar in Newcastle. Each group was in turn divided into a number of sectors with a sector HQ at each of the airfields. For instance, group 11 was divided into seven sectors. Group HQs had tactical control within their area and Sector HQs had control of pilots when airborne.

The second step in this process of achieving advantage was RAF fighter command constructing an effective system of 'information technology' that could sense the whereabouts of aircraft. This involved the establishment of 50 radar stations and 1000 observation posts stra-tegically placed around the coastline of Britain. There were actually two chains of radar station, one for detecting high-flying aircraft and one for detecting low-flying aircraft. These radar stations could detect air-craft flying at an altitude of as much as 30,000 feet and 150 miles dis-tant. This was supplemented with a chain of posts manned by civilian volunteers observing incoming aircraft, known as the Observer Corps. Radar stations, observer posts and fighter airfields were all connected to fighter command headquarters by dedicated Post Office tele-printer (tele-writer) and telephone lines.

Not surprisingly, in traditional accounts of this conflict, radar is portrayed as the 'killer application' which drove the strategy of air defence by the RAF (Grattan, 2005). This interpretation tends to under-emphasise the place of other important information technologies of the day. For instance, the data generated by radar such as height readings were often approximate. There was also a time lag of some four minutes between interpreting radar data and scrambling a fighter squadron and this compared to the six or so minutes it took for enemy aircraft to cross the English Channel.

Because of this radar, data was also supplemented and corrected by other communication channels. A chain of wireless listening stations known as Station Y and their control centre at Station X in Bletchley Park provided a significant channel of data for this purpose. These agencies, for instance, intercepted radio messages from Luftwaffe crews and this communication traffic frequently revealed the destination, size and timing of Luftwaffe raids. Another key advantage of this channel was that data was typically passed on to RAF fighter command within one minute of being heard (Puri, 2006).

The third crucial step was the creation of an effective system in which the 'information technology' could be utilised. During the summers between 1936 and 1939, a series of teams formed from physicists, engineers and RAF personnel engaged in a series of practical exercises with the aim of solving the fundamental problem of turning raw data received from radar, observer posts and other channels into information for pilots to fly to the precise point at which to intercept enemy raids. The teams were unable to be told of the development in RADAR at this time for security reasons. Hence, they were given the brief of designing an activity system and associated information system that could utilise data on the bearing, distance and altitude of enemy planes coming to them at regular intervals from a mysterious source. Their overall objective was to decide on the best way of turning such data into information in order that courses of interception could be established for fighter aircraft.

These 'experiments' established a quick and effective means of bringing two groups of aircraft travelling at different speeds together at the same point in the sky using something that became known as the 'Tizzy angle'. They also established the need for a filter room with its own 'map table' to ensure the accuracy of information passed to the operations room (see below).

The eventual system of air defence that was created was given a series of different names such as warning and control system, early warning network or the control and reporting system. We shall refer to it as the early warning network or Warning Network for short. Much literature portrays the Warning Network as allowing an initially under-strength RAF to successfully compete with a numerically greater force of enemy aircraft. While not denying the contribution of the Warning Network to RAF operations one should be careful not to over-play its importance. For instance, Puri (Puri, 2006) makes the point that the calculation of relative strength should discount bombers, dive-bombers and twin-engine fighters, all of which lacked the capability of speedy and rapid manoeuvre required of the dog-fighting that occurred during the Battle of Britain. If these aircraft are excluded, the RAF's 700 or so fighter force faced an opposition of 800 Luftwaffe single-engine fighters at this time.

Nevertheless, an effective system of sensing, interpretation and response was undoubtedly important to Dowding's strategy. Data from the two chains of radar stations were telephoned to Fighter Command HQ. This data went first to a filter room, manned 24 hours a day, where members of the Women's Auxiliary Air Force (WAAF) turned such data into useful information. Because of the possibility of human error in the use of RADAR detection equipment, the quality of the data was first assessed and if necessary corrections made to it. Radar plots and sightings were then turned into intelligence on the likely strength, position, height, speed and direction of both enemy aircraft and friendly aircraft. This filtered information was then passed on next door to the Fighter Command Operations Room (see Figure 9.1).

Within the operations room filtered information was coded onto a visual display by other members of the WAAF, whom we shall refer to as plotters. The display itself consisted of using wooden tokens and a large plotting table to model the disposition of aircraft, both enemy and friendly, in the sky.

The plotting table consisted of a large irregularly shaped table on which was painted a large-scale map of the parts of the UK controlled by the particular operations room. A small wooden block or token was used to represent a group of friendly and enemy aircraft, such as a RAF squadron. Such tokens were moved around on the plotting table by plotters using croupier sticks.

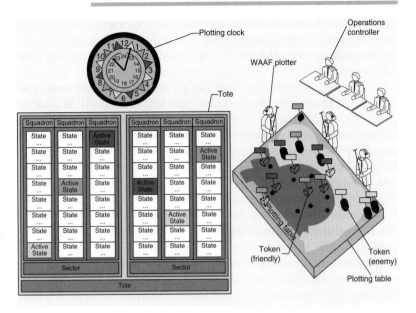

Figure 9.1   Elements of the operations room

The placement of tokens on the plotting table clearly indicated the last known position of groups of aircraft in the sky. The movement of tokens across the plotting table indicated the direction of the aircraft over a defined period of time. These tokens were also used to indicate the height and strength of aircraft units. RAF units were represented by triangular or wedge-shaped wooden tokens. Numerals slipped into tracks on the sides of such tokens revealed both the units' altitude in thousands of feet and the number of 'angels', or friendly fighters, in the formation. In contrast, disc-shaped tokens were used to represent German aircraft units. Each of these particular tokens showed a code number and the attack size of the unit, such as 30+ or 40+.

It was also possible to code the time a particular aircraft group had been in some area of air-space using such tokens. A specially built clock known as the plotting clock acted as a way of time-stamping the data represented on the plotting table within the operations room. Three colours – yellow, red and blue – were used on the clock-face to code five-minute intervals. On first identification a token was given the colour

207

associated with the current five-minute interval for example, red. This provided instant recognition of the recency of data recorded on the plotting table and by inference how long the aircraft group had been within airspace.

In addition to the plotting table and tokens, a display called the 'tote' was used to record the state of enemy raids and the state of readiness of particular RAF squadrons. For instance, particular states of readiness for a squadron included *available 30 minutes, available five minutes, take-off or cock-pit readiness – 2 minutes* or *in the air.* The actual state for a particular squadron was indicated by illuminating the particular area on the tote. The colour used for the illumination matched the time interval on the plotting clock in which the communication was received. A glowing white bar signified a communicated state more than ten minutes old. This rendered it unreliable.

One or more operations controllers were also present in the operations room, usually seated in an observation gallery above the plotting table and opposite the tote and plotting clock. They made decisions on the basis of the 'real-time' updates being made both to the plotting table and to the tote. Such decisions initiated the telephoning of instructions through to appropriate controllers at group and sector level, as well as other bodies such as Anti-Aircraft command, the Observer Corps, the BBC and civil defence organisations such as those sounding air-raid warnings. Hence, instructions could consist of commands for air-raid warnings to be sounded in threatened areas, fighter squadrons to be scrambled, and commands for air-sea rescue to pick up pilots ditched in the English Channel.

The operations room at group level worked in the same way except that the maps used represented the group air-space. Group HQs also received data (aircraft sightings) from Observer Posts. This was first filtered at group level and then passed on to command and sector HQs.

The sector operations rooms were set up as two units. The first unit duplicated the picture at command and group level by copying the positioning of counters and updates to the HQ tote and plotting table at sector level. This allowed operations controllers at sector level to continually sense their sector's place in the larger operational picture. The second unit plotted at sector level on the map the exact location of their own planes from their radio transmissions. From here aircraft were assigned to a particular raid and their interception courses were continually plotted using compass, ruler, pencil and paper. The sector operations controller scrambled selected aircraft on command from the group HQ. Once in the air, command passed over to the flight leader until combat was over.

The Warning Network described above contributed to successful action on the part of the RAF during the period from July to the end of October 1940 (Holwell and Checkland, 1998b). On Sunday 15th September 1940 the system was severely tested. A hundred German bombers crossed the Kent coast at 11:30 that day. Seventeen squadrons from three groups of the RAF went to intercept them. At 14:00 the same day a second wave came in and was met by 31 squadrons (over 300 planes in all). At the end of the day RAF losses were 27 aircraft with 13 pilots killed. The Luftwaffe lost 57 aircraft.

Informative acts

As we discussed in Chapter 8, a communicative or informative act is some aspect of performance designed by one actor, A, to influence the performance of some other actor, B. Searle (Searle, 1983) maintains that intentionality or 'aboutness' is expressed through illocutionary acts: acts of communication in which actors create and send messages in an appropriate context with certain intentions. The communication of such intentions is important for coordinated action. It also underlies the process of organising itself; particularly in relation to the way in which routines or repeating patterns of performance form in joint work.

We would argue that information systems consist of recurring patterns of communicative action. Such patterns arise from the 'game-like' character of human communication. A particular communicative act creates the possibility of usually a limited range of communicative acts as response. For instance, in verbal discourse between two human actors a question is normally responded to with an answer, an assertion with a statement of assent or disagreement, a statement of thanks with an acknowledgement and an apology with an acceptance.

The information system supporting the activity of Fighter Command could be interpreted as a number of inter-linked and recurring patterns of communication between actors within the different social groups involved in this joint endeavour: radar operatives, observation corps operatives, filter room staff, operations room plotters, operations room controllers, aircraft pilots and so on.

As mentioned in Chapter 8, Searle argues that a given communicative act consists of two main elements (Searle, 1970): a propositional attitude or illocutionary force and a propositional content. Hence, the communicative act 'I promise to write a letter' consists of the propositional attitude (to promise or commit something) and the propositional content [to write a letter].

Searle also refers to the *context* of some communicative act and uses this term to refer to the sender, receiver, time, place and the 'world' within which the illocutionary act takes place. Hence, the context defines a message from a sender S to a receiver R at time T and in place P. The term *world* is used to collect together a range of other features of context which are important for understanding the meaning of a message, such as channel (speech, writing etc.), code (language style) and message-form (chat, debate, sermon and so on). We find it more useful to segment off these aspects of a communication into their appropriate semiotic category. For instance, channel is a matter of empirics, code is a matter of semantics and message-form relates to matters of pragmatics.

He uses the notation F[p] to refer to a communicative act, where F stands for the illocutionary force of the communicative act and p its propositional content. As we have seen, he further formulates five key types of illocutionary or communicative act in terms of illocutionary force: assertives, directives, commissives, expressives and declaratives.

Assertives are communicative acts that explain how things are in the world and commit the speaker to the truth of the expressed proposition. We express an assertive as ⊢[p]. Examples of assertives within the case of the Warning Network particularly relate to various actors communicating their understanding of the current state of the world, consisting mainly of the positioning of friendly and enemy aircraft. Some examples are:

- A radar operator makes a statement of the expected strength, altitude, position and direction of an enemy aircraft group to filter room staff (/radar operator/⊢[an enemy aircraft group has strength X, is at position Y and is flying in direction Z] \filter room staff member\ @ time T & place P).
- A member of the observer corp. reports the expected strength, altitude, position and direction of an enemy aircraft group to filter room staff (/observer corp. member/⊢[an enemy aircraft group has strength X, is at position Y and is flying in direction Z] \filter room staff member\ @time T & place P).

- A station Y operative reports the content of signals intelligence to filter room staff (/station Y operative/⊢[signals intelligence] \filter room staff member\ @time T & place P).

Directives are communicative acts that represent the senders' attempt to get a receiver to perform an action, such as requests, questions, commands and advice. We express a directive as ?[p]. Examples of directives within the case of the Warning Network refer generally to commands issued by various actors to various other actors. Examples include:

- An operations controller requests a group controller to change the state of readiness of particular sectors (/operations controller/?[change of state to sector readiness] \group controller\ @time T & place P).
- A group controller requests a sector controller to change the state of readiness of a particular squadron (/group controller/?[change of state to squadron readiness] \sector controller\ @time T & place P).
- A sector controller instructs a squadron leader to change the state of readiness of his squadron (/sector controller/?[change of state to squadron readiness] \squadron leader\ @time T & place P).

Commissives are communicative acts that commit a speaker to some future course of action such as promises, oaths and threats. They are communicative acts that represent a speaker's intention to perform an action. We express a commissive as #[p]. Examples of commissives within the case of the Warning Network generally refer to acts of confirmation in response to directives. For example:

- A sector controller confirms that a squadron has scrambled to a group controller (/sector controller/ #[squadron to scramble] \group controller\ @time T & place P).
- A group controller confirms that a squadron has scrambled to a HQ controller (/group controller/ #[squadron to scramble] \HQ controller\ @time T & place P).

Expressives are communicative acts that represent the speakers' psychological state, feelings or emotions such as apologies, criticisms and congratulations. They express a speaker's attitudes and emotions towards some proposition. We express an expressive as ![p]. Many expressives are likely to have accompanied other communicative acts within the patterning of communication within the Warning Network.

Declaratives are communicative acts that aim to change the world through the communication itself, such as baptism, pronouncing someone husband and wife and sentencing a prisoner. Hence, they are usually communicated against a normative background and are frequently institutionalised. We express a declarative as ≡[p]. There are a number of key examples of declaratives within the Warning Network case. For instance:

- A filter room operative collates incoming data and declares the strength, altitude, position and direction of an aircraft group to members of operations staff and the operator of the tote (/filter room operative/ ≡[an aircraft group has strength X, is at position Y and is flying in direction Z] \tote operator\ @time T & place P).
- A plotter within the operations room declares the position of an enemy aircraft group by plotting it on the plotting table (/operations plotter/ ≡[an enemy aircraft group has strength X, is at position Y and is flying in direction Z] \operations controller\ @time T & place P).
- The operator of the tote declares the current state of a friendly aircraft group on the tote (/tote operator/ ≡[current state of friendly aircraft group] \operations room staff\ @time T & place P).
- A squadron leader indicating that an enemy squadron had been engaged to a sector controller (/squadron leader/ ≡[enemy engaged] \ sector controller\ @time T & place P).

Each of these types of communicative act can only occur at particular points within patterns of communication between radar operators, filter room staff, operations room plotters and various levels of operations controller. Each communicative act also calls into play a limited number of other communicative acts in response.

Hence, communicative acts such as the ones described above normally inter-relate in a network of precedence. By this we mean that one informative act normally precedes another in some regular and repeating sequence to form a coherent pattern. Part of such a pattern in the case of the Warning Network is illustrated in Figure 9.2; where dotted arrows represent the precedence of communicative acts.

In many information systems of this nature there is a natural sequence in which given communicative acts occur. On the left of Figure 9.2, we

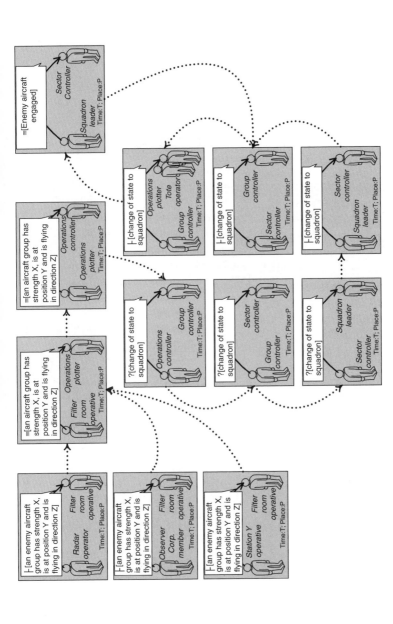

Figure 9.2 Informative pattern in the Warning Network

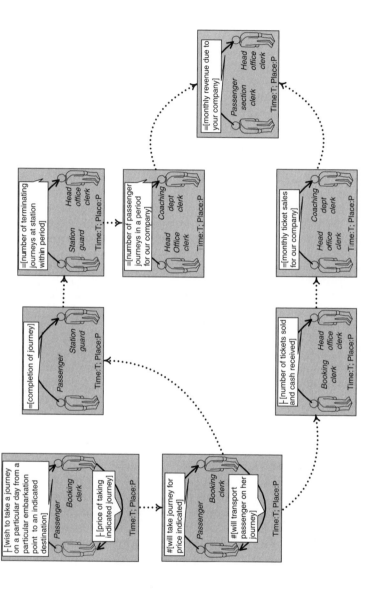

Figure 9.3 Informative pattern in the Railway Clearing House

have a number of assertive acts from various actors, stating their observations as to the state of the world. These observations are then collated by filter room and operations room staff and are used to declare the position of both enemy and friendly aircraft in the sky. Such declaration effectively serves to inform participants of the state of the world at a particular point in time. On this basis, actors make decisions and issue directives to respond to this state. Other actors in the chain of command then confirm that actions have been taken which hopefully match the directives issued.

Effectively this cycle of assertives, declaratives, directives and commissives implements patterns of in-forma underlying what many have referred to as a sense and respond strategy within organisations and which is similar to the control loop described in Chapter 5. Assertives and declaratives amount effectively to sensed signals within some social control system whereas directives and commissives effectively equate to effector signals.

Figure 9.3 illustrates another informative pattern, this time from the case of the Victorian Clearing House described in Chapter 2. Here again, a cycle of assertions, declarations and commitments supported the key decision-making involved with the calculation of revenues for particular railway companies.

Information systems and data systems

As argued in an earlier chapter, information systems rely in turn on data systems of various forms. In other words informa relies upon forma. Such forma in the case of the Warning Network includes non-persistent forma such as the spoken words of controllers and other staff. It also includes the techne evident in the situation – persistent forma. In the case of the Warning Network this persistent forma comprised radar, the telephony network and devices such as the plotting table, tokens, plotting clock and tote.

Many systems in organisations are examples of socio-technical systems. A socio-technical system is a system of technology used within a system of activity. Information systems are primary examples of socio-technical systems. Information systems consist of persistent data systems used within some activity system. They therefore span between 'information technology' and activity. Part of the activity will involve use of some persistent data system. The in-formation which emerges from the information system will

215

also drive decision-making leading to further action within some organi-sation. In other words, information systems constitute communication systems designed to support activity with the aid of technology.

Paradoxically, this definition of an information system conflicts with that typically used within the discipline that purports to study these systems and refers to itself with the label *Information Systems* or some-times *Management Information Systems*. Within this discipline, a com-mon definition of this term *information system* suggests that it refers to the interaction between people, processes, data and technology. This encompassing, well-established and well-used definition initially served the purpose of highlighting that an information system was a much larger construct than information technology. However, as Ray Paul (Paul, 2007) suggests, use of this encompassing definition now limits the intellectual capacity of the term because it does nothing to help answer important questions such as: how and why do people use data? Why is data important to processes and where does information fit in? Are processes different to technology? Are information systems different to organisations?

Some of the key lessons from the Warning Network case lie at the heart of the nature of an information system as a socio-technical sys-tem. An information system is fundamentally concerned with com-munication in support of activity using artefacts to represent, store, manipulate and transmit data. The essence of an information sys-tem therefore lies not purely in the technology or in the activity; it lies in the way in which technology is used in support of purposeful action.

For instance, radar by itself was not key to effective control of the skies over Britain during this period. Instead, it was the way in which the information technology was used within an encompassing informa-tion system to support purposeful action that proved important. Good information systems are therefore critical to effective human action. The information system within the Warning Network was set up by the RAF to enable them to better coordinate their actions in relation to beating off the mass raids of the German Luftwaffe. Hence, the key utility or value of this information system was established in relation to the effectiveness of action reliant upon it.

Information systems are systems of communication. They involve people in processes of in-formation. The information system of the Warning Network involved collecting data from channels such as radar, organising this data for military-decision-making and the dissemination of both decisions and data to airfields.

Consider the place of the operations room at RAF fighter command in this light. Here various elements such as the makeup and positioning of counters on the plotting table and the signals on the tote acted as a sign-system for relevant human actors. The state of such signs at any one point in time was used as a 'real-time' record or model of the disposition of aircraft within the air defence battle. On the basis of the key actors' continuous interpretation of this record, tactical decisions were made in relation to the deployment of fighter aircraft.

However, information systems are subtly different from general systems of human communication: an information system is a specialised sub-type of a communication system. The key difference between an information system and a communication system can be illustrated with an example. In the children's game 'telephone' a chain of children is required to pass on a verbal message. The 'sender' of the message whispers it in the ear of the first child. The first child then whispers it in the ear of the second child and so on down the chain until it reaches the ear of the 'receiver' child, the last person in the chain. Usually, the message is highly distorted by the time it gets to the end of the chain. Hence, a message like 'I love you' can end up as 'Joe hates Kate'. Therefore, this game normally demonstrates some of the limitations of human verbal communication in groups.

Communication theorists would explain the distortion in the message through the concept of 'noise' (Chapter 4). However, when substituting written for verbal communication the communication is less subject to distortion. Hence, getting each child to write the message transmitted separately each time and pass it on to the next child reduces problems for instance of poor hearing and misinterpretation. Passing of course the same written message along the line should minimise distortion. This highlights the usefulness of persistent forma in group communication. An information system is a communication system in which messages are encoded, transmitted and decoded in the form of persistent forma, particularly records. Such records have a life over and above the communication process within which they took part.

For example, the use of tokens on the plotting table of the operations room at RAF Fighter Command is an important example of the representation of data in 'records' of communication. The use of tokens upon the plotting table can be seen as a persistent data system which

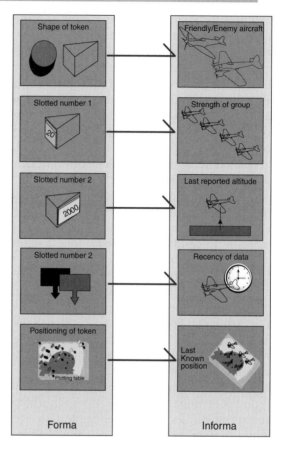

Figure 9.4 Signification of tokens

served to communicate a common understanding or world view of the situation amongst multiple actors within the operations room.

A given token was created by one of the plotters within the operations room as a record of a communication received from one of the WAAF operatives in the filter room. The makeup and use of a particular token upon the plotting table was used to signify a number of things to all present in the operations room (Figure 9.4):

- The shape of the token signified the type of aircraft. A triangular or wedge-shaped wooden block was used to represent a group of allied aircraft. A cylindrical or disc-shaped wooden block was used to stand for a group of enemy aircraft.

- The altitude and number of aircraft in a particular group was signified by annotations to the token. Two set of numbers were slotted into each triangular block: one on each face. One number referred to the altitude last reported for the group. The other number indicated the reported strength of the group.
- The recency of the record was indicated by the colour assigned to a token. The approximate time data was received about a particular aircraft group was coded in terms of a coloured flag attached to the token and calibrated against the plotting clock.
- The positioning of the token against the map of the plotting table signified the last known position of the aircraft group within the defined air-space.

Within the context of the operations room such symbols therefore were used to represent a shared intensionality: a common association between the tokens as symbols or designations and their meaning or intensions.

This example therefore highlights another key feature of an information system. An information system is characterised not only by one-to-one or dyadic communication. One particular advantage of the use of records within communication is that the presence of such persistent artefacts facilitates one-to-many and many-to-many communication within a group of actors over a period of time. As such, it turns individual memory into social or collective memory.

In terms of such many-to-many communication, an information system can be seen to 'model' critical aspects of its encompassing activity system. For instance, in a way the total collection of tokens on the plotting table, their makeup, and their positioning signified to both plotter and more importantly to operations controllers the current disposition of a particular air battle.

Conclusion

Some have argued for the critical significance of the Warning Network described in this chapter and made claims that this information system enabled Allied victory in the Battle of Britain and made possible the winning of World War II (Holwell and Checkland, 1998b). Others have rightly expressed concerns over this interpretation and argued in opposition that the linkages between the existence of the Warning Network, eventual victory of the Battle of Britain and successful invasion of continental Europe are subject to much historical debate (Robinson and Wilson, 2002).

For instance, success in the Battle of Britain was due to interaction of numerous factors, many of which were environmental or contextual in the sense that they occurred outside of the socio-technical system described in this section. For instance, significance has been attributed to the poor strategic decision-making by the Luftwaffe during this period as compared to an effective strategy produced and executed by the RAF. During early September of 1940 the Luftwaffe decided to switch from bombing military targets such as airfields to attacks on London. This, it is argued, provided Fighter Command with a much-needed breathing space in which to restore its strength. On the other hand, Dowding made the strategic decision to allow group 11 to bear the brunt of much of the fighting during the Battle of Britain. Other groups bolstered the defence when needed but also acted as a safe haven for squadrons in need of recuperation. The result of this strategy of rotation was a defence that never committed more than was necessary for the job at hand.

However, this is not to deny the contribution of the Warning Network to eventual success both in the Battle of Britain and as a platform for further Allied success in the war in Europe. As Robinson and Wilson cogently put it, the Warning Network *'played a necessary but not a sufficient role in the Battle of Britain'* (Robinson and Wilson, 2002). In a sense this interpretation is reminiscent of continuing arguments over the value of information technology and information systems to organisations. Both academics and practitioners in the area of information technology have a natural tendency to over-inflate the contribution of technology and information to organisational success. In contrast academics and practitioners within the business and management area frequently underestimate the role of technology and information to successful management. More generally, good information systems are a necessary but not a sufficient condition for organisational success. This is because the nature of information systems involves the complex intertwining of information, decision and action in continual interaction within some environment.

The logo for this chapter stands for the patterning of in-forma. Information systems consist of patterns of such informa: of in-form-ing. Information systems are systems for using signs in the sense that they act as a communication medium between different people, some-times spatially and temporally distant. Therefore, the sign-systems of relevance to information systems are best described as semi-formal sign-systems: some of their features are designed; some of their features emerge in continuous human interaction. Using this conceptual lens, information systems can be seen to consist of patterns of communica-tive or informative acts using semi-formal sign-systems to make deci-sions and as a consequence to create, control and maintain coordinated action between a multitude of actors.

On the one hand, an information system is tied to action – to *praxis*. On the other hand, an information system is normally tied to a sys-tem of artefacts – to *techne*. The 'language' of some information sys-tem includes formal messages that create, control and maintain social interactions in an organisational context. Such messages not only serve to make statements about the world. They are also used to give orders, make promises or commitments, classify things and so on.

In this chapter we have spent some considerable time unpacking the key elements of a communicative or informative act. In very broad terms, a communicative act is some aspect of human performance designed by one actor, A, to influence the performance of some other actor, B. Searle maintains that intentionality is expressed through such acts of communication in which actors create and send messages in an appropriate context with certain intentions. The communication of such intentions is important for coordinated action. We have used the five key types of communicative act defined by Searle to help build a conception of the patterning of human communication supporting instrumental performance. These types include: assertives, directives, commissives, expressives and declaratives.

We would argue that information systems consist of recurring pat-terns of communicative acts of such types. Such patterns arise from the 'game-like' character of human communication. A particular com-municative act creates the possibility of usually a limited range of com-municative acts as response. An information system can therefore be conceived as a semi-formal sign-system which supports human deci-sion-making and action on the one hand and utilises representation, particularly record-keeping, on the other.

The purpose of informative acts is to ensure coordination of activities. We have used the term performa to refer to this use of communication within social action. In-formation is critical to the control of mutual performance: acts of production or performative acts corresponding to the 'work' of people in collective interaction. It is to a consideration of such performative acts that we turn next...

References

Beynon-Davies, P. (2009d). The 'Language' of Informatics: the nature of information systems. International Journal of Information Management 29(2): 92–103.

Grattan, R. F. (2005). Strategy in the battle of Britain and strategic management theory. Management Decision 43(10): 1432–1441.

Holwell, S. and P. Checkland (1998b). An Information System Won the War. IEE Proceedings Software 145(4): 95–99.

Paul, R. J. (2007). Challenges to information systems: time to change. European Journal of Information Systems 16(3): 193–195.

Porter, M. E. (1985). Competitive Advantage: creating and sustaining superior performance. Free Press, New York.

Puri, R. (2006). The Role of Intelligence in Deciding the Battle of Britain. Intelligence and National Security 21(3): 416–439.

Robinson, B. and F. Wilson (2002). Soft systems methodology and dialectics in an information environment: A case study of the battle of Britain. Systems Research and Behavioural Science 20(3): 255–268.

Searle, B. J. R. (1970). Speech Acts: An Essay in the Philosophy of Language. Cambridge University Press, Cambridge.

Searle, J. R. (1983). Intentionality: an essay in the philosophy of mind. Cambridge University Press, Cambridge, UK.

10
Activity: Performa

Introduction

Within his comedy *As You Like It* Shakespeare has his character Jacques utter the following phrase: *'All the world's a stage, and all the men and women merely players; they have their exits and their entrances, and one man in his time plays many parts...'* Many years later the sociologist Erving Goffman played upon this idea in his classic work: *The Presentation of Self in Everyday Life* (Goffman, 1969). This led to what would become known as the dramaturgical perspective in sociology. The essence of this perspective is that we all perform every moment of our lives in the sense of enacting conventional patterns of behaviour. We all take on many roles in many continuing 'plays' with many other actors.

In a sense, we have considered action or activity at a number of points in our discussion within this book. This is because we have inherently tried to build an account of the nature of significance around the centrality of action. In doing so, we have explicitly made the distinction between three forms of inter-related action: performative, informative and formative action. We have argued that the patterning of such action within activity, information and data systems is the essence of what we mean by organisation, particularly human organisation. In previous chapters we have focused upon the nature of informative and formative action. In both the current and the next chapter we focus upon performative action.

Although the term performative action in the sense of performance could be taken to include all forms of action, we focus on a particular type of activity: that of productive acts or 'work', otherwise referred to as instrumental action. In a classic of the silent movie era, *Modern Times*, Charlie Chaplin satirises the instrumental activity system of the modern factory system. Within this system humans are portrayed as cogs in a mighty machine. Part of the blame for the invention of this system of work has been laid squarely at the door of Frederick Winslow Taylor and his creed of scientific management. We therefore use this as a key case to ground our consideration of 'work' as productive activity and relate this to the idea of performance. This enables us to build a critique of some of the central ideas arising from this movement which still have a resonance in many modern perspectives on the industrial organisation.

However, to build a coherent and effective account of performative action we have to formulate a place for the 'tool' or the 'machine' within activity. Such tools have traditionally been used to augment and improve human capacity for performing instrumental action. More recently, machines have attained the status of independent actors within significant activity systems.

The science of shovelling

Frederick Winslow Taylor was an American mechanical engineer who sought to improve industrial efficiency through an approach he referred to as *scientific management*. He was also one of the first to put the activity of consulting for management on a firm footing (Kanigel, 1997).

Taylor was born in 1856 to a wealthy Quaker family in Philadelphia, Pennsylvania. He studied for two years in France and Germany and during this period travelled widely throughout much of Europe. In 1872, he entered Phillips Exeter Academy in Exeter, New Hampshire and upon graduation Taylor was accepted at Harvard Law School. However, apparently due to rapidly deteriorating eyesight, Taylor decided to consider an alternative career within industry.

In 1873 Taylor became an industrial apprentice patternmaker, gaining shop-floor experience at the pump-manufacturing company Enterprise Hydraulic Works. In 1878, he became a machine shop labourer at Midvale Steel Works and rose rapidly to become gang-boss, foreman, research director and, finally, chief engineer. During his time at this institution, Taylor undertook evening classes at Stevens Institute of Technology and in 1883 obtained a degree in Mechanical Engineering through a series of correspondence courses.

From 1890 until 1893 Taylor worked as a general manager and a consulting engineer to management in the Manufacturing Investment Company, which operated a number of large paper mills in Maine and Wisconsin. Following his time there, Taylor opened an independent consulting practice in Philadelphia specialising in 'Systematizing Shop Management and Manufacturing Costs'. In 1898, Taylor joined Bethlehem Steel, where he and a team of assistants developed a process of treating high-speed tool steels.

Taylor eventually became a professor at the Tuck School of Business at Dartmouth College but in the winter of 1915 caught pneumonia and died in March of the following year, aged 59.

The essence of what became known as Taylorism consisted of the close and systematic study of work processes with the overall aim of improving such processes. Taylor thought that by analysing any form of work closely enough, that the *one best way* of achieving it could be determined. His form of work analysis involved breaking down an activity into a series of tasks or movements, each of which could be measured independently. One of the most important of such measurements was the time taken to make these movements – hence, such analysis became known as the *time and motion study*.

One of his most famous studies involved a close investigation of the activity of shovelling materials such as various grades of coal and coke from wagons into a steelworks. His way of analysing this form of work was described in his testimony to a special committee of the House of Representatives that was formed to investigate his methods in 1911 and 1912 (Copley, 1969).

In observing various workers, Taylor's team of researchers noticed that good shovellers owned their own shovels and preferred to use these tools rather than shovels supplied by the company. The researchers therefore recruited a team of what they referred to as these 'first-class shovellers' and subjected them to a series of experiments in which features of the shovels used for various materials were altered and the results noted. For instance, the team studied the number of shovel loads undertaken by 'first-class men' using a particular shovel when shifting iron ore. They found that the average shovel load was 38 pounds and that with this load a good shoveller could handle on average 25 tonnes per day. They then shortened the shovel so that it could handle 34 pounds of ore per shovel-full and found that the amount shovelled rose to 30 tonnes per day per man. They continued to do this until they found the point at which the amount shovelled per day started to diminish.

By this method they determined that a first-class shoveller would do his largest day's work when he used a shovel designed for a shovel load of twenty-one and one half pounds. This was therefore shown to be the optimal loading across various types of shovelled material.

Following this discovery, two changes were made to work practice. First, shovels were designed for each type of material to ensure this optimal loading. Second, workers were trained in the appropriate use of such shovels for the particular material worked with. Third, a planning process was instituted to ensure that at the start of each working day workers were assigned their particular task and provided with the appropriate tool for the job. Fourth, records were kept of each workers performance for each working day. Fifth, those workers found to be falling below expectation were expected to undergo further training on the job.

Taylor's scientific management was therefore founded on three principles. First, managers should be given total responsibility for the organisation of work; workers should concentrate on manual tasks. A 'thinking' department of managers should be set up responsible for task planning and design. Second, that all work tasks should be examined and if necessary re-designed to improve efficiency. By studying the approach adopted, the tools utilised and the fatigue generated for any task, an optimum procedure for the task can be determined. Third, methods should be adopted for the selection, training and monitoring of labour to ensure that work is done efficiently.

The underlying assumption of this approach is that the activities or performance of people within industrial organisations can be rationalised and closely defined or designed. This model of work clearly had its counterpart within the domain of office or administrative work in the system of bureaucracy. In a bureaucracy roles are precisely defined, tasks are explicitly documented and control of work is exercised in a strict hierarchical fashion.

Performative acts

Performa corresponds to the 'performance' of actors in various situations. We particularly focus on instrumental action in such terms. A performative act amounts to some transformation of the world undertaken by a particular actor at a particular time and in a particular place in an attempt to realise some particular goal.

To help understand the nature of performative action as individual action it is useful to turn to the work of the American pragmatic philosophers George Herbert Mead (Mead, 1934) and Charles Morris (Morris, 1946). For Mead and Morris behaviour is any change taking place in an organism. An organism begins to behave at the moment of its creation and its behaviour ceases only when it dies. Behaviour is hence continuous, patterned action. An action or act is a unit of behaviour with a clearly delineable beginning, end and goal, within the general patterned continuum of behaviour. The action is realised in relation to the attainment of some goal and the goal of some action is determined by an impulse.

Consider the simple case of shovelling in such terms. The actor in this case is the shoveller. The transformation of the world undertaken by this actor is the physical movement of some material from one place to another. The goal is to shift a quantity of this material in a working day and the stimulus to such action is most likely the payment received for such work by the shoveller.

There are numerous other examples of performative action in the cases we have considered in previous chapters. For example, within the Railway Clearing House there are various examples of performative action such as booking clerks issuing train tickets, passengers undertaking train journeys, train drivers driving trains on particular journeys, railway workers loading and unloading goods and parcels onto and off-of trains, train guards checking tickets, station guards collecting tickets and number-takers checking trains. We can take any of these performative acts and decompose them into its constituent parts. For example, in the case of a booking clerk issuing a train ticket, the actor is the booking clerk; the transformation is the issuing of a train ticket which takes place at a particular railway station at a particular time. The stimulus for the act is typically a request for a ticket from a customer.

For Morris, following Mead, any action can be analysed in terms of three phases which they call the perceptual, manipulatory and consummatory phases (Morris, 1964). These phases correspond quite closely with the classic elements of a control process as discussed in Chapter 5: sensors, effectors and comparators (Figure 10.1). In the perceptual phase, *'the organism must perceive the relevant features of the environment in which it is to act'*. The perceptual phase thus involves sensing relevant objects in the environment of the organism through its sensory apparatus. In

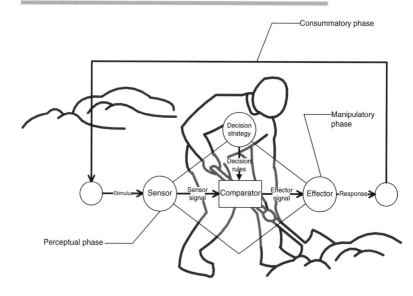

Figure 10.1   Psyche as a control system

the manipulatory phase, the organism *'must behave towards these objects in a way relevant to the satisfaction of its impulse'*. In other words the organism effects some change to the world through its effector apparatus to realise the possibilities offered by its perceptions. In the consummatory phase, the organism satisfies its impulse or realises its goal. It compares the consummation against its goal.

Hence, any performative act, such as that of shovelling, should be analysable in terms of these phases. In the perceptual phase, the shoveller senses elements of his environment like the location of the material and the quantity of material to be shifted. In the manipulatory phase, the shoveller moves the material using his brute strength and his tool: the shovel. In the consumatory phase, the shoveller confirms to himself that he has realised his goal of moving a target amount of material for his working day.

Tools in action

This conception of activity described in the previous section bears a family resemblance to that proposed within so-called activity theory

(Andersen, 2006). Within activity theory an activity is undertaken by a human actor (subject), motivated towards the solution of some purpose (object) and mediated by tools in collaboration with others. In this perspective, human beings do not interact with the world directly. Instead, such interaction is always mediated through the use of tools.

For example, a carpenter (subject) uses tools such as a saw and a hammer to build (activity) a timber-framed building such as a house (object). Building a house is normally not solely an individual activity, but a collective activity. Building workers have to coordinate their activity and to do so in terms of some division of this activity (labour).

Lev Vygotsky (Vygotsky, 1986), one of the Russian founders of activity theory, distinguishes between conventional physical or technical tools such as hammers or spades and psychological tools or signs which help people affect themselves or others such as symbols or maps. Both physical tools and psychological tools are mediators which help change the structure of activity.

In nature, activity is typically never mediated. A bird which picks a berry from a bush and eats it, engages in direct action. There is no mediation between subject and object. In the human context most of our activity is mediated in some way. Hence, most humans would not attempt to pick fungii in a forest and eat it without some recourse to collective knowledge, either by reading some form of field guide or communicating in some way with an experienced forager.

Tools therefore shape the way in which humans interact with reality. Tools reflect the experiences of other people who have tried to solve similar problems. Over time, the structural properties of the tool, as well as the knowledge as to how the tool should be used, will be shaped. Hence, tools are a means for the accumulation and transmission of social knowledge. Culture becomes embedded in a tool in the sense that the design or development of the tool as well as the knowledge as to its appropriate use is refined over time by numerous individuals.

The ways of doing work are shared amongst groups of workers and the application of ways of doing is referred to as praxis. Enacting praxis continues praxis while also opening up the possibility of changing praxis.

Consider our case in this light. Shovelling is an activity performed by a subject (shoveller) in terms of an object (such as a heap of iron ore) using some tool (shovel) in collaboration with others (other steel workers). The shovel is a tool which has developed for the specific purpose of performing certain types of praxis.

Consider two tools which have very similar structural properties: spades and shovels. Both are tools designed for some use by the human hand. Both consist of a long shaft, typically of wood, sometimes topped by a short cross-piece. Both end in a broad blade, typically constructed of metal, which is attached to the long shaft.

Where a spade differs from a shovel is in the shape of the blade. In a shovel, the cross-section of the blade is normally rectangular whereas in the spade the cross-section is typically pointed. These differences reflect the intended uses to which such tools are put. A shovel is 'designed' to lift material, usually some form of loose material. A spade, in comparison, is designed for digging or removing earth.

An experienced shoveller would never use a spade for his activity or an experienced gardener would never, through choice, use a shovel to dig his vegetable patch. The use of appropriate tools for particular activities is part of the praxis of shovelling. Such ways of doing also include skilled performance in relation to the use of the tool, the shovel.

Signs in action

We started this book by saying that signs mediate between the social and the physical world. Another way of saying this is that signs as 'tools' mediate between actors (subjects) and their environment (objects).

Action rarely occurs in isolated units. Instead, the action of a particular actor is normally taken in response to the action of many other actors. For George Herbert Mead (Mead, 1934), the basic model of social action or inter-action involves what he refers to as a *conversation of gestures*. In the conversation of gestures communication occurs merely in terms of stimulus and response. Communication takes place without awareness on the part of the organism of the response that its' gesture elicits in others. Since the actor is unaware of the reactions of others to the gestures it makes, it is unable to respond to its' own gestures from the standpoint of others. Hence, the individual participant in the conversation of gestures is communicating, but it does not 'know' that it is communicating. The conversation of gestures is therefore unconscious communication.

The dance of the honeybee described in Chapter 4 is a classic example of such a conversation of gestures (Beynon-Davies, 2010). The dance can be seen as a series of inter-related gestures between a scout bee and attending bees. The movements of the scout bee act as stimuli to the attending bees. Communication is evident when the attending bees respond appropriately to these movements. But there is no evidence that the bee is *conscious* of such communication. Instead, it is likely that the level of psyche active in such performance works perfectly adequately at an unconscious level – probably in terms of what we referred to in Chapter 5 as a Skinnerian psyche.

Such an example of unconscious psyche, communication and action is of course not unique to the animal world. There are also examples of such communication in the human sphere. Hence, facial expressions, as considered in Chapter 3, clearly constitute a mode of communication but such communication normally occurs at an unconscious level in terms of the 'society' of human psyche.

Mead is thus Darwinian in his approach in proposing that communication develops from more or less primitive toward more or less advanced forms of social inter-action through its reliance on a greater complexity of signification. In the human world, spoken language supersedes (but does not abolish) the conversation of gestures and marks the transition from non-significant to significant inter-action. Spoken language constitutes conscious communication and is communication through significant symbols. A significant symbol for Mead is a gesture (usually a vocal gesture) that calls out in the actor making the gesture the same (i.e., functionally identical) response that is called out in others to whom the gesture is directed. The implication is that the sender of some significant gesture is conscious of the meaning (intension) and intent of the gesture.

In terms of social interaction then, a significant gesture is one which not only causes a later phase of receiver action by referring the receiver to a later phase of the sender action; it also causes a later phase of the sender action by referring the sender to a later phase of the receiver action. In other words, the sender is interpreting another actor's behaviour as a continuation of its own. The actor will thus experience its behaviour as the earlier phase of a social action in which the later phase will be performed by its partner. In a significant gesture, a gesture takes over the role of a recipient of its own sign.

Significant gestures clearly demand a level of psyche that is self-aware (Gregorian psyche). The self arises when the individual becomes an object to itself with which it can interact. Self therefore constitutes the importation of the social process into the individual in which the 'I' and the 'Me' interact. The 'Me' is the social self and the 'I' is the individual self – the individual's response to the 'Me'. In other words, the 'I' is the response of an individual to the attitudes of others, while the 'Me' is the organised set of attitudes of others which an individual assumes. The 'Me' is the accumulated understanding of the generalised other: how one thinks one's group perceives oneself. The 'I' is the individual's impulses. In this conception, psyche contains a process of self-reflective interaction between the 'I' and the 'Me'.

The upshot of this conception is that action or activity can rarely be separated in practice from issues of communication and sometimes of representation. Hence, while for convenience we have separated out the ideas of forma, informa and performa in previous chapters, the three levels of patterning are necessarily intertwined or entangled in any truly accurate account of social inter-action.

Performa, informa and forma

As should be evident from the discussion above, we should beware of the tendency to discuss and analyse performative acts in isolation from communicative and formative acts. This is the mistake inherent in many existing approaches which attempt to model business processes or activity systems. On one level, performative acts amount to the reali-sation of intentions (Chapter 8). They also are the means for fulfilling the conditions of satisfaction of illocutionary or communicative acts (Chapter 9). But performative acts are likely to set up further cycles of informative and formative acts which form and inform performance. It is hence frequently difficult to conceive of performative action without some associated informative and formative action, if only because most performative action, at least as far as human beings are concerned, is social action.

In the way we have necessarily discussed the three patterns of organi-sation within this work, one would tend perhaps to assume that the direction of influence between such patterns is linear: from forma, through informa to performa. In actuality, these three patterns form a cycle of influence: that performa enacts forma which enacts informa and in turn enacts performa. This is illustrated in Figure 10.2.

Take, for example, the waggle dance of the honeybee in this light. A honeybee performs a number of actions on returning to the hive. Key aspects of this performa enact forma in the sense that these inten-sions serve to represent intentions. Hence, the degree of excitation in

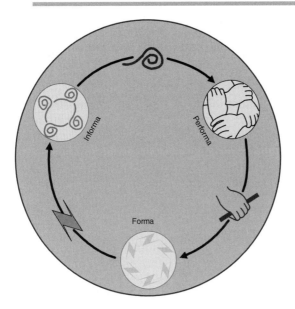

Figure 10.2   Cycle of significance

the straight part of the waggle dance is taken to stand for the quantity of some food source. The quantity of the food source thus represents the informa attempting to be communicated. This informa, in turn, if successful stimulates performa in attending bees: they leave the hive in the direction of the food source. On their return to the hive they are likely to construct a further cycle of significance.

Take also an example from the human domain: that of nursing in general hospitals. There are three basic models for organising nursing on a hospital ward: round nursing, primary care nursing and group nursing. *Round nursing* is very much task oriented. Each nurse has responsibility for one task on the ward. For example, one nurse is responsible for giving all patients their prescribed medicines. *Primary care* is patient-oriented. One nurse has the responsibility for carrying out all the tasks associated with one or a small group of patients. In primary care, for instance, one nurse is likely to be responsible for giving all medicines to her group of patients. *Group nursing* is a mixture of the above. A group of nurses have the responsibility for carrying out several tasks, but only tasks related to one group of patients. In group nursing, for example, one nurse may be given the responsibility for distributing regular medicines while all nurses give out additional medicines according to patient's needs.

Each of these systems of nursing activity demands a substantially different information system. In round nursing there is a need to exchange medical information such as which medicines have been given to which patients but there is little need for information to coordinate tasks between nurses. In contrast, within primary care there is very little exchange of medical information between nurses, but there is a need to know which nurses care for which patients. In group nursing there is need both to exchange medical information and for much information necessary to the effective coordination of nursing tasks. This last form of activity system therefore demands the most complex information system to support work.

Associated with each form of information system there is likely to be a distinct form of data system. Hence, in terms of round nursing acts of recording can focus on the patient and his care. In primary care nursing, we need to record not only patient details but which nurse undertook which aspect of care on which patient. In group nursing we need to record all this but also which nurses belong to which groups.

Within activity systems of healthcare such as nursing the focus is normally quite naturally upon performative activity: the treatment and care of patients. This is the most visible type of activity and is used almost to define what healthcare is about. What is frequently ignored is that much of such healthcare relies upon good communication and representation. Studies have shown that up to 40% of a nurse's time is taken up with communicative and formative acts (Beynon-Davies, 2009b). One suspects that doctors may spend even more of their time in such information and data handling. Hence, to build better systems of healthcare you cannot just focus on performative activity. You must also focus upon communication (informative activity) and representation (formative activity) as a means of building better organisation.

Hence, and ironically, to improve the 'performance' of some activity system you cannot focus solely upon performa. Indeed, it is dangerous to focus on any one of the three patterns of organisation without considering its relationship with the other two. For instance, there are numerous examples of large and expensive ICT systems (data systems) that have been introduced into organisations that have failed. When the reasons for such failure are investigated many place the blame squarely in the use of naive approaches to the design of data systems without adequate attention to the system of communication and system of performance into which they are introduced (Beynon-Davies, 1995).

Performance

It is no accident that the verb *to perform* and the noun *performance* have the same root. In systems terms the issue of performance is related to the idea of control. Within some control system, control inputs represent the purpose of some operational system being controlled. In such terms, control inputs effectively represent some defined measures of performance. A control process may only work effectively if there are defined levels of performance for the system being controlled. Such performance levels will be defined by higher-level systems.

For example, in terms of a manufacturing plant, a defined level of performance might be productivity level per manufacturing unit. In terms of a general hospital, certain levels of performance may be defined in terms of the size of waiting lists for specific treatments. In terms of shovelling, Taylor's research team defined an optimum level of performance for this activity across a number of different types of material.

If we consider networks of related activity as a system, the systems theorist Peter Checkland argues that there are three main types of performance measure appropriate to such systems which he refers to as efficacy, efficiency and effectiveness (Checkland, 1999). Not surprisingly, these he sometimes refers to as the three 'E's of performance. *Efficacy* is a measure of the extent to which a system achieves its intended transformation. Measures of efficacy consequently tend to focus on the outputs from some system. Hence, if a system fails to produce desired output, this is a problem of efficacy. *Efficiency* is a measure of the extent to which the system achieves its intended transformation with the minimum use of resources. Efficiency is primarily an attempt to address the balance of inputs to outputs in systems terms. Hence, a system might suffer from a problem of efficiency if it produces output but consumes excessive resources. *Effectiveness* is a measure of the extent to which the system contributes to the purposes of a higher-level system of which it may be a sub-system. Effectiveness is therefore always an attempt to relate the goals of some super-system with the goals for the sub-system. Hence, there is a problem of effectiveness if the output from some sub-system does not produce the required contribution to the wider system.

Consider the activity of shovelling in such terms. The efficacy of some observed shovelling activity clearly relates to the amount of material shifted from one place to another by a particular shoveller. The effectiveness of shovelling can only be determined by examining the contribution such shovelling activity makes to the overall performance of the steel mill within which it takes place. Efficiency is the primary focus of scientific management as conceived by Taylor and his associates. Efficiency was clearly measured in terms of the productivity of particular workmen: the amount of material shovelled by a particular workman in a specified period of time – the normal working day.

The cycle of significance discussed above has a basis in the control cycle discussed in earlier chapters. Performa constitutes instrumental action, which is frequently social action. Hence, certain aspects of performa become specialised to the function of attempting to influence the behaviour of other actors. Key aspects of performa enact forma in the sense that certain aspects of an actor's behaviour are used to stand for certain intensions. Such intensions in turn are used to build mutual intention through the enactment of informa. Such informa, in turn, will influence the next cycle of performa.

An actor will normally be stimulated to perform through some forma sensed through the actor's sensory apparatus. Such forma will enact informa through a process of interpretation which in turn will select amongst alternative courses of action. The actor will then act using its effector apparatus. The whole or part of such performative action may be directed to the purposes of communication in which the actor attempts to influence the behaviour of other actors. Hence, every individual pattern of action is enacted in a process of feedback within an encompassing environment of social action.

We recognise the unity of action by its repetitive nature. Control ensures that action is reproduced from one situation to another by actors. Such control is enacted at multiple levels by an actor. Consider the case of a man shovelling. Anybody who has performed prolonged physical work of this nature will recognise the performance of someone else who has performed such physical work. Hence, in cinema films it is apparent to anyone who has used a pick and shovel for a long period of time that actors are not specialists in this type of work. Their particular use of pick and shovel communicates that they are actors and not labourers. We can assess their performance against our own internal standards of performance.

This issue of performance then can be used to highlight some of the inherent strengths but also the deficiencies of Taylor's approach. In terms of strengths, Taylorism exploits the system characteristic of equi-finality: the idea that there is inherent flexibility in the way in which activity can be performed to achieve a certain goal. Taylor's aim was to determine the one best way of achieving some goal. However, in order to achieve this Taylorism needed to focus on relatively simple and individual tasks that could be re-designed. When such tasks were not individually based they were made individual through implementing some form of division of labour. In this attempt the need for communication and representation was constrained to defined channels – particularly along channels of management.

Such an approach may achieve short-term efficacy, efficiency and possibly effectiveness because it establishes clear regulatory processes within some system of activity. It defines clear measures for such performance and implements restricted channels of communication that implement sensing and effecting processes. However, in the longer term this restricted concept of control is likely to reduce the capacity of some system of organisation to adapt. This is because it reduces innovation and self-actuation processes amongst the actual actors performing work. As a consequence it reduces the amount of double-loop feedback that is experienced within a community of actors and consequently the ability of the overall patterns of organisation to learn and adapt.

Machines as actors

As we have seen, a fundamental presupposition of activity theory is that Homo sapiens as a species has always been a creator and user of tools – the species has shaped techne to help it transform aspects of the world. Most such tools are used to enhance human capability in particular areas. Hence, a shovel provides greater leverage in the movement of material; this tool is hence closely coupled to physical human performance.

More recently, with the aid of some of the key 'tools of thought' which we have described in this book – such as *system*, *communication* and *control* – humans have designed and built tools which can operate independently of human actors; they can act independently of human intervention. In the modern world, such tools are major actors in key systems of activity; particularly those associated with economic systems (Beynon-Davies, 2009b).

Take a key activity system supporting modern economies: that of the operation of security trading, collectively referred to as the stock market. The stock market is a market for the purchase and sale of securities which come in two major forms: stocks and shares. A stock, sometimes known as a gilt-edged security or gilt, is a security with an associated interest rate; the most important type of stock being the government bond. Shares are a type of security that pay no interest, but pay a dividend to shareholders at regular intervals. Shares are normally issued by companies to raise financial capital for investment.

Modern stock markets such as the UK stock market are no longer physical exchanges but are electronic markets. Such institutions are now composed of a network of economic actors that exchange securities over ICT infrastructure. Such economic actors are known as financial intermediaries and come in two main forms: brokers and market makers. Brokers act as intermediaries between investors and market makers and market makers act as intermediaries between corporations and brokers.

Securities are bought from certain registered market makers: financial institutions that opt to deal in a limited number of securities. The collection of such securities held by a market maker is known as the market makers' 'book'. All securities are initially placed on the stock market at an issue price. Once a share has been issued it can be traded: that is, bought and sold on the stock market.

Each market maker needs to define the state of each type of share it holds in terms of two prices: the offer price and the bid price. The offer price is the price a market maker is willing to sell a share; the price at which an investor will buy. The bid price is the price a market maker is willing to pay for a share; the price at which an investor can sell to him. The difference between the two prices is known as the market makers' *spread*. Different market makers will quote different spreads on shares depending on the state of their book. For example, market maker A might have an offer price of 102p and a bid price of 100p for Allied Metals. In contrast, market maker B might have an offer price of 103p and a bid price of 101p for Allied Metals.

Brokers purchase securities on behalf of investors, and/or sell securities to market makers on behalf of an investor. On both such transactions brokers normally charge a commission, normally a percentage of the cost of a particular deal: a sale or purchase of a nominated amount of shares.

The stock market is clearly an activity system which is heavily reliant upon both informa and forma. Securities are effectively records of information assets and deals are effectively records of security exchange. It should be apparent from this description that trading on the stock market effectively involves making rapid decisions on which securities to buy or sell and effecting deals to implement such decisions. Not surprisingly, security trading is one of the most technologically enabled activities in the modern world. Most modern security trading involves use of sophisticated data systems that sense movements in share price and enable rapid deployment of dealing amongst economic actors.

Therefore, particular national Stock markets, such as the UK Stock Market, form part of a global financial system. ICT infrastructure enables rapid flow of trading activity accompanied by rapid flows of money around the world, 24 hours a day. This is hence a critical enabler of globalisation. It also means that difficulties experienced in particular local markets more rapidly diffuse their effects to others than in the past.

Many of the ICT systems used for security trading by the big economic actors such as market makers have facilities which augment the trading activity of human actors. Such systems use complex algorithms or 'business rules' embedded within the systems to perform automatic trading of securities in certain situations. A simplification of one such a rule might be of the form: *if the offer price of share S amongst a group of market makers M falls below a certain specified level L then sell P percent of the security holding*. Depending upon the area of trading, the application of such automation can cover between 30% to 80% of normal trading activity. Much of this trading activity may be performed completely independently of human intervention. Hence, such trading 'machines' can undertake the perceptual, manipulative and consumatory phases of performative action demanded of security trading without any human input at any stage.

Now assume that a range of such machines maintain a similar range of such business rules. The sale of a particular security by trading machine A if done in sufficient quantity is likely to affect the average offer and bid price for this security amongst other market makers. It is also likely to trigger sales of such shares by other traders, both human and non-human, which has the consequential effect of lowering the share prices even further. Hence a positive or reinforcing loop is established between humans and machines within the trading network. This has much similarity with the herding or flocking behaviour characteristic amongst certain animals in which mass behaviour emerges without planned direction.

Some have argued also that the latency associated with automated trading has had a tendency to exacerbate the frequency and size of stock market bubbles and crashes. Latency refers to the time taken for a particular message transmitted from a sender to reach a receiver. The speed with which data such as the offer price of particular shares is transmitted has a direct effect on the speed with which a financial actor can respond. This speed – which in the case of automated trading can be measured in milliseconds – allied to common behaviour programmed into automated trading systems is seen to contribute to reinforcing cycles of selling behaviour (crashes) or reinforcing cycles of purchasing behaviour (bubbles).

As this example demonstrates, machines are clearly significant actors within the activity systems of the modern world. Machines are now commonplace in support of human activity, leading many to suggest that most modern-day activity systems are best described as socio-technical systems: social systems comprised of actors taking action through technology. Hence, the lone shoveller is now replaced by the bulldozer and pickup truck. Other machines automate much of performative action – the key example here being the robots which now work collectively on the automobile assembly line much pilloried by Charlie Chaplin. Machines such as automatic traders, engage in formative and informative action. However, the nature of the performative, informative and formative action of all such machines is limited – based upon algorithms and heuristics that collectively form 'business rules'. They are actors in modern activity systems but not full agents in this process.

However, a key problem is that it is difficult even for professional human actors within the domains that machines work to understand the basis for their action. This means that in Dennett's terms the majority of human actors find difficulty in understanding them as intentional systems and hence being able to predict the behaviour of such machine actors. Since they find them opaque, they find difficulty in interacting fully and effectively with such systems. Machines can clearly interact with one another – lending another layer of opacity. The speed of their interaction also makes them difficult to monitor and control by human beings. Some have even claimed that such complexity within the domain of security trading had a part to play in the so-called Credit Crunch of 2008.

Conclusion

The work of Frederick Taylor, although now frequently pilloried, set the scene for the development of management theory and its primary focus on performa. Taylor's scientific management had a great influence upon Henry Ford's design of mass manufacturing systems for automobiles, which acted as the blueprint for Chaplin's conception of the modern factory system which we alluded to in the introduction (Kanigel, 1997). It also had significant influence upon the so-called Japanese form of manufacturing that achieved such success after the Second World War. Despite much vilification many of the ideas underlying scientific management can be seen to have influenced more recent approaches to organisational design such as business process re-engineering or business process re-design. It also underlies the key idea of process analysis: the idea of building models of current and future industrial processes.

The logo for this chapter suggests *handedness* – our species ability to use our opposable thumb to grasp and use tools such as that of a shovel. This is clearly a crucial feature of a human's ability to perform – to take instrumental action or to transform the physical world. Performative acts focus on such transformation and correspond to human 'performance' in various areas of life. Performa stands for the 'work' of people in collective interaction and as such lies within the realm of an activity system.

On one level, performative acts amount to the realisation of intentions. They also are the means for fulfilling the conditions of satisfaction of illocutionary or communicative acts. But performative acts are likely to set up further cycles of communicative and formative acts which form and inform performance.

Performative acts are clearly both individual and social acts. An individual action or act is a unit of behaviour with a clearly delineable beginning, end and goal, within the general continuum of behaviour. The action is realised in relation to the attainment of some goal and the goal of some action is determined by an impulse. In such terms, any action can be analysed in terms of three phases (perceptual, manipulatory and consummatory) that correspond quite closely with the classic elements of a control system (sensors, effectors and comparators).

Social acts constitute inter-action between two or more organisms. In the simplest case of a social act – dyadic interaction – social acts rely on one organism reacting or responding to the acts of the other organism. The acts of one organism are therefore taken as stimuli by some other organism and vice versa. Communicative acts are a special case of social acts. Communicative acts form units within a conversation of significant 'gestures'. Such communicative acts serve to aid the coordination of performative acts.

To perform in either an individual or a social sense opens up questions of evaluation of performance. In terms of systems, control inputs effectively represent some defined measures of performance. A control process may work effectively only if there are defined levels of performance for the system being controlled. Such performance levels will be defined by higher-level systems.

Humans rarely interact with and transform the world directly. Tools mediate between human actors and their environment. Tools are significant elements of performative action and have traditionally been used to augment and improve human capacity for taking such action. More recently, machines have attained the status of independent actors within significant activity systems.

Within this chapter we have focused upon activity as individual performance. But clearly activities are not performed in isolation; activities form part of collective work or performance. Collective work demands coordination amongst multiple actors to achieve collective goals. This is the primary essence of an activity system, the topic of the next chapter.

References

Andersen, P. J. (2006). Activity-based Design. European Journal of Information Systems 15(1): 9–25.

Beynon-Davies, P. (1995). Information systems 'failure': the case of the London Ambulance Service's Computer Aided Despatch System. European Journal of Infomation Systems 4(1): 171–184.

Beynon-Davies, P. (2009b). Business information systems. Palgrave, Houndmills, Basingstoke.

Beynon-Davies, P. (2010). Dances with bees: exploring the relevance of the study of animal communication to informatics. International Journal of Information Management 30(1): 185–198.

Checkland, P. (1999). Soft Systems Methodology: a thirty year retrospective. John Wiley, Chichester.

Copley, F. B. (1969). Frederick W. Taylor: father of scientific management. Augustus M Kelly, New York.

Goffman, E. (1969). The Presentation of Self in Everyday Life. Penguin, Harmondsworth, Middx.

Kanigel, R. (1997). The One Best Way: Frederick Winslow Taylor and the Enigma of Efficiency. Viking, New York.

Mead, G. H. (1934). Mind, Self, and Society. University of Chicago Press, Chicago.

Morris, C. (1964). Signification and Significance. MIT Press, Cambridge, Mass.

Morris, C. W. (1946). Signs, Language and Behavior. Prentice-Hall, New York.

Vygotsky, L. (1986). Thought and Language. MIT Press, Cambridge, Mass.

11
Activity systems: Patterns of performa

Introduction

The sociologist Norbert Elias (Elias, 1978) published a fascinating and accessible book some time ago entitled, *What Is Sociology?* As part of his answer to this question he considered the related question of what is society and came fundamentally to the conclusion that society is much more than a mere aggregation of individual actors. Instead, society is a system consisting of the multitude of individual actors, relationships and actions. Such actors through their relationships and actions produce and re-produce patterns (Elias refers to them as figurations), which in turn serve to constitute society. In such terms, society is considered an emergent phenomenon of a complex system of activity.

As we have seen in Chapter 10, the term activity covers all aspects of human performance. Human activity or action is normally directed at some goal and does not occur in isolation. Human activity is normally undertaken in response to other actors and activities. When the activities of two or more actors are directed towards a common goal then issues of coordination come into play. If multiple actors pursue a common goal they have to organise their joint actions. This extra layer of organisation we refer to as coordination. Such coordinated action typically relies on convention, which provides the motor for the regularity or patterning of activity. When it is possible to set a coherent boundary around such patterning then we can speak of an activity system.

Activity systems are clearly social systems; they consist of patterns of coordinated action between multiple actors. But within human organisation we take a particular interest in 'designed' social systems. In other words, those systems designed to achieve some purpose, usually as part of some more encompassing form of human organisation.

We start with a case from healthcare – that of the emergency ambulance service – as a means of helping refresh our understanding of the nature of activity systems and their relationship to information systems and data systems. We particularly use the case to highlight the close coupling of these three forms of patterning and the difficulties of making changes to any one pattern independently of any changes made to others. In other words, we want to use this chapter to set the scene for some of the difficulties of designing and introducing organisational change without understanding and managing the issues of significance covered in this book.

The emergency ambulance service

Within modern healthcare an effective system is required for responding to emergency health incidents. Most countries in the world rise to this challenge by establishing and maintaining specialist staff such as paramedics and specialist equipment such as ambulance vehicles to enable emergency response.

Getting specialist ambulance staff in their vehicles to an incident in the shortest period of time is a key goal for such an ambulance service. This demands effective coordination and control of activity amongst multiple actors to ensure that resources such as ambulances and paramedics are used most effectively, and patients receive appropriate emergency healthcare as promptly as possible.

In 1996 a review of ambulance service performance in the UK concluded that more clinically relevant performance measures were needed for the service. It suggested that the focus should be on the potential for saving lives with shorter response times to patients suffering life-threatening conditions. Over the last decade demand for emergency ambulance services in the UK has increased by over 50% whilst funding has increased by only 17.5%. The review recommended a long-term performance target of 90% of life-threatening calls responded to within 8 minutes. Subsequently, an interim target of 75% of life-threatening calls to be responded to within 8 minutes was introduced and ambulance services were required to achieve this target by 2001.

Until 1997 the ambulance service in the UK worked using a first-come, first-served basis in terms of responses to emergency calls. However, to achieve targets set by the performance review, most ambulance services have now instituted a process of 'triage' to enable prioritisation of response to incidents.

Ambulance services in the UK have the freedom and responsibility to establish their own forms of activity and technology. This means that there is variation amongst activity systems, information systems and data systems within ambulance services in the UK. The description below is therefore based on a composite of the systems experienced amongst a number of such services.

The service is first aware of an incident when telephone operators take an emergency call and identify the caller's area code or closest mobile phone cell from the call. The call is then routed to the ambulance control call centre. A call-taker matches the number calling with an address using a computerised gazetteer and then asks a set series of questions prompted by a set of rules embedded in the ICT system. On the basis of answers to the questions supplied, the system suggests appropriate action.

A dispatcher will have been listening to the call since the location was identified. If the call is category A (life threatening) or category B (serious) then a paramedic dispatcher may have been asked for assistance. Some ambulance services employ paramedics within the control room who can be consulted in the case of any doubt as to the priority of the incident. The dispatcher assesses manually the nearest appropriate ambulance by using a number of computer screens: a screen indicating a plan designed to maximise the efficient use of resources (known as the system status management or SSM plan), a screen listing the status of all current resources and a screen which plots the current location of ambulance resources against a computerised map and a touch-screen telephone. The SSM plan is an attempt to dynamically deploy vehicles around the area covered by the ambulance service according to demand patterns established for day and time, geographical area and clinical urgency. As part of the functionality of the ICT system the SSM plan is capable of prompting control room staff to shift resources such as ambulances on a continual basis to stay within plan.

Using this technology and her knowledge of the local area the dispatcher assigns an ambulance to the incident. This means that the dispatcher does not always send the nearest ambulance in terms of distance to an incident. For example, it would be inappropriate to dispatch a spatially near ambulance if the incident is called in during rush hour and the ambulance would need to travel in the direction of the major traffic flow. In this case, it is preferable to send a slightly more distant ambulance that can travel against the primary traffic flow. Not surprisingly, many ambulance services institute a policy of recruiting control room staff from their pool of operational ambulance crews because of the critical importance of such domain knowledge to effective dispatch.

During this process the call-taker will be giving pre-arrival advice to the caller prescribed both by the software and their own training. While the call-taker continues with this interaction the dispatcher typically uses a radio message to alert the chosen ambulance crew that they are required to attend an incident. Details of the location of the incident (including a grid reference) and the reported details of the patient's condition are also transmitted in this way. Some ambulance services also employ communication systems enabling control staff to page information as to incidents to ambulance crews.

A member of ambulance crew presses a button on their communication set indicating the point at which they go mobile. Ambulances are fitted with global positioning system equipment that updates the dispatch system every few seconds with the location of ambulance crews. Crews are guided by satellite navigation to the incident location, supplemented with radio communication with the control room. When the crew arrive at the incident they press an *arrive* button on the communication set. They press a *leave scene* button when leaving the incident and an *at hospital* button when arrived at the hospital. Finally, they press a *clear* button when they are available to be allocated as a resource again.

Performative patterns

Performative acts such as the shovelling of coal considered in the last chapter, the issuing of train tickets considered in Chapter 2 or the response to emergency incidents considered in this chapter do not occur in isolation. Performative acts normally correspond to the 'work' of people in collective interaction, typically using 'tools' to transform 'objects' in the world.

Hence, performative acts typically occur in sequences where one performative act is reliant upon the completion of one or more other performative acts: in performative patterns. There is thus a clear relationship between the idea of a performative pattern and that of an organisational routine. Brian Pentland and Martha Feldman (Pentland and Feldman, 2008) argue that organisational routines are generative systems that produce recognisable, repetitive patterns of interdependent actions, carried out by multiple actors. They also explain the generative nature of routines by making the distinction between the ostensive and performative aspects of such routines. *'On the one hand, routines consist of abstract regularities and expectations that enable participants to guide, account for, and refer to the specific performances of a routine'*. These they refer to as the ostensive aspects of a routine. *'On the other hand, routines also consist of actual performances by specific people at specific times, in specific places'*. They refer to this as the performative aspect of routines. The ostensive aspect constrains and enables the performative aspect. The performative aspect in turn creates and re-creates the ostensive aspect.

Performative acts therefore tend to occur in conventional patterns that repeat across situations, which we shall refer to as a performative pattern. This means that a performative pattern is an abstraction of the regularity of performance; an ostensive specification of how to behave in particular situations. A coherent collection of such performative patterns we refer to as an activity system.

Hence, the performative act of a particular shoveller shifting his targeted amount of coal takes place within a more encompassing pattern. Fellow shovellers clearly engage in their own work in continual and parallel patterns. To keep the steelworks continually supplied with coal, iron ore and coke, trains and trucks were continually driven into the yard to replenish supplies. The coke moved by shovellers was likewise used by foundrymen to re-stock the furnace and produce steel. The interaction of all these performative patterns formed a coherent activity system.

Take also a simple example of a performative pattern from the Railway Clearing House case as illustrated in Figure 11.1. A passenger makes payment for a railway ticket which is in turn issued by the booking clerk. The passenger then proceeds to make her journey with the ticket. At some point during her journey the ticket will be checked by a train guard. When the passenger has completed her journey she hands over her ticket to a station guard at her terminal station. The station guard creates a batch of such used tickets received during a particular day.

This example contains all the features of a performative pattern. Performative acts are performed by particular actors, in this case by passengers, booking clerks, train conductors and station guards. Acts

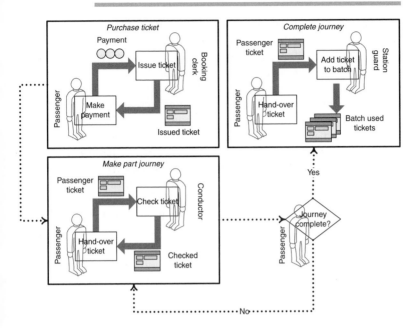

Figure 11.1   A performative pattern

involve some transformation such as making payments or issuing tickets. Such transformations typically involve the use of 'tools' – artefacts for doing things. The passenger, for instance, uses money as a 'tool' of exchange. In response, the booking clerk issues a ticket, which is a 'tool' of commitment. Performative patterns normally contain points of decision-making performed by the actors involved which determine different routes through the inter-linked sequences of performative acts.

Performative acts are therefore repeating and conventional patterns of behaviour evident amongst a particular population of actors. As we argued in Chapter 6, a pattern is any modulated aspect of the world. A repeating pattern is any regular pattern which is reproduced across more than one situation. Actors within a population re-create such patterns by reproducing performative acts from one situation to the next. This is important to the intentional ordering of mutual action.

For example, within the Clearing House case many different actors enacted the performance of issuing tickets to passengers. Such performance was therefore predictable by other actors in the sense that the intentions of the actors in this situation could be inferred with some accuracy. In such situations sociologists and social psychologists denote the common package of actions or behaviour associated with particular types of actor/situation as a *role*. In a sense, we have already established this practice by denoting actors within cases such as the Clearing House with labels such as *train guard* or *passenger* or *shoveller* or *plotter*. When making a train journey we enact the role of *passenger* by reproducing as behaviour our understanding of the performative pattern associated with this role. The shoveller in the Taylor case enacted and re-enacted on a daily basis the expectations of behaviour made of him by the work system of the steel yard. Within the UK most people are able to perform in response to an emergency incident by dialling 999; in the United States by dialling 911.

However, as argued previously, a pattern is only conventional if its reproduction is reliant purely upon precedent and is unlikely to be reproduced by any other means. David Lewis (Lewis, 2002) describes a convention as a regularity in the behaviour of a population and argues that it serves a key function for such a population. For Lewis, conventions solve coordination problems. A coordination problem arises when people have a purpose or goal in common which must be achieved by joint action. In other words, achieving the goal cannot be achieved by the action of a single individual. Instead, two or more actors must coordinate their actions to achieve the goal.

For example, within emergency response various actors have a purpose or goal in common: to provide effective healthcare at the point of incident. This goal cannot be achieved by any one particular actor. Instead, the actions of a multitude of different actors have to be coordinated in achievement of the collective goal.

There are also a number of other properties associated with a coordination problem. First, the contribution that each actor makes towards achieving some collective purpose will vary depending upon the contribution of others to producing a successful outcome. Two or more actors therefore must each choose one of several alternative possible actions. Second, the outcomes that the actors want to produce are determined jointly by the actions of all the actors involved. So the outcome of any action an actor might choose depends on the actions of the other actors in some situation. Hence, each actor must choose what to do according to his or her expectations about what other actors will do.

A classic example here is the activity of driving an automobile or perhaps an ambulance along some road network. If two drivers are approaching each other along some road they both have a common goal: that of passing each other safely. To achieve this there are actually alternative options to achieving a successful outcome: car A can pass on the left while car B can pass on the right; alternatively car A can pass on the right while car B can pass on the left. However, to achieve either of these successful outcomes each driver must engage in joint action with the other; the successful action of actor A depends on the successful action of actor B.

When an ambulance of course sets off its alarm in responding to an incident this initiates enactment of conventional patterns of performance amongst other road users. There is an expectation that fellow road uses will coordinate their driving to open up a free and safe route of passage through traffic.

This means that in system terms such features of coordination are subject to the property of *equifinality*. This means that a system – such as a performative pattern – can achieve its goals or purpose in a number of different ways. In terms of the coordination of the activities of multiple actors equifinality means that there is normally more than one acceptable way of combining the contributions of such actors to produce a successful outcome. Also, the set of combinations of actions which work fails to determine what any one actor's contribution should be in isolation from the actions of others.

In the last chapter this was actually the motive force behind Taylor's intention within his 'scientific management'. Taylor was attempting to breakdown conventional patterns of action within defined work situations and subject such action to close scrutiny. Through such scrutiny he attempted to weigh up the utility of particular performative acts and performative patterns in terms of some defined measures of performance. Taylor was therefore attempting to deliberately remove any decision-making on the part of the worker and place such decision-making in the hands of, or more precisely the thoughts of, the manager.

Coordination and communication

As a by-product of this approach Taylor was attempting to remove any need for communication and indeed representation in the activity of work except for the need to direct each individual worker in his or her individual actions. Wherever coordination was necessary such coordination was achieved by imposing some rationally designed coordination conventions. Coordination conventions are conventional patterns of activity that proliferate because they act as solutions to coordination problems. In our terms, performative patterns undertaken by actors are key examples of coordination conventions.

However, Ruth Millikan (Millikan, 2005), as we have already seen, argues that not all coordination relies on convention. If the parties to some joint action are able to gain evidence of each other's likely actions then coordination can be negotiated. Only when each partner in a joint action must act before having evidence concerning the likely behaviour of the other actor are coordination conventions necessary. Hence, when two drivers approach each other along a road they need to adopt a convention of either driving on the right or the left. In fact, this extends to most driving behaviour where convention is formalised in the UK in a 'Highway code'. It also underlies other less formal conventions such as the expectation that drivers should make every effort to facilitate the passage of an emergency vehicle in response to an incident.

Lewis not surprisingly argues that communication can be used as a major mechanism to negotiate coordination. The actors can reach agreement on coordination through communication rather than convention. Interestingly however, as we hope we have argued sufficiently in previous chapters, communication itself relies on sign-systems, which are in themselves sets of conventions. Hence, social action is typically conventional but not all social action relies on convention for effective coordination. In fact, most so-called social action relies upon symbolic inter-action.

Hence, in the case of walking, as considered in Chapter 5, although in many public settings attempts are made to provide a convention in the sense of walking on the right in a particular direction and on the left in another, much of the navigational activity essential to walking is performed 'on the fly'. This is because when we perambulate we travel at low speed and can directly observe the behaviour of other walking actors. We can then adjust our activity to reflect our 'reading' of the situation. In contrast, walkers and automobiles do not usually coordinate their activity through negotiation very successfully. This is at least partly because it is difficult to 'read' the intentions of people sitting in metal boxes and travelling at high speed.

Within the ambulance case performing Triage frequently relies upon convention in the sense that there will be defined routines for assigning commonly occurring incidents to particular categories of response. In some situations however matters of judgement will need to be made on the part of control room paramedics and such judgement will need to be communicated to an ambulance dispatcher.

Activity system

To refresh, a performative pattern is a recognisable, recurring, network of performative acts undertaken by two or more actors. An activity system is therefore an organised patterning of acts of performance. This means that the mutual action within an activity system is coordinated in order to achieve some common purpose or goal for the participating actors.

Therefore, when we speak of activity being coordinated, we normally presume a number of things: a set of two or more actors, a set of activities, a set of dependencies between activities, in pursuit of one or more joint goals. As discussed above, in attempting to achieve common goals through sets of dependent activities actors meet coordination problems. Such coordination problems arise from the way in which the dependencies between activities constrain the achievement of goals. Coordination is therefore fundamentally about managing the dependencies between activities. Within so-called coordination theory, such dependencies are managed by what are referred to as coordination mechanisms. This idea has much similarity with the idea of a control process as discussed in Chapter 5.

However, such coordination mechanisms or control processes do not need to be imposed, they can be negotiated in action. This explains how many acts of performance are coordinated through symbolic inter-action. In such instances, human actors inter-act with each other by interpreting each other's actions. However, the responses of two actors in inter-action are not made directly to the actions of one another but instead are based on the meaning which actors attach to such actions. Thus, human inter-action is mediated by the use of signs within processes of signification and interpretation. This is what we referred to in chapter 8 as in-formation.

Take another simple and 'strange' example. Sea shanties were work songs performed on sailing ships such as fishing boats, whalers and

253

men-of-war. Many such songs were used during the 18th and 19th centuries to coordinate collective activity, particularly repetitive activity, performed by a multitude of actors in pursuit of some common goal such as hauling up the anchor or hoisting the mainsail. The rhythm of the shanty sung in unison set the tempo for collective performance such as the pulling of a sail rope or the pushing of a capstan. Certain shanties were also sung in association with particular phases of performance. Hence, outward bound shanties were never sung when homeward bound and homeward bound shanties were never sung when outward bound.

Hence, when the actions of two or more individuals are coupled we speak of coordinated action. Coordination is normally achieved through the imposition of convention, either through specifying some procedure to be followed in relation to a particular situation or in terms of conventions of communication and representation. Communication therefore facilitates coordinated action, which in turn is sometimes facilitated by representation.

Again, we have explicitly attempted to use the term actor rather than person when referring to an activity system. Within the human sphere, our use of tools in performative acts has therefore progressed to a level where certain super-tools become significant and independent actors within contemporary activity systems. Certain 'machines' are clearly actors within many activity systems in the modern world since they can act independently of any particular person's immediate control and have the capacity to interact with other actors in the activity system. Some have therefore described the activity systems in many aspects of the modern organisation as humanchine networks (Atkinson and Brooks, 2005), emphasising by this the close coupling of humans with machines. In such cases of course, the activity system is no longer purely a human activity system.

Activity and organisation

However, a <u>human</u> activity system is what Peter Checkland refers to as a 'soft system' (Checkland, 1999). It is a type of social system that is 'designed' to meet certain defined objectives. Activity systems are soft for a number of reasons. First, the boundaries or scope of the activity system may be fluid. Second, the purpose of the activity system is likely to be open to interpretation and certainly reliant on the viewpoint or world view of differing actors. Third, the definition of precisely what control means in terms of the activity system and hence exact measures of performance for the activity system are both dependent on the world views of actors.

If activity systems are designed there must be someone doing the designing: defining the boundary of such a system as well as the structure of activities within the system. Following conventional practice we shall say that such design should take place by those actors who have some 'stake' in the system. Hence, we refer to them as stakeholders in the activity system.

One of the earliest definitions of the concept of stakeholder is that supplied by Richard Mason and Ian Mitroff (Mason and Mitroff, 1981). They define stakeholders as being *'all those claimants inside and outside the organisation who have a vested interest in the problem and its solution'*. The term *problem* within this definition, Checkland refers to as a *problem situation*: a situation in organisational life that is regarded by at least one person as being problematical. Facing up to the problem situation are some 'would-be-improvers' of it, people looking for a solution to the problem situation; these are the stakeholders for the activity system in question.

'Beauty is in the eye of the beholder'. Likewise, the decision as to what is contained within an activity system and what forms part of the environment of some activity system is dependent on the viewpoint of the stakeholder in such a system. Stakeholders normally exist as groups of actors to which a particular activity system is relevant. Different stakeholders may hold different viewpoints as to the boundaries of systems and the key elements of systems. There may also be conflict over perceptions as to the intended purpose of some system. Such differences are likely to reflect the differing *world views* of different stakeholders.

Consider the ambulance service as an activity system. From the point of view of the 'customer' – the patient – this form of organisation might be described as a system designed to offer quality emergency healthcare at the point of incident. From the viewpoint of the manager it might be seen as a system to achieve optimal utilisation of a limited healthcare resource in fulfilment of targets.

Considered as a whole, an organisation can be seen as a complex system of human activity. Applying the principle of system hierarchy, an organisation consists of a collection of inter-related and inter-dependent sub-systems, each of which could be considered an 'organisation' in its own right.

As we alluded to in Chapter 2, systems are inherently processes of organisation (order) in a universe of disorganisation (disorder). Systemic thinking is interested in the process of organising as well as the entity of organisation. The entity of organisation (noun) arises from the process of organising (verb). Like a river, an organisation as entity is in a continual state of flux. Organisational actions continually re-create the organisation. Organisational action also is the motor for organisational change.

As we have seen, in a typical organisation the predictability of organisational action is reliant on a defined structure of organisational roles and procedures, routines or patterns for doing things. This is the essence of what we mean by performative action. In the process of performing their roles and adhering to routine organisational actors re-create the organisation. However, innovation in action always occurs, and is particularly evident in times of environmental disturbance. At such times, organisational action has to change or adapt to environmental change if it is to remain viable.

Organisations are different from mere collections of people or social groups in general in the sense that they are normally established for some purpose, usually to produce some form of value such as goods or services. Organisations are typically seen as needing clear identities to establish a context for action. However, organisational purpose is a dynamic not a static issue. Purpose is continually negotiated, understood and disseminated throughout the organisation by its actors.

It should be evident from the above that identifying the actors, particularly the stakeholders, in a system is critical to understanding the system itself. Different actors will have different world views as to what constitutes the system – its purpose and key activities. The definition of what constitutes the activity system is hence relative to the actor. However, building a coherent and inter-subjective world view (in management parlance – vision) is important to organisation. To facilitate this, models of activity systems are useful.

Modelling activity systems

The language of systemics is useful as a means of building models of reality. It thus acts as a tool-kit of concepts and components for engaging with and making sense of the complexity of reality. The process of modelling is undertaken for a number of reasons. First, it allows the modeller to abstract certain features of some situation or phenomenon and in this sense simplify some real-world situation. Second, it enables the modeller to represent these key features in some agreed sign-system. Third, the model promotes communication of a set of common understandings about some phenomenon amongst a group of persons.

A good example of the value of a model is a tube or metro map. The first diagrammatic map of the London underground was designed by Harry Beck in 1933. Beck was an employee of the London Underground who realised that the physical locations of Underground stations were irrelevant to the traveller wanting to know how to get from one station to another. What matters to the user of the Underground is the topology of this system; in other words, how the stations are connected. Such a map is hence a model of the actual underground railway network. It highlights or abstracts the key features of the network for its users. It represents these features as a series of circles (for stations) and coloured line segments (for tube lines). This map communicates to potential users of the tube which stations are connected to which and thus acts as an aid to performance, to travel.

There is hence a clear relationship between models and signs. Models need sign-systems in the sense that models are created through signs and effectively act as an external communicative resource. Natural language is clearly the richest of sign-systems with which we model our world. For the design of activity systems, more restricted and formalised sign-systems are typically used.

The main activities of modelling systems in this way are three-fold. First, we need to define the boundary of a system in the sense of what is considered part of the system and what is considered part of the environment of the system. Second, we need to define the hierarchy within the system itself – in terms of assigning structure and behaviour to sub-systems and sub-sub-systems and so on. Third, the modeller needs to define the elements of the system such as activities and control as well as the relationships between elements.

The ideas that stakeholders hold of a particular activity system can be modelled more precisely using the idea of a 'root definition'. A root definition expresses the core purpose of an activity system, in terms of the classic input-process-output model of a system discussed in Chapter 2. Checkland (Checkland, 1999) has suggested that most useful root definitions consist of six elements making up the acronym CATWOE. C stands for Customers: the victims or beneficiaries of the transformation of the system. A stands for Actors: those who would do the transformation. T stands for the Transformation itself: the conversion of input to output. W stands for World view: that which makes the transformation meaningful. O stands for Owners: those that could stop the transformation. Finally, E stands for Environmental constraints: elements outside the system which it takes as given.

The core of CATWOE is the pairing of Transformation with the World view, which makes it meaningful. For any activity system there will always be a number of different transformations by means of which it can be expressed, these deriving from different interpretations or world views of its purpose. The other elements of the mnemonic add ideas of key stakeholder types and their role in the system: someone must undertake the purposeful activity (Actors), someone could stop it (Owners) and someone will be its victim or beneficiary (Customer). The system will also take some Environmental constraints as a given.

Consider the ambulance service as an example. From our description of this case we can see that a number of stakeholders exist within this system such as patients, ambulance staff and control room staff. Each stakeholder will potentially hold a different world view as to the purpose of this 'system'. For example, a patient's world view might be translated into a CATWOE root definition as follows.

- Customer = Myself as a patient.
- Actors = Other patients, ambulance staff and control room staff.
- Transformation = Providing rapid response to incidents and providing appropriate emergency healthcare at the point of incident.
- World view = That effective emergency healthcare is critical to my health.
- Owners = Ambulance service management, National Health Service management, Politicians.
- Environment = The system of healthcare in the UK: other healthcare providers both public and private.

As models for management, root definitions provide the material for constructing conceptual models of purposeful activity. These represent graphical representations of key relationships between the minimum necessary activities needed to support the key transformation process

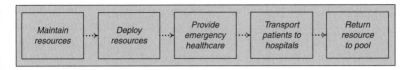

Figure 11.2   Starting a conceptual model of an activity system

specified in a root definition. Such an activity model can be constructed in the following manner.

The modeller starts with the key transformation of the system. In our sample root definition this was expressed as: *providing rapid response to incidents and providing appropriate emergency healthcare at the point of incident*. We thus represent this transformation as an activity or a series of performative activities on our diagram (Figure 11.2) – in this case as *provide emergency healthcare*.

The modeller works out from the central activity to consider activities that input into the central transformation and those which output from the central transformation. Activity boxes are joined with dotted arrows to indicate dependencies or precedence of activities. Hence, in Figure 10.2, to provide emergency healthcare in response to incidents we first need to maintain resources such as ambulances and paramedics and to deploy such resources at ambulance stations and hospitals such that they are likely to be close to the point of incident. These are input activities. Once emergency healthcare has been delivered at an incident the patient is likely to need to be transported to the nearest general hospital and following this the ambulance needs to return quickly to its base of operation. These are output activities.

We next need to consider the issue of control. By this we need to answer the question of how does one assess the key purpose of our activity system? Also, how do we implement this purpose in terms of the three Es of performance discussed in the previous chapter: efficacy, efficiency and effectiveness? This involves specifying four additional types of activity familiar to the idea of a control process discussed in Chapter 5. First, we need to consider planning activities which supply criteria for assessing performance in terms of the resources to be used and how they will be measured. This effectively means specifying control inputs. Second, we need to specify control processes that need to be in place to assess performance against criteria set. Such processes

implement decision-making strategies necessary to assess the performance of some operational process and as such represent comparators.
Third, we need to consider monitoring processes which collect measurements of activities against performance criteria set. Such processes
are necessary to supply performance information to control processes
and effectively amount to sensors. Finally, we need to consider change
processes necessary to enact regulation of operational activities, which
amount to effectors.

These processes need to be joined together with appropriate dependencies. Hence, in terms of our example (Figure 11.3), each of these main
operational activities may need to be controlled. Hence, for instance,
to deliver rapid emergency healthcare at incidents we first need to
define what we mean by rapid, perhaps by implementing targets such
as response times to incidents (control inputs). We then need to identify the geographical location of incidents (sensors) and dispatch ambulances to incidents (effectors). We may then monitor the degree to
which target response times are being met.

Within software development it has become accepted that many common features of algorithms occur across a variety of programming situations. Hence, there has been increasing interest in documenting such

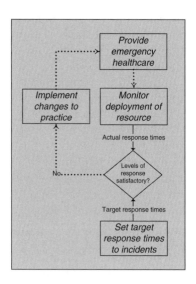

Figure 11.3   Example of ambulance service control

features as software patterns. More recently researchers have attempted to identify common patterns associated with business processes. Hence, it will come as no surprise that the patterns evident in the system of performative activity underlying the organisation of the ambulance service bears a resemblance to performative patterns evident in other organisational settings such as the Warning Network case as described in Chapter 9.

In Chapter 9 we considered the Warning Network as an information system. But implicit in the case is the idea that this information system was used to support a critical activity system: a set of actors engaging in coordinated and collaborative action. In the case of the Warning

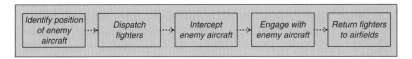

Figure 11.4   The activity system of fighter command

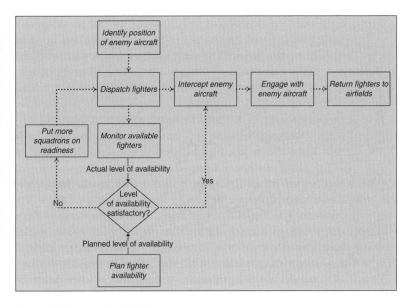

Figure 11.5   Control of fighter command

Network the activity system consisted of the operation of the fighter aircraft of the RAF in air defence of the UK. From our description of the major strategy of fighter command, the key purpose or transformation of this activity system was to intercept enemy aircraft.

This central transformation relies on a number of input and output activities (Figure 11.4). In terms of input, the position of incoming aircraft needed to be determined accurately. Following this, sufficient aircraft needed to be dispatched from airfields to intercept the enemy. In terms of output, the enemy aircraft needed to be engaged effectively by fighter squadrons and fighters needed to be able to return to their base airfields.

To reiterate, all activities whether they be individual or group activities are clearly subject to some form of control. For instance, if we are to dispatch fighters to intercept incoming bombers, we need to know the numbers, positioning and state of readiness of friendly fighters (Figure 11.5).

Activity systems, information systems and data systems

However, there is a danger in this approach to modelling activity systems. We should not forget that the diagrams in the previous section represent abstractions. The model is not the reality. We need to always keep in mind that an activity such as *dispatch fighters* or *dispatch ambulances* actually comprises a complex, entangled network of performative acts which is reliant in turn on networks of informative and formative acts.

Take Figures 11.5 and 11.3 which describe aspects of control associated with the Warning Network and ambulance service cases. Each of the control loops drawn against these activity systems is actually a high-level description of informative and formative action.

Within Figure 11.5, for instance, the control loop was enacted within the informative and formative action of the operations room of the Warning Network. The actual number of friends and fighters in the sky was represented as forma by the positioning of particular tokens on the plotting table. The actual number of available fighters was represented on the tote. Operations controllers were able to use this forma to enact informa: to make decisions to increase or decrease the availability of fighters by issuing directives to change the states of readiness of fighter squadrons at airfields.

Within the ambulance service case, much of the forma is now enacted in ICT systems. On the basis of the forma recorded in such systems, dispatchers within the control room take informative action to attempt to maintain performance such as response times within targeted levels – deciding on which resource to dispatch to which emergency incident.

William Edwards Deming is widely credited with improving activity systems both in the United States and particularly in Japan during the Cold War period through application of quality management principles to industrial processes. His adage – *'If you can't describe what you are doing as a process, you don't know what you're doing.'* – underlines the importance of modelling activity systems within organisations; both to understand how they work and with the aim of improving how they work. This idea, as we have seen, has a long history dating back at least to Taylor's scientific management. It also underlies many modern approaches to management.

A branch of management arose during the 1990s, initially promoted by Michael Hammer (Hammer, 1990), which concerned itself with the design of so-called business processes and referred to itself as business process re-engineering or business process re-design – BPR for short. Within this approach a business process was described as a set of activities cutting across the major functional boundaries of organisations by which organisations accomplish their missions, particularly the key one of delivering value to the customer.

Soft Systems Method – SSM for short – is an approach developed by Peter Checkland and a whole host of associates at the University of Lancaster over a number of decades (Checkland, 1999). This method has been refined in a number of industrial and public sector projects since the 1970s. The key concept within SSM is a human activity system; as we have seen, a type of social system that is 'designed' to meet certain defined objectives.

Despite claims by proponents of each approach to the uniqueness of their perspective, there are a number of inherent similarities between SSM and BPR. Both utilise a systems model of organisations, BPR implicitly and SSM explicitly. Both focus on the issue of business change and assume that organisations or parts of organisations can be designed. Both see technology, particularly ICT, as key enablers of business change. Both maintain that the design of organisational work and the design of technology systems must be considered together. Hence, they both can be seen as founded in the socio-technical tradition of organisational thinking which we described in the last chapter. Both SSM and BPR also implicitly assume one of the fundamental premises of scientific management as considered in the last chapter: that the design of work can be optimised.

There are also some key differences between SSM and BPR. BPR had its genesis in the business arena, particularly the US business arena. BPR in its original form focused on radical business transformation, revolutionary change in organisations. BPR, at least in its original guise, is therefore interventionist and top-down. It works with the premise that change should be initiated by managers planning and introducing transformation into organisations. In contrast, SSM had its genesis in the academic arena and focuses more on evolutionary forms of business change. As a result, SSM aims to be consultative and bottom-up. It works with the assumption that representatives of various stakeholder groups, particularly those affected by business change itself, should participate in the re-design of organisational activity.

Both these approaches have experienced notable success as well as failure, particularly in the case of BPR. In a sense, we take from both these approaches the notion that a systems perspective on the nature of organisation is important, particularly because of the way in which it emphasises an active or dynamic viewpoint upon organisation. However, both approaches have little place for the consideration of signs and as a result communication and representation are seen within these design methods as if to magically emerge from a consideration and proper ordering of activities or processes.

Our aim has been to demonstrate the necessary inter-connection between performance, communication and representation. We would go further and argue that part of the reason both SSM and BPR have experienced difficulties in application is because they lack a coherent conceptualisation of the linkages between performance, information and data. For instance, part of the reason the business process movement experienced such high rates of failure was that they focused upon re-designing activities (performa) and assumed that informa and forma (particularly in the shape of information technology) would take care of themselves.

Our aim has been to highlight the advantage of augmenting a clear conceptualisation of activity systems with that of information systems and data systems. In doing so we have attempted to illustrate the way in

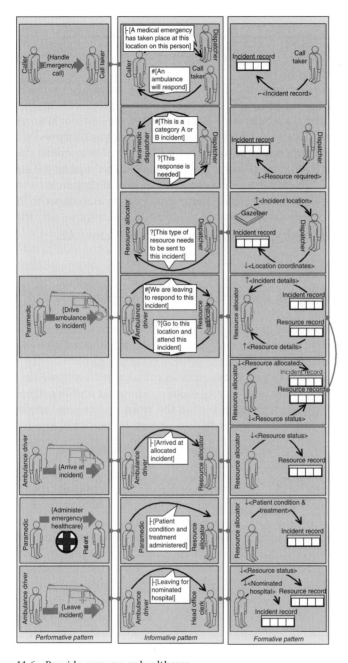

Figure 11.6 Provide emergency healthcare

which such systems inherently relate to issues of control, communication and organisation.

We can illustrate this in relation to the ambulance services case. Figure 11.6 illustrates that part of the activity system of this organisation in which ambulances are dispatched to incidents. It is an attempt to model the way in which performative actions as contained within a coherent performative pattern are closely coupled to a parallel stream of informative and formative action. Without such coupling the effective coordination of the activity of a multitude of dispersed actors would not be feasible. Hence, the activity of driving an ambulance to an incident will necessarily involve a range of communicative acts which in turn are likely to be reliant upon a series of formative acts.

Conclusion

The logo for this chapter is a set of inter-linked hands. This is meant to illustrate the essence of an activity system – the mutual coupling or binding together of the activities of multiple actors. Each actor within an activity system must coordinate his performative activity with that of his fellow actors in order to achieve collective goals.

Hence, within emergency response ambulance crews have to coordinate their activity with control room and hospital staff in fulfilment of effective patient treatment. Within the Warning Network the activities of pilots had to be coordinated in pursuit of victory in the Battle of Britain. Within Victorian Britain, a complex of activities performed by railway companies had to be coordinated through the Railway Clearing House.

The need for the coordination of performance stimulates the patterning of performance. Performative acts therefore tend to occur in conventional patterns that repeat across situations; what we have referred to as performative patterns. A performative pattern is therefore an abstraction of the regularity of performance, used as a resource by individual actors. In referring to such patterns we inherently acknowledge that similarity in performance is likely across different situations. Hence, there are clear similarities between the ways in which the control of resources within the Warning Network were organised and the ways in which modern ambulances are controlled within emergency response.

Performative acts tend to occur in conventional patterns because such patterns solve coordination problems. A coordination problem arises when people have a purpose in common which must be achieved by joint action. The contribution that each actor makes to achieving collective purpose will vary depending upon the contribution of others to producing a successful outcome. There is also more than one acceptable way of combining actor contributions to produce such a successful outcome. The set of combinations of actions which work fails to determine what any one actor's contribution should be in isolation from the actions of others.

Whenever the actions of two or more actors are coordinated we may speak of the presence of an activity system: a coherent collection of performative patterns. An activity system constitutes the order or organisation of such action which is reliant upon the organisation of communication and the organisation of representation. It is therefore to this overarching issue of organisation that we turn next.

References

Atkinson, C. and L. Brooks (2005). In the Age of the Humanchine. Proceedings of the International conference on information systems. Las Vegas.

Checkland, P. (1999). Soft Systems Methodology: a thirty year retrospective. John Wiley, Chichester.

Elias, N. (1978). What is sociology? Hutchinson, London.

Hammer, M. (1990). Re-Engineering Work: don't automate, obliterate. Harvard Business Review July-August: 18–25.

Lewis, D. (2002). Convention: a philosophical study. Blackwell, Oxford.

Mason, R. O. and I. I. Mitroff (1981). Challenging Strategic Planning Assumptions: theory, cases and techniques. John Wiley, New York.

Millikan, R. G. (2005). Language: a biological model. Clarendon Press, Oxford.

Pentland, B. and M. S. Feldman (2008). Designing routines: On the folly of designing artifacts, while hoping for patterns of action. Information and Organization 18: 235–250.

12
Organisation: Viable patterns

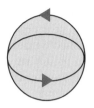

Introduction

The term organisation is normally associated with the social world. In the immediate post-war period the influential sociologist William H. Whyte published an influential book known as *The Organization Man* (Whyte, 1956). The central theme of the book considered the rise of the modern organisation and the effects of organisations upon individuals, particularly those living in the United States. It chronicled how individuals not only worked for organisations but in many ways 'belonged' to such organisations.

Although Whyte's analysis is still a matter of controversy, it is undoubtedly true to say that organisations as institutions dominate the modern day. People worldwide now spend a substantial proportion of their life either working within or interacting with organisations of various forms. Much of modern-day life is therefore organisational life.

But organisation is also a term that has importance in the physical sciences. For instance, Tom Stonier (Stonier, 1996) argues for information to be treated as a basic property of the universe as are matter and energy. Just as energy is defined in terms of its capacity to perform work, so information is defined in terms of its capacity to organise a physical system. For instance, deoxyribonucleic acid (DNA) is a nucleic acid that contains the genetic 'instructions' used as the motor of organisation amongst all known living organisms. DNA is often considered a code, since molecules of this acid contain instructions needed to construct other components of cells, such as proteins and RNA molecules.

But what do we mean when we say a system, whether physical or social, is organised?

In a similar manner to the way in which we considered the concept of information, organisation can be considered both a noun and a verb. As a noun, organisation is evidence of pattern in some aspect of the world. In these terms, organisation is another word for the emergent effect of patterning. The patterning of performance, communication and representation amongst a group of human actors is what we mean by human organisation. However, such patterning is only evident in action. We speak of organisation when patterns of performance, communication and representation are enacted and reproduced. In this sense organisation is best treated as a verb – as *poesis* – as a process of continual production (Maturana and Varela, 1987).

The conceptual framework which we have built within previous chapters is an attempt to provide a coherent and accessible explanatory framework for the central phenomena considered in this book, which we have referred to as the *enactment of significance*. Organisation is continuously produced or constructed through such enactment which consists of the complex entanglement of performative, informative and formative action. Such entangled action produces and reproduces viable data, information and activity systems.

Within this chapter we revisit a number of the cases discussed in previous chapters to help illustrate the nature of human organisation as the viable patterning of performance, communication and representation. But first, we provide a summary of the key elements of our conceptual framework.

Enactment of signs

Figure 12.1 acts as a composite illustration of the elements and inter-relationships of the three facets of our conceptual framework. Fundamentally, our framework attempts a unification of organisational semiotics on the one hand with organisational systemics on the other. The unity amongst these phenomena, which we summarise here, we refer to as the *enactment of significance* (Beynon-Davies, 2010). In the epilogue we shall argue that the proper study of this unity, at least as it concerns human organisation, is best denoted by the term *organisational informatics*.

269

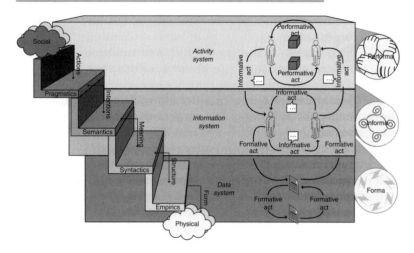

Figure 12.1   The conceptual framework

In Chapter 2 we defined signs as being units of significance. Signs are significant because they mediate between the social world on the one hand and the physical world on the other. Semiotics, the study of signs, can be seen to have four branches which offer four perspectives on the sign and act as a 'ladder' between the physical world and the social world through the psychological world. *Pragmatics* considers the relations between signs and actors and is concerned with the purpose or intentionality of a sign. *Semantics* considers the relations between signs and objects and is concerned with the meaning or intensionality of a sign. *Syntactics* considers the relations between signs and other signs and is concerned with the structure of some sign-system. Finally, *empirics* considers the relations between signs and matter or energy and is concerned with the physical form or representation of a sign.

A pattern is a coherent set of differences – a modulated aspect of the world. A repeating pattern is any regular pattern which is reproduced across more than one situation. In such terms, signs consist of significant patterns. Signs are repeating patterns treated by two or more actors as significant. Most signs are conventional patterns. A pattern is only conventional if it is reproduced purely by weight of precedent and only if it is unlikely to emerge or re-emerge in the absence of such precedent.

270

Conventional patterns are arbitrary patterns: patterns for which other patterns might well be substituted except for historical accident.

Signs are conceptual 'glue' which interconnect various levels of systems. This means that signs take their shape within systems of various forms. Systems constitute the continuing patterning of order or organisation in the world. The term system is used to refer not only to the patterning of signs. It is also used to denote the patterning of activity, communication and representation.

Signs inter-relate between and within three different patterns of order: forma, informa and performa. Forma constitutes the substance or representation of signs, informa the content or communication of signs and performa the use of signs in coordinated action. The patterning of order characteristic of human organisation is enacted through three inter-related forms of action. Formative acts amount to the enactment of forma: acts of data representation and processing. Informative acts constitute the enactment of informa: acts of communication involving message-making and interpretation. Performative acts constitute the enactment of performa: the performance of coordinated action amongst a group of actors.

These patterns of order and action allow us to more clearly define three levels of system of interest to human organisation: activity systems, information systems and data systems. Activity systems consist of the patterning of performa: of regular and repeating patterns of performative acts. Information systems consist of the patterning of informa: of regular and repeating patterns of informative or communicative acts. Finally, data systems consist of the patterning of forma: of regular and repeating patterns of formative acts.

Signs do not exist in isolation. They form part of complex wholes which we refer to as sign-systems. A sign-system is any organised collection of signs and relations between signs. Sign-systems amount to the patterning of signification in the world: distinct domains of signs which interact and inter-relate. The term sign-system is used to refer to any resource used in communication. It encompasses all forms of such resource used in human communication, animal communication and machine communication.

As a system, a sign-system consists of some organised pattern of signs. By organised we mean that each sign within the sign-system has coherence. A sign-system displays a certain stability or viability of signification. This means that signs can be expressed and interpreted in a standard way amongst some group of actors. Sign-systems can be distinguished on a number of levels, such as in terms of the actors involved, the medium or mode of communication, the level of formality associated with the sign-system and the level of complexity of the sign-system. Most sign-systems within the human domain are arbitrary – the relationship between symbols and what they signify relies on convention. When we say that a pattern is conventional we mean it amounts to a regularity in the behaviour of some population of actors.

Significance clearly relies upon communication and communication involves the use of signs for in-formation. The standard way of discussing communication is in terms of a classic model due to Claude Shannon, which focuses solely upon the medium of communication. We have argued that a satisfactory and augmented model of communication must include other layers of the semiotics ladder. Hence, communication is not only a matter of forma, it is also a matter of informa and performa. In other words, messages within communication are used not only to inform but to perform.

Communication is seen as a process involving the interaction of a number of elements: actors, messages, signals and communication channels. Actors are the senders of communication or the receivers of communication. The intentions of a sender will be encoded in a message using elements from a particular sign-system. The message will be transmitted by the sender in terms of signals along some communication channel. One or more of the other parties to some communication will be a receiver, which have the ability to decode signals to reveal the meaning of the message.

Within face-to-face (embodied) human and animal communication the communication process is framed by the sensory modality and sensory apparatus of the actors involved. The physical makeup of the actors in some communication determines a limited range of sensory modalities. These modalities determine what the actors are capable of sensing: the range of phenomena that can be discriminated using a particular sense.

Communication is important because it acts as a critical process for ensuring organisation or order. Internal or endogenous communication is essential for the regulation and adaptation of the behaviour of a particular actor. External or exogenous communication is critical to ensure effective coordination between multiple actors.

Systems of whatever sort must maintain their identity through time through processes of continuous re-creation. Control is the process by which a system remains viable at the current time and sustainable through time. The idea of control and control processes has relevance for understanding how order or organisation emerges not only in systems of performance, communication and representation but also in the intentional systems of psyche.

A given control process has sensors, comparators and effectors and works with feedback. *Sensors* are processes that monitor changes in the environment of some system or in the system itself (sensed signals) and send further signals to comparators. *Comparators* compare signals from sensors against control inputs and on the basis of some decision strategy send signals to effectors. Sometimes referred to as actuators or activators, *effectors* cause changes to a systems' state. Control is normally exercised within a system through some form of feedback. Control outputs from the process of a system are fed back to the control process. The control process then adjusts the control signals to the operating process on the basis of the information it receives.

Data or forma is a phenomena primarily of concern to the empirics level on the semiotics ladder and refers to the physical characteristics of signs. It is concerned with how signs are represented or stored using various different media as well as the traditional concern with how signs are coded as signals which travel along various communication or sensory channels.

Forma is thus concerned with the way in symbols are 'formed' from signals. Signals relate to patterns of energy or matter in the environment and as such are physical, objective constructs. In contrast, symbols relate to sensation and as such are perceptual, cognitive and subjective constructs. Signs relate symbols to meaning and to eventual action and as such are social, inter-subjective constructs.

As mediating constructs symbols point both to the physical world and to the social world. A symbol is any aspect of the world that can be modulated as a signal and hence used in communication. Modulation is the process by which variety is introduced into a signal.

Organisms exist in a surrounding environment of energy and matter. Ambient energy in this environment is continually signalling. Any form of energy propagation can be used for signals. A signal therefore consists of the patterned modulation of energy or matter along some communication channel. Signals have an existence independent of any sensing agent: they are objective. However, to become symbols we must have some sensing actor that is able first to sense the signal, second to interpret the signal and third to use this interpretation as a stimulus to behaviour. This assumes that critical processes of perception are involved in turning a signal into a symbol and critical processes of cognition are involved in turning a symbol into a sign.

The range of features in the world that can be modulated (that make differences) is potentially infinite. Different cultures choose different aspects, features or facets of the world as significant. A finite set of facets derived from the infinite variety in the world is used to code a conventionally organised set of symbols necessary for communication. Therefore, whereas symbols are sensed by humans through human perception, what is regarded as the meaning of a symbol will be determined within the context of some culture. By this we mean that cultures develop <u>conventional</u> expectations of significant patterning in the world.

Data systems are systems of forma. As such they cross over from empirics into syntactics. Within a data system we are interested not only in the formation of symbols but also how such symbols relate in larger structures. Symbols relate together and are operated upon in such data systems: a data system being a physical symbol system consisting of physical patterns (symbols) which can be combined into structures and manipulated to produce new structures.

We suggest a particular interest in those data systems in which symbols have some persistence. By persistence we mean that symbols exist for some duration over and above the communication within which the symbols were used. A persistent data system has the key advantage that external objects can be manipulated independently by multiple actors, at different places and at different times.

The syntax of some data system may be expressed in terms of a data model: a 'meta-language' for representing, organising and manipulating data. A data model can be seen to consist of two sets of primitives: representors and operators. Representors are primitives of data representation or organisation: operators are primitives of data manipulation or processing.

In terms of data representation, a data model can be described at a high level of abstraction in terms of a hierarchy of data items, data elements and data structures. A data item is the lowest-level of data organisation. A data element is a logical collection of data items and a data structure is a logical collection of data elements.

In terms of data processing we defined a number of core types or classes of formative act from which all forms of such processing can theoretically be built: create, read, update and delete. A formative act consists of the operation of one or more operators on one or more representors. Create or 'write' actions involve creating new data structures, elements or items (⊢<d>). Update actions involve changing the value of existing data representors in the sense that the symbols appropriate to representors such as data items are changed (↓<d>). Delete actions involve removing data items or data elements from data structures (¬<d>). Retrieval or 'read' actions involve accessing data from data items, data elements and data structures (↑<d>).

As mentioned above, a symbol points in two directions. On the one hand, it points to the physical world and relates to signals emanating from the ambient environment. On the other hand, a symbol points to the social world: it relates to effects such as individual and social actions. Interposing between these two is the realm of cognition, mind and more generally the issue of meaning. The term informa is used to refer to this latter pattern of organisation.

Informa is concerned with the content or meaning of signs used within the message conveyed in a communicative act. The meaning of a message is not a given but is a continuing accomplishment of intentionality (with-a-t) and intensionality (with-an-s). Intentionality is 'aboutness' – the relationship between mental acts/states and the external world, and in terms of semiotics is largely a matter of relevance to pragmatics. However, since intentionality relates to the issue of how symbols can have meaning it overlaps somewhat with the notion of intensionality. Intensionality is defined by the stands for relation between the symbol (designation) and its concept (intension) and is hence largely a concept of relevance to semantics.

Information relies on the patterning of the world in symbols; but information is not a given in the presence of such symbols. Instead, information is a process of sense-making within acts of communication. As such, it should be rewritten as a verb – *in-formation* because it is an inward-forming in terms of the organisation of a particular actor.

The *in* within in-formation actually refers to two things. On the one hand, *in* refers to intentionality and intentions. On the other hand, *in* refers to intensionality and intensions. In-formation is therefore a process in which intentions and intensions merge. In-formation is an entangled accomplishment involving the mix of individual (internal)

and social (external) representations of the 'world'. On the one hand, in-formation can be seen to rely upon ex-formation – the expression of symbols in forma. On the other hand, whereas informa relies upon forma, it is directed upon performa.

Information systems consist of patterns of informa: of in-forming. Information systems are systems for using signs in the sense that they act as a communication medium between different actors, sometimes spatially and temporally distant. Therefore, the sign-systems of relevance to information systems are best described as semi-formal sign-systems: some of their features are designed; some of their features emerge in continuous human interaction. Using this conceptual lens, information systems can be seen to consist of patterns of communicative or informative acts using semi-formal sign-systems to make decisions and as a consequence to create, control and maintain social action.

On the one hand, an information system is tied to action. On the other hand, an information system is tied to a system of artefacts. The 'language' of some information system includes formal messages that create, control and maintain social interactions in an organisational context. Such messages not only serve to make statements about the world. They are also used to give orders, make promises or commitments, issue feelings and classify things.

A communicative or informative act is some aspect of performance designed by one actor, A, to influence the performance of some other actor, B. Intentionality is expressed through illocutionary acts: acts of communication in which actors create and send messages in an appropriate context with certain intentions. According to John Searle, communicative acts come in various forms such as assertives, directives, commissives, expressives and declaratives.

We would argue that information systems consist of recurring patterns of such communicative action. A particular communicative act creates the possibility of usually a limited range of communicative acts as response. An information system can therefore be conceived as a semi-formal sign-system which supports human decision-making and action on the one hand and utilises representation (particularly record-keeping) on the other.

Performative acts deal with performa and correspond to the 'performance' of actors in various situations. A performative act amounts to some transformation of the world undertaken by a particular actor at a particular time, in a particular place in an attempt to realise some goal. Such acts of transformation are typically mediated through tools.

Performative acts do not occur in isolation but correspond to the 'work' of people in collective inter-action. Hence, they normally occur in sequences where one performative act is reliant upon the completion of another. Such acts therefore tend to occur in conventional patterns which we refer to as performative patterns. A performative pattern is therefore an abstraction of the regularity of performance and a coherent collection of such performative patterns we refer to as an activity system.

There is a tendency to discuss and analyse performative acts in isolation from communicative and formative acts. This is the mistake inherent in traditional approaches which attempt to model business processes or activity systems. On one level, performative acts amount to the realisation of intentions. They also are the means for fulfilling the conditions of satisfaction of communicative acts. But performative acts are likely to set up further cycles of communicative and formative acts which form and inform performance.

Performative acts tend to occur in conventional patterns because such patterns solve coordination problems. A coordination problem arises when actors have a purpose in common which must be achieved by joint action. The contribution that each actor makes to achieving this purpose will vary depending upon the contribution of others to producing a successful outcome. There is also more than one acceptable way of combining contributions to produce a successful outcome. The set of combinations of actions which work fails to determine what any one actor's contribution should be in isolation from the actions of others.

We have used the term actor deliberately in our definition of a performative act and a performative pattern. This is meant to imply that an actor may be human, animal or machine. Hence, a performative pattern may refer to aspects of animal behaviour or it may consist of a divisioning of activities between human, animal and machine. Hence, what we term as agriculture can be seen to consist of performative patterns that, for many thousands of years, involved the coordination of the work of human and animal actors. Over the last century or so this form of organisation has been replaced with activity systems that involve the performative interaction of humans with machines.

There is considerable debate about the degree to which we can assign agency to various actors within particular performative patterns. This relates to the complexity of psyche as a control system for behaviour. Only when a sufficiently complex mind mediates between perception and action in terms of a particular actor should we speak of agency. Hence, neither a thermostat nor a plant displays agency. However, humans and many classes of animal display various levels of agency. This is because such organisms maintain an internal environment which enables them to react flexibly in terms of their external environment.

On one level a performative act can be considered individual action. An individual action or act is a unit of behaviour with a clearly delineable beginning, end and goal, within the general continuum of behaviour. The action is realised in relation to the attainment of some goal and the goal of some action is determined by an impulse. Any such action can be analysed in terms of three phases (perceptual, manipulatory and consummatory) that correspond quite closely with the classic elements of a control system (sensors, effectors and comparators).

On another level performative acts take place within a larger complex of such acts. Social acts constitute inter-action between two or more organisms. In the simplest case of a social act – dyadic interaction – social acts rely on one actor reacting or responding to the acts of some other actor. The acts of one organism are therefore taken as stimuli by some other organism and vice versa. Communicative acts are a special case of social acts. Communicative acts form units within a conversation of significant 'gestures' and such communicative acts serve to aid the coordination of performative acts.

Performative acts tend to occur in coordinated patterns which we refer to as performative patterns. A performative pattern is a recognisable, recurring, network of performative acts. Such patterns are conventional patterns of behaviour and serve to facilitate coordinated behaviour amongst multiple actors.

An entangled web of such patterns forms an activity system. Activity systems are clearly social systems; they consist of patterns of coordinated action. But we take a particular interest in 'designed' social systems. In other words, those systems designed to achieve some purpose, usually as part of some more encompassing human organisation.

Human organisation

So having summarised our framework, what value does it have in illuminating the nature of human organisation.

Generally speaking, there are two major ways in which we may view human organisation. We may examine organisations in a top-down way as institutions with their own particular characteristics and behaviour. This is typically referred to as the *institutional perspective* on organisations. Alternatively, we may consider an organisation in a bottom-up fashion as formed from the everyday engagement of people in the process of organising joint action. This is typically referred to as the *action perspective* on organisations.

In essence, the institutional perspective focuses on the unit of organisation and is interested in the features of organisations as wholes. The institutional perspective views organisations as entities which exist independently of the humans belonging to them. Human actions are directed or constrained by such larger social structures and institutions have a life over and above the life of their members. In this sense human organisations are objective structures and can be studied in terms of patterns or features representative of these institutions.

In contrast, the action perspective focuses on the process of organising rather than the unit of organisation. In opposition to the institutional perspective, the action perspective maintains that social institutions are fundamentally constructed in action performed by human beings. The critical interest here is in how humans generate structures of coordination and cooperation in work: how organisations are formed and re-create themselves through the inter-action of their component parts. This means that social institutions such as organisations do not exist independently of the humans belonging to them. Consequently, organisational reality is subjective: different for each individual and the only valid way of studying organisational reality is through the interpretation of human action.

For much of its history, the study of human organisation – otherwise known as Organisation Theory – has tended to portray the institutional and action perspectives on organisations as mutually exclusive. Whole schools of social science became established which took as their orienting principles one or other of these positions. In practice, of course, each is a legitimate or valid position. We all act and interact with fellow human beings within organisations and appreciate the fluidity of organisational life. We all also experience the monolithic nature of organisations and the constraints imposed upon our actions by these institutional structures.

Structuration theory was created by the sociologist Anthony Giddens (Giddens, 1984) as an attempt to reconcile the action and institutional perspectives. Structuration theory speaks of the 'duality of structure'. On the one hand, the structure of social institutions is created by human action and is only evident in human action. Through human interaction, social structures are reproduced but may also change. On the other hand, human action is constrained by the way in which humans utilise institutional structure as a resource in interpreting their own and other people's actions. Institutionalised patterns exist only as human actors enact them. This cyclical process Giddens calls the process of structuration.

Figure 12.2 illustrates the process of structuration. Social structure both informs and constrains human action. In turn, human action both produces and reproduces social structure.

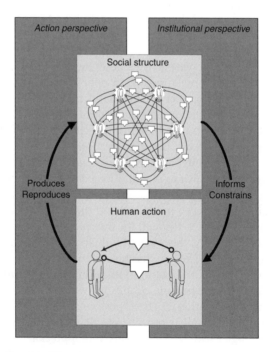

Figure 12.2   Structuration

One of the central concepts considered in this book, a sign-system, can be seen as having many of the features of a social institution, since it is a necessary pre-condition for formative, informative and performative acts amongst a group of persons. In this sense a sign-system can be seen to have an existence independent of the humans using it. It also means that the patterning of signs can be described and studied somewhat independently of the given enactment of signs. However, a sign-system is only really evident in actual sign acts. People use a sign-system as a resource for representation, communication and action. This sign-system is produced and re-produced through sign acts. Over time, sign acts may change the structure of the sign-system itself leading to a new basis as a resource.

We would argue that there is a similarity between the notion of structuration and considering organisations as complex, adaptive systems. Traditionally, the system perspective on organisations has been seen as a top-down, institutional perspective. In other words, its interest has been in the concept of organisation as a whole and the ways in which this institution regulates itself. More recently, a systems perspective has become interested in how organisation occurs through the complex interaction of multiple actors. This bottom-up perspective offers useful insight into how human organisations adapt and change.

A systemic conception of organisations is therefore useful in a number of ways (Jackson, 2003). First, it has clear ways of addressing some classic concerns of Organisation Theory such as decision-making, coordinated action and communication. Second, the conceptual tools of systemics offer managers practical ways of engaging with or intervening in organisations for which they are responsible, not only in terms of ensuring operational effectiveness but also understanding environmental uncertainty, planning strategy and managing change.

From our perspective, and at a broader level, the organisation of phenomena is evident in the patterning of such phenomena. Within human organisation we are interested in three inter-related forms of patterning: patterning of performance, patterning of communication and patterning of representation. Such patterning is evident in the enactment of signs within systems of activity, communication and representation. In such terms, significance is both a resource and an accomplishment.

The enactment of significance

Within Chapter 2 we introduced the term enactment to help us relate systems of signs to systems of representation, action and communication. This term has found use within Organisation Science, Cognitive Science and Computer Science. For Karl Weick (Weick, Sutcliffe et al., 2005), enactment is a social process, central to sense-making within organisations. For Francisco Varela (Varela, Thompson et al., 1993), enactment is an individual process, used to describe the structural coupling between human and environment through means of human interpretation. Within Computer Science the term enactment is used particularly to refer to the execution of business processes (OMG, 2007). Our view of enactment attempts a unification of these viewpoints. We have tried to unpack how enactment makes social, individual and computational sense through utilising the concepts of signs and systems.

Weick uses the term enactment to refer to the process by which individuals bring structures and events into existence and set them in action within an enacted environment: *'...people enact the environments which constrain them'* (Weick, 1995). Enactment therefore involves both a process and a product, an enacted environment. The enacted environment is described as *'...the residuum of changes produced by enactment'*. It is also described as a *'material and symbolic record of action'*. This suggests that Weick is struggling to encapsulate both technology and action within his conception of an enacted environment.

In terms of our conception we see the enacted environment as composed of the patterning of performance, communication and representation. Such patterns form resources and constraints for performative, informative and formative action. People, on the basis of established understandings of the significance of things, will perform in some situation. Patterns of communication will be important to the coordination of such performance. Individuals and groups may choose to make persistent representations of certain aspects of both communication and performance. Such representation as social memory, combined with individual memory, will help constitute the enacted environment for further cycles of the enactment of significance.

We have attempted to build a clear conceptualisation of the nature of organisation with the explicit purpose of explaining the entanglement of such organisation with communication and technology. In doing this we have adhered to three principles suggested by Brian Pentland

and Martha Feldman for building any satisfactory account of organising (Pentland and Feldman, 2007). First, we need to foreground action and explain how technology enters the social world through action. Second, we need to explain how patterns are important to joint action. Third, we need to demonstrate how patterns are contingent: how they are resources which influence but do not determine behaviour. At any point in the enactment of a pattern a human actor can choose to act differently.

The enactment of significance, conceived of as a complex adaptive system, is in continuous interaction with an enacted environment through a process of feedback. Such feedback ensures the continuity or viability of such enactment; it is also critical to change in the sense that enactment and environment are in a continuous process of mutual adaptation. The enacted environment consists of a complex mesh of patterns. Such patterns input as resources and constraints into the process of enactment. Enactment is a continuing accomplishment of actors which serves not only to reinforce patterns but to introduce changes to such patterns. Such enactment therefore changes the enacted environment over time.

Consider an example of such enactment within the case of Inka. The entanglement of communicative acts with performative acts and formative acts within this case is illustrated in Figure 12.3 and comprises one part of the enacted environment evident within the case of the Inka described in Chapters 6 and 8. The vertical dimension in the figure expresses a number of performative, informative and formative patterns. The entanglement between such patterns is indicated by connectors between the various types of acts on the horizontal dimension.

A number of performative patterns were important to sustaining the Inka Empire such as activities of agriculture, textile manufacture, mineral extraction, road building and census-taking. Each of these activity systems was reliant on a complex network of communicative or informative patterns. Hence, within the account detailed in Chapters 6 and 8, there is evidence to suggest that khipu were used to represent certain facets of a number of different types of communicative act. For instance, a particular pendant cord would be used to assert that a province had so many people of working age (⊢[this province has 2801 males of working age]). Alternatively, a pendant cord might be used to record the commitment of a defined amount of labour from a tributary unit for use by the Inka hierarchy (#[this ayllu will pay 54 units of

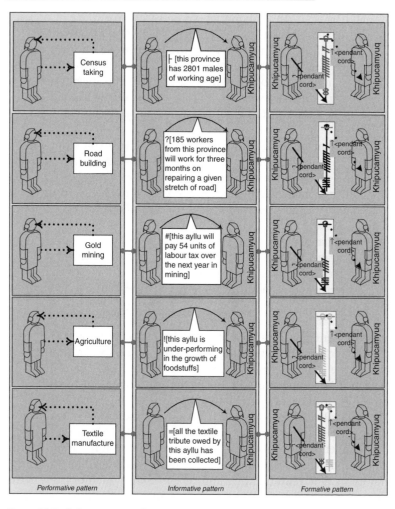

Figure 12.3   Inka patterns of enactment

labour tax over the next year in mining]). Khipu might also have been created in formative acts to record opinions about the performance of some group of workers (![this ayllu is under-performing in the growth of foodstuffs]), document orders to specific tributary units (?[185 workers from this province will work for three months on repairing a given stretch of road]) and to declare events, such as when tribute had been fully paid by a tributary unit (≡[all the textile tribute owed by this ayllu has been collected]). In each case, the data element produced by one khipucamayuq would be read by another khipucamayuq, normally displaced in time and space.

Consider a further example of such enactment within the case of the Railway Clearing House, as described in Chapter 8. The entanglement of communicative acts with performative acts and formative acts is indicated in Figure 12.4 and comprises a small part of the enacted environment evident within this case. Again, the vertical dimension in the figure expresses a number of performative, informative and formative patterns, entangled together and represented through connectors.

In this figure, a communicative pattern initiates enactment. A passenger asserts her intention to a booking clerk: ⊢ [wish to take a journey on a particular day from a particular embarkation point to an indicated destination]. A booking office clerk then asserts to the passenger:⊢[the price of taking the indicated journey].

Following this a passenger commits herself to the booking clerk: #[taking the indicated journey for the price indicated]. In turn, the railway company, in the form of the booking clerk, commits itself to the passenger: #[transporting the passenger on her journey for the fee agreed]. Such joint commitment causes a formative act to occur, namely, the creation of an appropriate data structure, a railway ticket: ⌐<Railway ticket>. It also initiates acts of performance: the payment of a fee by the passenger and the issuing of a ticket by the booking clerk.

During part of her journey a passenger performs the act of producing a ticket, handing it over to a railway conductor. This is taken as evidence of her entitlement to travel: ⊢[entitlement to travel]. The railway conductor conducts a formative pattern: reading and checking it is a valid ticket (↑<passenger ticket>) and updating the railway ticket by clipping it with a snippers (↓<Passenger ticket>) to indicate that a passenger has travelled on a particular part of the railway network: ≡[passenger has undertaken a part journey]. The railway conductor then performs the act of returning the clipped ticket to the passenger.

At some point a passenger disembarks from a train and attempts to perform the act of leaving the railway station by handing over a valid used ticket to a railway guard. This is taken to signify that the passenger has completed her journey: ≡[completion of journey]. The railway ticket is read and checked by the railway guard (↑<used ticket>) and added as

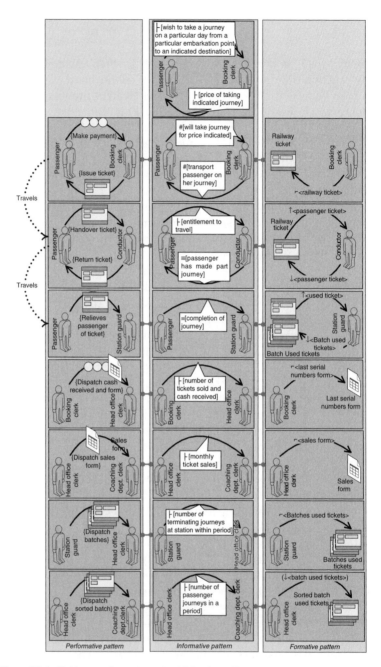

Figure 12.4 Patterns of enactment within the railway case

a data element to a data structure consisting of a batch of such used tickets (↓<Batch used tickets>)

A booking office clerk asserts on a daily basis tickets sold and cash received (⊢[number of tickets sold and cash received]) by writing the last serial numbers from ticket batches on a form (⊢<last serial numbers form>. The booking clerk then performs the act of sending the form with cash received to a head office clerk.

The enacted pattern ends with three segments of situated entanglement. A head office clerk asserts monthly sales (⊢[monthly ticket sales]) on a form (⊢<sales form>) and dispatches this to a coaching department clerk. A railway station guard indicates passenger-journeys terminating at their station (⊢[number of terminating journeys at station within period]) through return of batches of used tickets (⊢<batches used tickets>) to a head office clerk. A batch of tickets sorted by destination (↓<batch used tickets>) is sent to a clerk within the coaching department by a railway clerk to indicate the range of passenger-journeys terminating at a particular station during a particular period (⊢[number of passenger-journeys in period]).

Conclusion

The conceptual framework described in this book and summarised within this chapter is deliberately not an attempt to 're-invent the wheel' but to synthesise thinking from a number of areas which helps illuminate a number of enduring and wicked problems within organisation, information and computer science. The framework centres an appropriate locus for understanding certain problems such as that of information technology and organisation at the intersection between signs and systems; what we have referred to as the enactment of significance. This concept of enactment suggests a broadening of our sense-making to consider the complex entanglement of significance within the nature of human organisation.

We conclude the chapter with some of the key value which our conceptual framework supplies. In other words, we attempt to answer the key question set in the prologue: what's significant about the enactment of significance?

First, it provides greater clarity to the nature of information, particularly the apparent paradox between the subjective, objective and inter-subjective nature of this phenomenon. Our conception of information can be seen to build and expand upon the work of both Fred Dretske (Dretske, 1981) and John Mingers (Mingers, 1995). Both criticise the established 'engineering' model of information in communication as we have done so in Chapter 4 and like us wish to include semantics within any definition of information. Both also lay claim that information is both an objective and subjective phenomenon. Information is objective in the sense of comprising physical signals as we indicated in Chapter 6. It is subjective in the sense of relating to interpretation and meaning as discussed in Chapter 8. Mingers also importantly points to the inter-subjective nature of information because meaning is expressed in and conditioned by language, or in our terms, sign-systems (Chapter 3).

However, we believe that using the same term – *information* – for each of these perspectives actually serves to obscure the multi-faceted nature of information and as a consequence helps preserve many of the entrenched connotations of the term which as we have seen in Chapter 8, Richard Boland challenged some decades ago. We have therefore attempted to demonstrate the utility of segmenting out the forma, informa and performa of significance. Forma can be seen to encapsulate the objective nature of information, informa its subjective nature and performa its inter-subjective nature.

Hence, to take one of our examples, knot groups within khipu are clear examples of forma. The physical structure of a given knot group has an independent existence over and above the actor who created it. The meaning of such knot groups was clearly a critical and continuing accomplishment within acts of intentional communication and interpretation (informa) in the Inka Empire. Such signification relied upon conventional or inter-subjective agreement concerning not only the intensions associated with knot groups but also the intentions supporting coordinated activity.

Second, the framework helps to breakdown our established current conceptions of the nature of 'information technology' and as such supplies a more historically encompassing and less culturally-centric conception of such technology. It also allows us to relate the development of such technology to forms of embodied human communication. As we have seen, forma is a term we use to stand for the physical aspect of a sign. Hence, we can speak of the forma of human speech or the forma of non-verbal human communication. Such examples of forma are *embodied* in the sense that human actors communicate by manipulating aspects of their physical makeup directly, whether this be in terms of bodily movement or manipulating internal organs such as the larynx. Such embodied forma can be seen to involve 'writing' to a particular sensory modality such as the human auditory channel and 'reading' from this channel.

However, restricting forma to the vehicles of embodied communication excludes consideration of 'techne' in sign-systems – the activities involved in producing signs using 'tools' which persist beyond the body and beyond any one communication. Such 'technical' activity involves manipulation of a persistent rather than a non-persistent data system. Defining the essence of 'information technology' in the concept of a persistent data system allows us to make sense of a vast array of artefacts used across time, space and human cultures for physical symbol representation and manipulation.

Hence, within this conception, even though the clay tokens discussed in Chapter 1 and the khipu discussed in Chapter 6 would not traditionally be considered a form of 'writing', there is substantial evidence to suggest the use of such artefacts as forms of persistent data system. Indeed, this allows us to push back the idea of information technology to the first use of such persistent data systems, perhaps as far back as the Upper Palaeolithic (35,000–10,000 B.C.) period.

Third, we would suggest that the term *information system* as currently used within many areas, such as in the discipline of Information Systems, is overloaded. Within this discipline an information system has traditionally been defined as consisting of people, processes, data and technology. This definition was initially useful in suggesting that information systems were significantly different from information technology. However, more recently, many (Paul, 2007) have suggested that this definition is limited because it fails to help answer a number of important questions such as: What is information and why is it so important? How does information relate to language and communication? In what sense do animals and machines communicate? Are computers the only information technology? What is the value of information systems to organisations?

It is probably because of the entangled and overloaded nature of this conception that much Information Systems literature paradoxically does not study information systems as such. Instead, this work tends to take one of two polar positions. One method of interpretation, characteristic of *technological determinism*, tends to portray innovations in information technology as a critical force or driver shaping innovations in social systems. Another method of interpretation, characteristic of the *social construction of technology*, tends to portray information technologies as fundamentally shaped by social forces. It should be apparent from our method of exposition that we believe that a more sophisticated and accurate view is to portray the relationship between information technology (data systems) and activity systems as being much more dialectical in nature. Data systems and activity systems exist in a reinforcing cycle of interaction and creation through the mediating position of information systems.

In one sense our definition of an information system as a specialised form of communication system appears much narrower in scope than the encompassing definition and looks, at first glance, to provide little to understanding the exigencies of modern digital computing systems. In another sense, we would argue, that our conception of an information system when placed within the wider conceptual framework described actually provides more intellectual capacity and greater applicability than the encompassing definition. It not only allows us to provide a clearer conception of what an information system constitutes; it also addresses the problematic raised by Paul: how such systems differ from information technology on the one hand and activity systems or business processes on the other. In doing so, it provides preliminary answers to the questions provided in the previous paragraph. For instance, it allows us to appreciate the functional role that information systems play within human societies of various forms. As suggested within the Inka case and other such cases discussed in this book, many societies invent various forms of information system and their associated technologies to address crises in the control of activity. In the case of the khipu, for instance, the manipulation of such artefacts appears to have been critical to communication between dispersed communities making up the Inka empire. This communication was essential to ensuring the coordinated performance of dispersed groups across the high Andes.

Fourth, the framework provides a new rendering of information systems as socio-technical systems. Rather surprisingly, although digital computers have been applied for over fifty years within organisations we still lack a coherent conceptualisation of the value that such technology has for organisations. This enduring problematic of information technology and organisation has been highlighted in recent literature within the discipline of Organisation Science. Zammuto et al. (Zammuto, Griffith et al., 2007), for instance, argue that '*the relationship*

between technology and organizational form and function has been of interest to organization scientists for over 50 years…[However,] organization science's interest in this relationship has declined significantly over the past thirty years, a period during which information technologies have become pervasive in organizations and brought about significant changes in them.' They further suggest that *'a conceptual shift – from 'organizational form' to 'forms of organizing' – is needed…viewing the social and technological systems of organizations in concert, which was a critical part of sociotechnical systems theory in the 1950's, is a perspective that the field needs to rediscover because IT has become inextricably intertwined with social relations to weave the fabric of organization.'*

The practical effect of utilising our conceptual framework means that any coherent account of a particular information system cannot be provided without considering the information technology used, the communication this enables and the activities supported. For instance, the utilisation of khipu as a mechanism for data representation and transfer only makes sense in the context of the information specialists of the Khipucamayuq. It also is only significant in the context of the tributary systems of the Inka and their need to manage the distribution of labour, land and produce throughout their empire.

Fifth, a more precise rendering of the essence of information systems provides a firmer basis for studying and unpacking what Wanda Orlikowski (Orlikowski, 2007) has recently referred to as the nature of sociomaterial practice within organisations: the way in which *'the social and the material are constitutively entangled in everyday life'*. The concept of sociomaterial is intellectually seductive but actually extremely difficult to pin down. We believe that our framework provides a path to understanding the nature of the constitutive entanglement proposed as underlying the nature of the sociomaterial. In our terms, performing, communicating and representing are undoubtedly entangled within cycles of enactment. It is through such enactment that the value of 'information technology' is accomplished. Hence, the value of khipu as artefacts only makes sense within the situated context of the communicative and performative needs of the Inka empire. Or within the case of the Warning Network the value of the plotting table, tote and the plotting clock was continuously enacted in supporting the command and control of RAF fighter command.

However, this does not mean that we cannot for the purposes of analysis separate out the forma, informa and performa of the enactment of significance within both historical and contemporary domains. Nor should it prohibit us from suggesting approaches that attempt to model formative, informative and performative patterns within organisational settings, perhaps with the aim of re-designing such systems.

Overall, our critique suggests the need to re-orient the disciplinary locus within those disciplines which focus around the problematic of 'information', and it is to this challenge we turn in the epilogue ...

References

Beynon-Davies, P. (2010). The enactment of significance: a unified view of information, systems and technology. European Journal of Information Systems 19(4): 1–20.

Dretske, F. I. (1981). Knowledge and the flow of information. Blackwell, Oxford.

Giddens, A. (1984). The Constitution of Society: outline of a theory of structuration. Polity Press, Cambridge, UK.

Jackson, M. C. (2003). Systems Thinking: creative holism for managers. John Wiley, Chichester.

Maturana, H. R. and F. J. Varela (1987). The Tree of Knowledge: the biological roots of human understanding. Shambhala, Boston, Mass.

Mingers, J. (1995). Information and meaning: foundations for an intersubjective account. Information systems journal 5(4): 285–306.

OMG (2007). Business Motivation Model (BMM) Specification, Object Management Group.

Orlikowski, W. J. (2007). Sociomaterial Practices:exploring technology at work. Organization Science 28(9): 1435–1448.

Paul, R. J. (2007). Challenges to information systems: time to change. European Journal of Information Systems 16(3): 193–195.

Pentland, B. and M. S. Feldman (2007). Narrative networks: patterns of technology and organization. Organization Science 18(5): 781–795.

Stonier, T. (1996). Information as a basic property of the universe. Biosystems 38(2): 135–140.

Varela, F. J., E. Thompson, et al. (1993). The Embodied Mind: cognitive science and human experience. MIT Press, Cambridge, Mass.

Weick, K. E. (1995). Sensemaking in Organizations. Sage Publications, Oxford.

Weick, K. E., K. M. Sutcliffe, et al. (2005). Organizing and the process of sensemaking. Organization Science 16(4): 409–421.

Whyte, W. H. (1956). The Organization Man. Simon & Schuster, New York.

Zammuto, R. F., T. L. Griffith, et al. (2007). Information technology and the changing fabric of organization. Organization Science 18(5): 749–762.

Epilogue: The nature of informatics

Introduction

Within the prologue we posed the question: what's significant about the enactment of significance? Remember also the 'ticket home' initiative we described? We raised this as an example of the 'magical' nature of signs within systems. Let us return to this case and try to infer why a particular sign was so magical within this situation by applying some of the conceptual tools we have developed throughout this book.

The *ticket home* initiative involved the introduction of a piece of laminated card on which was printed the patient's name, clinical consultant and their expected date of discharge. This initiative, which had the simple intended purpose of making information more visible to patients, had an unexpected side-effect of improving patient discharge rates.

The activity system in this case included a vast range of performative patterns performed by a multitude of healthcare actors – from orthopaedic surgeons through nurses, administrative staff, hospital porters and cleaners. We should also not forget the focal actor in this system – that of the patient herself, since much modern healthcare is founded on the importance of patient involvement in their own 'treatment'.

As we have seen, the key difficulty in any complex activity system such as the one described is that of coordinating the multiple activities of diverse actors. For such coordination effective communication is needed – particularly for the communication of collective goals and for the communication of the degree to which such goals have been achieved. It is physically impossible for such information to be imparted through face-to-face communication amongst all the actors within this activity system. Hence, persistent records of communication are required – recorded in persistent data systems.

But the problem is that each set of actors frequently maintain their own records in their own data systems. Hence, clinicians are likely to

293

maintain their medical records, nurses their care plans and administrators their records of patient admission. Also, of course, the patient rarely has access to the data held about them in any of these data systems. This turns the patient into a passive actor in their own treatment. There is little feedback for the patient about the progress of their own recovery.

The beauty of the 'ticket home' initiative is that it uses a simple but effective way of representing a common goal or collective intention for all actors within the activity system – the effective treatment of a named patient in a prescribed period of time. It also goes some way to representing the degree to which the goal is being achieved. In this sense, statements written on the ticket acted in the capacity of what we referred to in Chapters 8 and 9 as a commissive communicative act. It represented a collective promise amongst the actors involved.

Of course and most importantly this sign included the patient as an actor within this sign-system. The patient is given the capacity to not only read the representation and communicate about the representation with other actors but to communicate about it with herself. In this sense the patient is given the power in a certain respect to 'act' to achieve the goal herself.

So signs such as the 'ticket home' are magical, but only because they entangle action, communication and representation. It is to the proper and systematic study of such entanglement that we propose the term *informatics* be applied.

Informatics

Walter Bauer (Bauer, 1996) claims to have invented the term *informatics* in the United States in 1962, around the same time that Phillipe Dreyfus started using the term *informatique* in France. Because it was used as a company name in the United States, Bauer's company blocked its more general application. Meanwhile, in France the name took on the meaning of *'the modern science of electronic information processing'* and was eventually accepted by L'Academie francaise as an official French word. The word Informatique has now been adopted and adapted in various European languages: Informatik, Informatica and so on.

Within the United Kingdom, Informatics has been treated by many in recent years as synonymous with the discipline of Computer

Science. However, some have begun to see informatics as being something inherently larger in nature but with the study of computation still at its core. Saul Gorn (Gorn, 1983), for instance, defines informatics as *'computer science plus information science'*. On this basis, there has been a tendency to rename computer science schools or departments, at least within the UK, as departments or schools of informatics in recent times.

Much more recently some of the larger ambition which is reflected in the current book appears to be starting to influence such schools of computation. For instance, the University of Edinburgh defines informatics as *'the study of how natural and artificial systems store, process and communicate information'* while the University of Manchester describes it as *'a multi-disciplinary approach to information and information systems'*.

Informatics as an area of study certainly must include the study of computation per se. However, the nature of information, information systems and information technology as described in this book emphasises the need to take what we might call a trans-disciplinary approach. As an attempt to demonstrate this we have deliberately referenced literatures from disciplines as diverse as archaeology, social anthropology, linguistics, communication theory, philosophy and logic within this work, to name but a few. All of these areas have formed facets of the prism we have used to build what we feel has the beginnings of a more productive conceptualisation for the field of informatics.

We would therefore like to avoid the boundary wars inherent in debates about distinctions between information management, information systems, computer science and information technology. Gammack et al. (Gammack, Hobbs et al., 2007) get closer to our conception in defining Informatics as *'the art and science of information'*. We would propose a broader definition for informatics as being the study of the intersection between signs and systems, because we know from a reading of this work that both signs and systems are high-level concepts that encompass a vast array of phenomena. In this sense, informatics is something of a meta-discipline or perspective and as such has much to offer as a distinct area of study and practice.

There is already evidence of this conceptual drift occurring in that informatics as a core sense-making space has already found application to numerous areas. Consistent with a division highlighted in Chapter 1, broadly we may distinguish between the application of informatics

295

to the physical world and the application of informatics to the social world. For instance, in terms of the physical world, informatics has been applied in medicine and healthcare (health informatics), in biology (bio-informatics), in physical geography and geology (geo-informatics), and even more recently within chemistry (chem-informatics).

Our emphasis has mainly been on the use of informatics to help understand particular areas of human social life (social informatics). Within this focus we have applied it in helping us understand the interaction between signs and systems within organisations in general (organisational informatics) and business organisations in particular (business informatics).

Within the current text our interest has been to try to tease out some of the essence of the nature of organisational informatics: a discipline

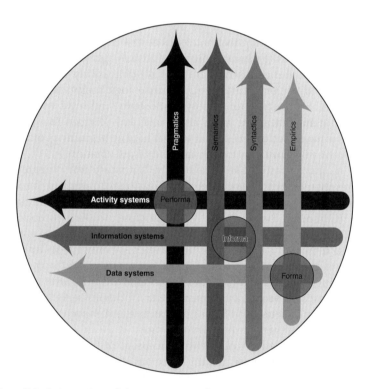

Figure E.1   Intersection of signs, systems and patterns

which is necessarily interdisciplinary in nature because its area of concern bridges between the physical/technical and the social. Another way of thinking about the nature of human and organisational informatics is that it engages with three types of 'science'. From one direction organisational informatics is inherently a social science in that it is interested in organisational behaviour. From another direction it is inherently a physical or natural science in that it is interested in the makeup of physical artefacts such as electronic computing devices. In terms of its third face it is what has been referred to as a design science (Hevner, March et al., 2004) in the sense that it is interested in the productive application of information technology to organisations and their management.

Therefore, to think informatically (Bryant, 2008) about an issue and attempt to resolve such an issue in informatics terms means applying a particular sense-making stance in which the issue of *significance* assumes centre stage. The phenomenon of significance is naturally located at the intersection of signs, systems and patterns (Figure E.1). *Signs* are critical to sense-making because they encapsulate issues of intentions (pragmatics), meaning (semantics), structure (syntactics) and form (empirics). Such signs are enacted through three *patterns* of organisation: forma (the substance of a sign), informa (the content of a sign) and performa (the use of signs in coordinated action). Such a conception of enactment allows us to define more clearly and to relate three classes of *system* important to human organising: activity systems, information systems and data systems. Such systems consist of the patterning of performa, informa and forma.

The infinity of lists

As we mentioned in a previous chapter, the semiotician Umberto Eco (Eco, 2009) in a recent work has focused upon the way in which various societies use lists as part of their attempt to impose forms of ordering on the world. The ubiquity of lists across time and human culture suggests that they serve some critical function amongst human society. But what is such a function? What does the imposition of order or control through list-making mean in this context? To help answer this question we consider the place of the list within our conceptual framework. This framework allows us to understand the way in which lists play different roles in the construction of significance. Lists relate both to representation and action. Lists are important as records of our understanding of world order as well as guides to action in the world. This conception allows us to understand not only the key functions that lists play but also some of the inherent dangers that lie within any attempt at list-making.

Modern Information and Communication Technology (ICT) has made the making of and use of lists much easier. However, the increasing ease with which we can create and manipulate lists frequently masks much of the nature of lists as significant artefacts. Lists as forma always lie within an encompassing context of informative and performative action. However, elements of such context frequently become disentangled within many modern organisations leading to a number of potential dysfunctions.

The Ticket home initiative with which we began this chapter demonstrates the positive nature of signs as the motive force in representation, communication and action. But this motive force also contains inherent dangers if not used appropriately. Let us, therefore, conclude this book with an examination of two inter-related cases, which we use here to highlight some of the dangers inherent in failing to think informatically about the nature of human organisation.

The Criminal Records Bureau

The Criminal Records Bureau (CRB) is an Executive Agency of the UK Home Office. Its purpose is to provide access to criminal records for public, private and voluntary sector organisations and particularly to enable them to use this information to make more effective recruitment decisions. The service is hence particularly designed to identify candidates who may be unsuitable for certain work, especially that involving children or vulnerable adults.

The CRB was established under Part V of the United Kingdom Police Act of 1997. However, it took until 2002 for the service to be launched, mainly in response to increasing public concern about the safety of children, young people and vulnerable adults. It was felt at the time that British police forces did not have adequate capability or resources to routinely process and fulfil the large number of criminal record checks requested in a timely fashion. Hence, a dedicated agency was set up to service this function.

The CRB is run by the private company Capita who initially promised to respond to 90% of high-level enquiries, such as those required for the teaching profession, within three weeks. However, the increasing volume of such checks has led to some difficulties. In 2002, 1.5 million persons were checked. By 2007 the CRB processed 3.4 million checks and this had gone up to 4 million checks in 2008–2009, partly in response to a larger range of activities that are now classed as needing such checks.

In 2009, a new Vetting and Barring Scheme was created as a partnership of the Independent Safeguarding Authority and the CRB. This scheme requires all adults who teach, train, supervise or care for children or vulnerable adults on a frequent or intensive basis to register with the scheme. The population covered by the scheme is therefore expected to rise to something of the order of approximately 11.3 million people over the next few years: a quarter of the adult population in England and Wales.

The process by which the CRB provides criminal record data is called 'disclosure'. There are two levels of such disclosure: standard and enhanced. Checks cannot be obtained by members of the public directly but are only available to registered organisations and only in relation to a defined set of professions, offices, employments, work and occupations listed in the Exceptions Order to the Rehabilitation of Offenders Act, 1974.

An organisation must first register with the CRB before they can request disclosure data about an applicant. The individual then applies to the CRB with their application countersigned by the organisation. The applicant is then checked against criminal records maintained on the Police National Computer (PNC). If appropriate, applicant's details may also be checked against records held of people considered unsuitable to work with children and vulnerable people maintained by a number of organisations such as the Independent Safeguarding Authority. Copies of completed disclosures are sent to the applicant and the requesting organisation.

The standard disclosure is primarily for positions involving regular contact with children or vulnerable adults, but can also be used for some other professions of high responsibility. Since 2009 the standard disclosure is checked only against the Police National Computer. Standard disclosures reveal details of any convictions, cautions, reprimands and final warnings that the applicant has received, regardless of length of time that has elapsed since the incidents have been recorded. It also provides details of whether a person is banned from working with children or vulnerable adults.

The enhanced disclosure is for positions that involve work which involves regularly caring for, supervising, training or being in sole charge of such children or vulnerable adults. Such positions include nurses, doctors, social workers and teachers. In addition to the information provided for a standard disclosure, enhanced disclosure involves two additional checks: a check of Children and/or Vulnerable Adults barred lists maintained by the Independent Safeguarding Authority; a check with police forces in every area of the country in which the applicant has lived or worked for details of any relevant information. In the latter check, the police themselves decide what (if any) additional information will be added to the disclosure.

The fact of suicide

There are elements of the CRB case, particularly the formative nature of deviance, that bear a family resemblance to analyses of suicide. Over one hundred years ago one of the founding fathers of sociology, Emile Durkheim, published an influential book simply entitled *Suicide* (Durkheim, 1976). He intended this book as an example of how sociology should focus upon the study of what he referred to as social facts. This was a term he used to describe phenomena which are external to individual experience; having an existence in and of themselves and not bound to the actions of particular individuals.

Hence, even the most apparently individualistic phenomena, such as suicide, were regarded by Durkheim as objective social facts. Sociology's task was to discover the qualities and characteristics of such social facts, primarily through quantitative means. Statistics implicitly rely on the idea that the social world can be relatively easily quantified on the basis of 'facts' collected about it. Hence, Durkheim pioneered the analysis of statistics in support of sociological reasoning. In *Suicide*, for instance, Durkheim explored the differing suicide rates among Protestants and Catholics, and explained the lower suicide rates amongst Catholics at the time in terms of the stronger levels of integration and social cohesion among Catholics than amongst Protestants.

Within organisations records are equally and typically treated as 'facts' about areas of the world of interest to the organisation. Many years after the work of Durkheim a branch of sociology known as *ethnomethodology* started to emphasise that social facts are not objective but are reliant upon a set of subjective human accomplishments and practices (Cicourel, 1974). As evidence of this they particularly focused upon the practices or 'methods' people use in record-keeping of various forms. They argued that the process of producing a record of something is an accomplishment or a set of practices which actually serves to create the social order. Practical reasoning is utilised by relevant actors, for instance, in decisions pertaining to defining delinquent behaviour in the creation of criminal records by police officers or the registration of a person's death as a suicide by Coroners.

Hence, a social fact such as a suicide rate, which Durkheim took to be objective, is in fact reliant on what we have referred to as the enactment of significance. In the case of suicide various professional groups accord the status of suicide to suspicious deaths. In the process they assign an intension to this event based on an interpretation of the likely intentions of the dead actor. Such an interpretation is based in them applying rules of inference associated with collective intentionality to the evidence associated with a particular death.

Consider the case in which a given police officer or medical practitioner is called to the scene of a death. Such actors are imbued by society with the authority to make the key decision as to whether or not the death was 'suspicious'. In coming to this decision they look for 'evidence' that accords with their 'common sense' definitions about what constitutes a 'suspicious' death. Hence, they might ask themselves the following questions:

- How did the person die?
- Was the victim alone at the time of death?
- Was there a note left with the body?
- What was the victim's 'state of mind' immediately prior to death?
- Were elaborate preparations made by the victim?

If answers to such questions confirm the conception of 'suspicious death' which such officials hold then an inquest into the death is called at a Coroner's Court. The Coroner then becomes the most important actor, insofar as he or she now has to come to a decision about whether or not the death was a suicide.

The Coroner is likely to engage in similar forms of practical reasoning to actors such as the police or the medical profession. Hence, if a person was found hanging and alone, had left a note explaining his actions, and was suffering depression prior to his death, the Coroner is probably likely to declare such a death to be a suicide. Such practical reasoning is built around notions of collective intentionality, particularly about the likely causes of suicide and the expected behaviour of a suicidal person.

If one or more of the answers to such questions cannot be determined, then the coroner has to weigh the evidence in favour of a suicide verdict, or not. For example, consider the case of a woman in which there appears to have been a history of depression as well as evidence of suffering financial problems. The person's death was caused by a head-on car crash with a wall but no note was found with the victim. However, the victim is a Catholic and she comes from a Catholic family. The coroner herself is a Catholic and the court is being held in a Catholic country. All parties are therefore aware that the Catholic Church views self-murder as a sin.

In such a situation the Coroner may not declare a suicide, perhaps explicitly citing the lack of clear evidence but also implicitly taking into account the likely consequences of her decision upon the victim's relatives. A record is therefore made in this case of death by misadventure. Of course, individual formative acts such as this, when manipulated as aggregates may serve to communicate certain things about the state of the world. When all such communicative and formative acts are aggregated together in state-istics it might appear evident that Catholic countries have lower suicide rates than Protestant countries.

Forming order

Modern society relies upon lists for effective communication and performance in many and varied areas of life. Fields, records and files build up to form complex lists of things. However, it is frequently forgotten that each individual record in a list has a life-history consisting usually of a complex sequence of formative acts situated within an even more complex nexus of communicative and performative acts. We might even argue that making a record about an object, person or event is a significant part of the way in which modern reality is constructed.

Take the example of criminal records. Criminal records are created in formative acts – people deciding what is significant to represent as well as how to represent such significance. Hence, a given act of performance, might be labelled in this manner as an act of deviance. Such records are later used as a resource within communicative acts. They are particularly used to communicate the belief (assertion) that a particular deviant act has taken place and on this basis to (declare) that somebody is a criminal or not. On this basis certain persons make decisions and take action such as accepting or prohibiting someone from taking on a job as a teacher or a nurse.

Lists therefore take central place in the way in which organisations and society at large form order through the construction of 'facts' – assertions and declarations about the state of the world. Such 'facts' are used as a key resource in communicating and reinforcing the nature of order. In the case of the CRB, the appearance of certain properties associated with a particular person upon one of the many lists used by this organisation serves to establish expectations as to the level of safe behaviour likely from represented persons in the presence of children. This in turn is used to establish or prohibit enrolment within a growing range of activity systems in contemporary UK society. The list is therefore a key 'tool' through which our activity within many aspects of modern society is mediated.

Therefore, the value of our framework lies in the way in which it highlights the necessary entanglement of action, communication and representation. Unfortunately there are many examples in the modern world of the dis-entanglement of these essential patterns. This is particularly evident in the way in which many organisations form order through 'facts'.

Creating forma

Forma, as evident in some persistent data system, has the key advantage that external objects can be manipulated by multiple actors, at different places and at different times. Such persistent data systems achieve particular usefulness as systems of 'record'-keeping within processes of communication. First, the number of actors involved in communication is no longer limited to those immediately present within the communication situation. As a consequence, a persistent data system turns one-to-one or one-to-many communication into many-to-many communication. Second, the senders of a communication can be physically dis-located in time and space from the receivers of a communication. This extends the capacity for memory beyond that of any particular individual actor involved in communication; forming collective memory available to multiple actors.

Therefore, the forma utilised by organisations such as the CRB serve a necessary function in acting as a collective memory which can be used to inform and perform. However, one of the inherent dangers in making records of things is that the cycle of action from performa, through informa to forma is a necessary process of abstraction. This is because patterns of significance inherently form an inverted pyramid: *what I communicate is always less than what I do; what I represent is always less than what I communicate.* In systems' terms, the variety (Ashby, 1956) of an activity system is always greater than the variety of an information system, and the variety of an information system is always greater than the variety of a data system.

This means that the potential danger in any forming of records is that much of the performa and informa is typically lost within the process of creating persistent forma. Hence, in the process of creating a record of some event, for instance, the richness of the event itself as well as much of how people communicate the event is lost. This also has something to do with the way in which forma inputs into and outputs from in-forma. The way in which a person's intentions are represented as intensions is reliant upon an interpretive process by particular actors which is in itself not represented within records.

For instance, within the case of suicide the richness inherent in the process of classifying a suspicious death as a case of suicide is typically lost in the record of death. This led to some mistaken inferences being made on the basis of the aggregation of such records by persons such as Durkheim. Within the CRB case the process by which people become 'listed' is frequently opaque. Within enhanced checks the police are able to utilise evidence relating to all records of convictions held about an individual, even those not directly pertaining to child protection, such as theft, when replying to a criminal records check.

There is also some evidence of cases of people being 'listed' within police records on the basis of hearsay or third party accounts of behaviour held by the police. For instance, a person might report to police officers that their neighbour has been seen naked in their back garden. The incident is recorded by the police but they decide to take no further action. However, some time later this list-item is used within a decision to fail a CRB check for this person under enhanced disclosure.

Through cycles of significance records may also potentially misrepresent aspects of the 'world'. It is entirely likely within a database of the size required for use by the CRB that there are mis-representations – inaccurate records. This situation is not without precedent. For example, the UK National Insurance database currently has 20 million more personal records on it than the UK population (Beynon-Davies, 2007a). Part of this situation has arisen because as workers move around the country undertaking different occupations they may have made more than one application for a national insurance number. This has made the association between person and record extremely difficult for this organisation.

Creating informa

However, difficulties may not only arise from formative acts of creation. They may also arise from other forms of data manipulation. Hence, for example in the case of suicide, inferences may be made upon the aggregate formation of data structures as statistics, which disconnect with the acts of significance undertaken upon original records. In the case of the CRB, reading similar patterns of data might cause communication mistakes and eventual mistaken performance.

There may also be cases in which the records are mis-communicated, causing mis-information. In either case, performance is likely to be undertaken in terms of such mis-representation and miscommunication. Hence, in 2006 it was reported that some 2,700 people had been wrongly labelled as criminals by the Criminal Records Bureau (BBC, 2010). Such mistakes led to some people being turned down for jobs. The UK Home Office explained that the errors arose when the personal details of the persons checked were similar to but not identical with those of people with a conviction.

The case of the CRB is thus a classic example of an organisation set up to use forma to communicate informa and in turn to enable and to prevent performa. The case is particularly useful as a means of highlighting the difficulties of using forma to record and communicate forms of deviance, and on this basis to enact behaviour.

The CRB case is also a more recent example of the danger of ignoring the place of formative acts in a wider nexus of communicative and performative acts. In this case, the very act of making records of things and relying unquestioningly upon such records for communication and decision-making has the potential for a range of potential side-effects. Lyon (Lyon, 1994), for instance, has pointed to the dangers of what he refers to as *social sorting*: the way in which contemporary institutions make life-critical decisions about individuals on the basis of data profiles created on the individual.

Creating performa

In terms of performa, there may thus be an over-reliance placed upon the records themselves by society in terms of organisations such as the CRB. Maintaining and utilising a criminal register in and of itself is no guarantee that the phenomena it was designed to order and control will be ordered and controlled. There is evidence to suggest for instance, that the majority of child abuse occurs between children and adults with which the children are familiar. Although such incidents achieve rightful prominence, comparatively less child abuse appears performed by strangers and particularly by professionals (NSPCC, 2010). Hence, a CRB check is only likely to be useful in the control of a limited range of such deviance; albeit an extremely important form of such deviance to prevent. This means that the process of CRB checking is a necessary but not a sufficient condition for preventing this particularly loathsome form of deviance.

More worryingly, the very act of creating and maintaining such a data system may have unforeseen side-effects in that many people may be dissuaded from performing in the particular area covered by the process of list-making. The sociologist Frank Furedi (Furedi and Bristow, 2008), for instance, argues that the use of the CRB to ensure the safety of children and vulnerable adults has created an atmosphere of suspicion within UK society. He believes that most adults now think twice before telling off children who were misbehaving, or helping children in distress for fear of the consequences. Further, many people may decide not to interact with children in situations such as work within the voluntary sector because of the complexities of the informative and formative action involved; the need to have a CRB check done.

Conclusion

In writing this book I have attempted to form a preliminary framework which attempts to explain some of the essence of what I like to refer to as organisational informatics. I acknowledge that this conceptualisation is still only a framework and does not constitute a full theory. There is of course nothing new under the sun. The framework is deliberately and explicitly an attempt to unify positions, concepts and descriptions from a number of areas. My aim has not been to re-invent the wheel but to demonstrate how to build a more effective wheel from existing materials; also, that this wheel, fitted to suitable vehicles, can be used to travel further than existing conceptions.

At a very high level, the framework is very much centred around the notion of activity or action. As such, the framework can be seen to have been influenced by various action-oriented philosophies such as American pragmatism, the philosophy of Jürgen Habermaas and to some extent Russian activity theory. At a more concrete level, elements of the framework have been informed by a diverse set of literatures. Semiotics and its application in Organisational semiotics provides the idea of signs and sign-systems. Organisational systemics, and soft systems theory in particular, has helped us formulate the distinction between activity systems and information systems. We have used both information theory and communication theory as a baseline to expand upon the nature of human communication. Information theory contributes the classic model of the communication process while communication theory helps us expand upon the nature of information technology and its basis in control. Evolutionary anthropology informs the conception of Homo sapiens as a symbol-manipulating ape and evolutionary biology along with zoosemiotics helps provide ideas relating to the nature of sensing and the idea of sensory modalities. Conceptual modelling, from Computer Science, has helped us define the notion of ontology, that of a data model and the idea of formative acts. From the language-action tradition we have adapted the idea of communicative acts and we have used symbolic interactionism and the dramaturgical perspective from sociology to help inform the notion of performative acts.

In utilising and integrating such material, I have deliberately tried to write an accessible book as possible. It seems to me that many writers in many disciplines make a blessing of their inaccessibility. The excuse is frequently provided that their writing is complex because their subject matter is complex. However, one suspects that there is often a hidden agenda. Presenting something in complex ways makes it difficult to understand; it also makes it easier to defend.

I do not want intellectual walls around the work I have presented here. I want my errors and misinterpretations to be as apparent as possible; so that others can correct them or improve upon them. Only in such a way can this description of the enactment of significance itself participate in the enactment of significance.

This book is my attempt at making sense of issues I have had to grapple with in over thirty years of both academic and industrial experience. In a sense I am trying to open up a dialogue about some of the essential nature of not only the modern world but also aspects of the historical world. I am particularly interested in how our modern 'information society' is a reflection of and an evolution from themes that are evident in our prehistory and may be associated with our very nature as a species.

But of course the test of any pill is in the swallowing. I would hope that you the reader have found some value in this work and are able to take the ideas expressed and apply them to understanding your own organisational situations and experiences. Please let me know of the results both positive and negative.

 beynon-daviesp@cardiff.ac.uk

References

Ashby, W. R. (1956). An Introduction to Cybernetics. Chapman Hall, London.

Bauer, W. F. (1996). Informatics and (et) Informatique. IEEE Annals of the History of Computing 18(2): 323–334.

Beynon-Davies, P. (2007a). Personal identity management and electronic government: the case of the national identity card in the uk. Journal of Enterprise Information Management 20(3): 244–270.

BBC. (2010). Criminal records mix-up uncovered. Retrieved 3rd March, 2010, from http://news.bbc.co.uk/go/pr/fr/-/1/hi/uk/5001624.stm.

Bryant, A. (2008). The future of information systems: thinking informatically. European Journal of Information Systems 17(6): 695–698.

Cicourel, A. V. (1974). Police practices and official records. Ethnomethodology: selected readings. R. Turner. Harmondsworth, Middx, England, Penguin.

Durkheim, E. (1976). Suicide: a study in sociology. Free Press, New York.

Eco, U. (2009). The Infinity of Lists. Maclehase Press, New York.

Furedi, F. and J. Bristow (2008). Licensed to Hug: How Child Protection Policies Are Poisoning the Relationship Between the Generations and Damaging the Voluntary Sector. Civitas, London.

Gammack, J., V. Hobbs, et al. (2007). The Book of Informatics. Thomson Learning, Australia.

Gorn, S. (1983). Informatics (computer and information science): its ideology, methodology and sociology. The study of information: interdisciplinary messages. F. Machlup and U. Mansfield. New York, John Wiley: 121–140.

Hevner, A. R., S. T. March, et al. (2004). Design science in information systems research. MIS Quarterly 28(1): 75–105.

Lyon, D. (1994). The Electronic Eye: the rise of surveillance society. Polity Press, Cambridge.

NSPCC. (2010). Facts and figures about child abuse. Retrieved 11th June, 2010, from http://www.nspcc.org.uk/news-and-views/media-centre/key-information-for-journalists/facts-and-figures/Facts-and-figures_wda73664.html.

Bibliography

Alexander, C. (1964). Notes on the Synthesis of Form. Harvard University Press, Harvard, Mass.

Andersen, P. J. (2006). Activity-based design. European Journal of Information Systems 15(1): 9–25.

Arrabales, R., A. Ledezma, et al. (2010). ConsScale: a pragmatic scale for measuring the level of consciousness in artificial agents. Journal of Consciousness Studies 17(3/4): 131–164.

Ascher, M. and R. Ascher (1978). Code of the Quipu: Data Book. University of Michigan Press, Ann Arbor.

Ascher, M. and R. Ascher (1997). Mathematics of the Incas: Code of the quipu. Dover Publications, New York.

Ascher, R. (2002). Inka Writing. Narrative Threads: accounting and recounting in Andean Khipu. J. Quilter and G. Urton. Austin, Texas, University of Texas Press: 103–118.

Ashby, W. R. (1956). An Introduction to Cybernetics. Chapman Hall, London.

Atkinson, C. and L. Brooks (2005). In the Age of the Humanchine. Proceedings of the International conference on information systems. Las Vegas.

Austin, J. L. (1971). How to Do Things with Words. Oxford University Press, Oxford.

Austrian, G. (1982). Herman Hollerith: forgotten giant of information processing. Columbia University press, New York.

Bagwell, P. S. (1968). The Railway Clearing House in the British Economy 1842–1922. Allen and Unwin, London.

Bateson, G. (1972). Steps to An Ecology of Mind. Balantine books, New York.

Bauer, W. F. (1996). Informatics and (et) Informatique. IEEE Annals of the History of Computing 18(2): 323–334.

BBC. (2010). Criminal records mix-up uncovered. Retrieved 3rd March, 2010, from http://news.bbc.co.uk/go/pr/fr/-/1/hi/uk/5001624.stm.

Beer, S. (1966). Decision and Control: the meaning of operational research and management cybernetics. John Wiley, Chichester.

Beer, S. (1972). Brain of the Firm: the managerial cybernetics of organisation. Allen Lane, London.

Beniger, J. R. (1986). The Control Revolution: technological and economic origins of the information society. Harvard University Press, Cambridge, Massachusetts.

Berlin, B. and P. Kay (1969). Basic Color Terms: their universality and evolution. University of California Press, Berkeley and Los Angeles, California.

Beynon-Davies, P. (1995). Information systems 'failure': the case of the London Ambulance Service's Computer Aided Despatch System. European Journal of Infomation Systems 4: 171–184.

Beynon-Davies, P. (2007). Informatics and the Inca. International Journal of Information Management 27(5): 306–318.

Beynon-Davies, P. (2007a). Personal identity management and electronic government: the Case of the National Identity Card in the UK. Journal of Enterprise Information Management 20(3): 244–270.

Beynon-Davies, P. (2009b). Business Information Systems. Palgrave, Houndmills, Basingstoke.

Beynon-Davies, P. (2009c). Formated technology and informated action: the nature of information technology. International Journal of Information Management 29(4): 272–292.

Beynon-Davies, P. (2009d). The 'Language' of Informatics: the nature of information systems. International Journal of Information Management 29(2): 92–103.

Beynon-Davies, P. (2009e). Neolithic Informatics: the nature of information. International Journal of Information Management 29(1): 3–14.

Beynon-Davies, P. (2009f). Neolithic Informatics: the nature of information. International Journal of Information Management 29(1).

Beynon-Davies, P. (2009g). Significant threads: the nature of data. International Journal of Information Management 29(3): 170–188.

Beynon-Davies, P. (2010). Dances with bees: exploring the relevance of the study of animal communication to informatics. International Journal of Information Management 30(1): 185–198.

Beynon-Davies, P. (2010). The enactment of significance: a unified view of information, systems and technology. European Journal of Information Systems 19(4): 1–20.

Biles, G., A. A. Bolton, et al. (1989). Herman Hollerith: inventor, manager, entrepreneur – a centennial remembrance. Journal of Management 15(4): 603–615.

Black, E. (2002). IBM and the Holocaust. Time Warner.

Boland, R. J. (1987). The In-formation of Information Systems. Critical Issues in Information Systems Research. R. J. Boland and R. A. Hirschheim. New York, John Wiley.

Bryant, A. (2008). The future of information systems: thinking informatically. European Journal of Information Systems 17(6): 695–698.

Campbell-Kelly, M. (1994). The Railway Clearing House and Victorian Data Processing. Information Acumen: the understanding and use of knowledge in modern business. L. Bud-Frierman. London, Routledge.

Carroll, J. B. (1956). Language Thought and Reality: selected writings of Benjamin Lee Whorf. MIT Press, Boston, Massachusetts.

Checkland, P. (1987). Systems Thinking, Systems Practice. John Wiley, Chichester.

Checkland, P. (1999). Soft Systems Methodology: a thirty year retrospective. John Wiley, Chichester.

Cheney, D. L. and R. M. Seyfarth (1985). Vervet monkeys alarm calls: manipulation through shared information. Behaviour 1/2: 150–166.

Cicourel, A. V. (1974). Police Practices and Official Records. Ethnomethodology: selected readings. R. Turner. Harmondsworth, Middx, England, Penguin.

Codd, E. F. (1970). A Relational Model for Large Shared Data Banks. Comm. of ACM 13(1): 377–387.

Conklin, W. J. (2002). A Khipu Information String Theory. Narrative Threads: accounting and recounting in Andean Khipu. J. Quilter and G. Urton. Austin, Texas, University of Texas Press: 53–86.

Copeland, J. B. (2004). The Essential Turing. Oxford University Press, Oxford.

Copley, F. B. (1969). Frederick W. Taylor: father of scientific management. Augustus M Kelly, New York.

Crist, E. (2004). Can an insect speak?: the case of the honeybee dance language. Social studies of science 34(7): 7–43.

D'altroy, T. N. (2002). The Incas. Basil Blackwell, Oxford.

Darwin, C. (1998). The Expression of Emotions in Man and Animals. Oxford University Press, Oxford.

Dawkins, R. and J. R. Krebs (1978). Animal Signals: information or manipulation. Behavioural ecology: an evolutionary approach. J. R. Krebs and N. B. Davies. Oxford, Oxford University Press.

de Saussure, F. (1964). Course in General Inguistics. Peter Owen, London.

Delgado, A. (1979). The Enormous File: a social history of the office. John Murray, London.

Dennett, D. C. (1987). The Intentional Stance. MIT Press, Cambridge, Mass.

Dennett, D. C. (1996). Kinds of Minds: towards an understanding of consciousness. Weidenfield and Nicholson, London.

Dewey, J. (1916). Essays in Experimental Logic. University of Chicago Press, Chicago.

Dick, P. K. (1978). Do Androids Dream of Electric Sheep? Gollancz, New York.

Dietz, J. L. G. (2006). Enterprise Ontology: theory and methodology, Springer-Verlag, Berlin.

Dretske, F. I. (1981). Knowledge and the Flow of Information. Blackwell, Oxford.

Dretske, F. I. (1999). Machines, Plants and Animals: the origins of agency. Erkenntnis 51: 19–31.

Durkheim, E. (1976). Suicide: a study in sociology. Free Press, New York.

Eco, U. (1977). A Theory of Semiotics. Macmillan, London.

Eco, U. (2009). The Infinity of Lists. Maclehase Press, New York.

Ekman, P. (1998). Afterword. The expression of emotions in man and animals. C. Darwin. Oxford, Oxford University Press.

Ekman, P. (2003). Emotions Revealed: understanding faces and feelings. Weidenfield and Nicholson, London.

Ekman, P. and W. V. Friesen (1971). Constants across cultures in the face and emotion. Journal of Personality and Social Psychology 17(2): 124–129.

Ekman, P. and W. V. Friesen (1978). Facial Action Coding System. Consulting psychologists press, Palo alto, Calif.

Elias, N. (1978). What Is Sociology? Hutchinson, London.

Ezzamel, M. (2009). Order and Accounting as a Performative Ritual: Evidence from Ancient Egypt. Accounting, Organizations and Society 34: 348–380.

Furedi, F. and J. Bristow (2008). Licensed to Hug: how child protection policies are poisoning the relationship between the generations and damaging the voluntary sector. Civitas, London.

Gammack, J., V. Hobbs, et al. (2007). The Book of Informatics. Thomson Learning, Australia.

Gardenfors, P. (1995). Cued and detached representations in animal cognition. Behavioural processes 35: 263–273.

Gawande, A. (2010). The Checklist Manifesto: how to get things right. Profile books, New York.

Giddens, A. (1984). The Constitution of Society: outline of a theory of structuration. Polity Press, Cambridge, UK.

Goffman, E. (1969). The Presentation of Self in Everyday Life. Penguin, Harmondsworth, Middx.

Gorn, S. (1983). Informatics (computer and information science): it's ideology, methodology and sociology. The study of information: interdisciplinary messages. F. Machlup and U. Mansfield. New York, John Wiley: 121–140.

Gould, J. L. and C. G. Gould (1995). The Honey Bee. Scientific American, New York.

Grattan, R. F. (2005). Strategy in the Battle of Britain and Strategic Management Theory. Management Decision 43(10): 1432–1441.

Hammer, M. (1990). Re-Engineering Work: don't automate, obliterate. Harvard Business Review July-August: 18–25.

Harris, R. (1986). The Origin of Writing. Duckworth, London.

Hevner, A. R., S. T. March, et al. (2004). Design Science in Information Systems Research. MIS Quarterly 28(1): 75–105.

Hobart, M. E. and Z. S. Schiffman (1998). Information Ages: literacy, numeracy and the computer revolution. John Hopkins University Press, London.

Hockett, C. F. (1963). The Problem of Universals in Language. Universals of Language. J. H. Greenberg. Cambridge, Mass., MIT Press.

Holwell, S. and P. Checkland (1998a). Information, Systems and Information Systems. John Wiley, Chichester, UK.

Holwell, S. and P. Checkland (1998b). An Information System Won the War. IEE Proceedings Software 145(4): 95–99.

Jackson, M. C. (2003). Systems Thinking: Creative holism for managers. John Wiley, Chichester.

Kanigel, R. (1997). The One Best Way: Frederick Winslow Taylor and the Enigma of Efficiency. Viking, New York.

Le Guin, U. (1993). The Earthsea Quartet. Puffin books, London.

Lewis, D. (2002). Convention: a philosophical study. Blackwell, Oxford.

Locke, L. (1923). The Ancient Quipu or Peruvian Knot Record. The American Museum of Natural History, New York.

Lyon, D. (1994). The Electronic Eye: the rise of surveillance society. Polity Press, Cambridge.

Marshack, A. (2003). The Art and Symbols of Ice Age Man. Communication in History: technology, culture and society. Boston, Pearson Education.

Mason, R. O. and I. I. Mitroff (1981). Challenging Strategic Planning Assumptions: theory, cases and techniques. John Wiley, New York.

Mattesich, R. (1989). Accounting and the Input-Output Principle in the Prehistoric and Ancient World. ABACUS 25(2): 74–84.

Mattesich, R. (2000). The Beginnings of Accounting and Accounting Thought. Routledge, London.

Maturana, H. R. and F. J. Varela (1987). The Tree of Knowledge: the biological roots of human understanding. Shambhala, Boston, Mass.

McGowan, B., S. F. Hanser, et al. (1999). Quantitative tools for comparing animal communication systems: information theory applied to bottlenose dolphin whistle repertoires. Animal Behaviour 57(3): 409–419.

313

Mcluhan, M. (1994). Understanding Media: the extensions of man. MIT Press, Cambridge, Mass.

Mead, G. H. (1934). Mind, Self, and Society. University of Chicago Press, Chicago.

Mead, M. (1962). Keynote address. Approaches to Semiotics: transactions of the Indiana university conference on paralinguistics and kinesics. Indiana University, US.

Millikan, R. G. (1984). Language, Thought and Other Biological Categories: new foundations for realism. MIT Press, Cambridge, Mass.

Millikan, R. G. (2005). Language: a biological model. Clarendon Press, Oxford.

Mingers, J. (1995). Information and meaning: foundations for an intersubjective account. Information systems journal 5(4): 285–306.

Minsky, M. (1988). The Society of Mind. Simon and Schuster, New York.

Mithen, S. J. (2006). The Singing Neanderthals: the origins of music, language, mind and body. Weidenfeld & Nicolson, London.

Morris, C. (1964). Signification and Significance. MIT Press, Cambridge, Mass.

Morris, C. W. (1946). Signs, Language and Behavior. Prentice-Hall, New York.

Morris, D. (1979). Manwatching: a field guide to human behaviour. Harry N. Abrahams, London.

Newell, A. and H. A. Simon (1976). Computer Science as Empirical Inquiry: Symbols and Search. Comm of ACM 19(3): 113–126.

NSPCC. (2010). Facts and figures about child abuse. Retrieved 11th June, 2010, from http://www.nspcc.org.uk/news-and-views/media-centre/key-information-for-journalists/facts-and-figures/Facts-and-figures_wda73664.html.

Ogden, C. K. and I. A. Richards (1923). The Meaning of Meaning. Routledge and Kegan Paul, London.

OMG (2007). Business Motivation Model (BMM) Specification, Object Management Group.

Orlikowski, W. J. (2007). Sociomaterial Practices:exploring technology at work. Organization Science 28(9): 1435–1448.

Paul, R. J. (2007). Challenges to Information Systems: time to change. European Journal of Information Systems 16(3): 193–195.

Pentland, B. and M. S. Feldman (2007). Narrative networks: patterns of technology and organization. Organization Science 18(5): 781–795.

Pentland, B. and M. S. Feldman (2008). Designing routines: On the folly of designing artifacts, while hoping for patterns of action. Information and Organization 18: 235–250.

Pierce, C. S. (1931). Collected Papers. Harvard University Press, Cambridge, Mass.

Pinker, S. (2001). The Language Gene. Penguin, Harmondsworth, Middx.

Placer, J. and C. N. Slobodchikoff (2004). A method for identifying sounds used in the classification of alarm calls. Behavioural Processes 67(1): 87–98.

Porter, M. E. (1985). Competitive Advantage: creating and sustaining superior performance. Free Press, New York.

Porter, M. E. and V. E. Millar (1985). How Information Gives you Competitive Advantage. Harvard Business Review 63(4): 149–160.

Puri, R. (2006). The Role of Intelligence in Deciding the Battle of Britain. Intelligence and National Security 21(3): 416–439.

Ravilious, K. (2010). The writing on the cave wall. New Scientist. 2748: 12–14.

Robinson, B. and F. Wilson (2002). Soft Systems Methodology and Dialectics in an Information Environment: A Case Study of the Battle of Britain. Systems Research and Behavioural Science 20(3): 255–268.

Rose, J. and J. G. Gamble, Eds. (1994). Human Walking. Baltimore, Williams and Wilkins.

Rowland, W. D. (2003). Foreword. Communication in History: technology, culture, society. D. Crowley and P. Heyer. Boston, Pearson Education.

Rudgley, R. (1999). The Lost Civilisations of the Stone Age. Simon and Schuster, New York.

Ryave, A. L. and J. N. Schenkein (1974). Notes on the art of walking. Ethnomethodology: selected readings. R. Turner. Harmondsworth, Middx, England, Penguin.

Ryle, G. (1949). The Concept of Mind. Hutchinson, London.

Schmandt-Bessarat, D. (1978). The Earliest Precursor of Writing. Scientific American 238(6).

Schmandt-Bessarat, D. (1992). Before Writing. The University of Texas Press, Austin, Texas.

Schmandt-Bessarat, D. (1996). How Writing Came About. The University of Texas Press, Austin, Texas.

Searle, B. J. R. (1970). Speech Acts: An Essay in the Philosophy of Language. Cambridge University Press, Cambridge.

Searle, J. R. (1975). A Taxonomy of Illocutionary Acts. Language, Mind and Knowledge. K. Gunderson. Minneapolis. Volume 7.

Searle, J. R. (1983). Intentionality: an essay in the philosophy of mind. Cambridge University Press, Cambridge, UK.

Searle, J. R. (1995). The Construction of Social Reality. Penguin, London.

Sebeok, T. A. (1972). Perspectives in Zoosemiotics. Mouton, The Hague.

Sebeok, T. A. (1976). Contributions to the Doctrine of Signs. Indiana University Press, Bloomington, Indiana.

Shannon, C. E. (1949). The Mathematical Theory of Communication. University of Illinois Press, Urbana.

Slater, P. J. B. (1983). The study of communication. Animal Behaviour: Volume 2: Communication. T. R. Halliday and P. J. B. Slater. Oxford, Blackwell.

Slobodchikoff, C. N., B. S. Perla, et al. (2009). Prairie Dogs: communication and community in animal society. Harvard University Press, Cambridge, Mass.

Smith, M. (1998). Station X: the code breakers of Bletchley Park. Channel 4 books, London.

Smith, M. E. (2003). The Aztecs. Blackwell, Oxford.

Snowdon, C. T. (2002). From Primate Communication to Human Language. Tree of Origin: what primate behavior can tell us about human social evolution. F. B. M. deWaal. Cambridge, Mass., Harvard University Press.

Spencer-Brown, G. (1969). Laws of Form. Allen and Unwin, London.

Stamper, R. K. (1973). Information in Business and Administrative Systems. Batsford, London.

Stamper, R. K. (1985). Information: Mystical Fluid or a Subject for Scientific Enquiry? The Computer Journal 28(3).

Stonier, T. (1994). Information and the internal structure of the universe: an exploration into information physics. Springer Verlag, Berlin.

Stonier, T. (1996). Information as a basic property of the universe. Biosystems 38(2): 135–140.

Stonier, T. (1997). Information and Meaning: an evolutionary perspective. Springer-Verlag, Berlin.

Tapscott, D. and A. D. Williams (2006). Wikinomics: how mass collaboration changes everything. Atlantic Books, London.

Tomasello, M. and M. Carpenter (2007). Shared intentionality. Developmental Science 10(1): 121–125.

Tomasello, M., M. Carpenter, et al. (2005). Understanding and sharing intentions: the origins of cultural cognition. Behavioral and Brain Sciences 28: 675–735.

Tsitchizris, D. C. and F. H. Lochovsky (1982). Data Models. Prentice-Hall, Englewood-Cliffs.

Urton, G. (2003). Signs of the Inka Khipu: binary coding in the Andean Knotted-String Records. University of Texas Press, Austin, Texas.

Urton, G. and C. J. Brezine (2005). Khipu Accounting in Ancient Peru. Science: 1065–1068.

Varela, F. J., E. Thompson, et al. (1993). The Embodied Mind: cognitive science and human experience. MIT Press, Cambridge, Mass.

Vedral, V. (2010). Decoding Reality: the universe as quantum information. Oxford University Press, Oxford.

Von Baeyer, H. C. (2003). Information: the new language of science. Weidenfeld & Nicolson.

Vygotsky, L. (1986). Thought and Language. MIT Press, Cambridge, Mass.

Waddington, C. H. (1977). Tools for Thought. Jonathan Cape, St Albans, Herts.

Webber-Maybank, M. and H. Luton (2009). Making effective use of predicted discharge dates to reduce the length of stay in hospital. Nursing Times 105(15): 20–21.

Weick, K. E. (1995). Sensemaking in Organizations. Sage Publications, Oxford.

Weick, K. E., K. M. Sutcliffe, et al. (2005). Organizing and the process of sense-making. Organization Science 16(4): 409–421.

Whyte, W. H. (1956). The Organization Man. Simon & Schuster, New York.

Wiener, N. (1948). Cybernetics. Wiley, New York.

Wiener, N. (1950). The Human Use of Human Beings: cybernetics and scoiety. Discuss books, Boston, Mass.

Wilson, B. (1990). Systems: concepts, methodologies and applications. John WIley, Chichester, UK.

Wolmar, C. (2007). Fire and Steam: a new history of the railways in Britain. Atlantic Books, London.

Yates, J. (1989). Control through Communication: the rise of system in American management. John Hopkins University Press, London.

Zammuto, R. F., T. L. Griffith, et al. (2007). Information Technology and the Changing Fabric of Organization. Organization Science 18(5): 749–762.

Zipf, G. F. (1965). The Psycho-Biology of Language: an introduction to dynamic philology. MIT Press, Cambridge, Mass.

Index